Archaeology and the Media

Timothy Clack
Marcus Brittain
editors

**Left Coast
Press** Inc.
Walnut Creek, California

Left Coast
Press Inc.

Left Coast Press, Inc.
1630 North Main Street, #400
Walnut Creek, CA 94596
http://www.lcoastpress.com

Copyright © 2007 by Left Coast Press, Inc.

ISBN 978-1-59874-233-6 hardcover
ISBN 978-1-59874-234-3 paperback

Library of Congress Cataloging-in-Publication Data

Archaeology and the media/Timothy Clack, Marcus Brittain, editors.
    p. cm.—(Publications of the Institute of Archaeology, University College London)
  Includes bibliographical references and index.
  ISBN 978-1-59874-233-6 (hbk. : alk. paper)
  ISBN 978-1-59874-234-3 (pbk. : alk. paper)
  1. Archaeology—Social aspects. 2. Mass media—Social aspects. 3. Clack, Timothy.
4. Brittain, Marcus.
  CC175.A725 2007   930.1—dc22   2007025129

Printed in the United States of America

♾ The paper used in this publication meets the minimum requirements of American National Standard for Information Sciences—Permanence of Paper for Printed Library Materials, ANSI/NISO Z39.48–1992.

09 10 11 5 4 3 2

CONTENTS

LIST OF ILLUSTRATIONS

Figures

Table

PREFACE

Archaeology is more prevalent in the media today than ever before. Likewise, the media is more prevalent in archaeology than has previously been experienced. Media is both the means to mass communication and the material agency by which that communication is transmitted, transferred, or conveyed. Different media have impacted upon archaeology in different ways, and a future relationship with the media lies in an uncertain balance with the emergence of the digital era of technology. What has archaeology's relationship with the media looked like in the past, what are the issues at stake in this relationship today, and is archaeology suitably equipped for this partnership in a future of increasingly rapid information transfers?

Written by internationally acclaimed scholars directly engaged with 'the media' and archaeology, the chapters that have been brought together in this volume explore these questions with a varied range of styles and approaches, original research and ideas, and personal and critical evaluations.

The media infiltrate every facet of archaeological practice. Increasingly, this is becoming reflected in a growing focus on media-related issues in archaeological teaching and research throughout the world, particularly in Europe and the United States. Issues of representation, communication, accountability, and multivocality are fundamental areas that are addressed throughout this volume with the successes, failures, potentials, and challenges of the media-archaeology interaction in the past, present, and future placed under scrutiny.

The volume is divided into five parts that we believe represent the core concerns of a relationship that is recursive in nature. In many cases, the order of the chapters could have been different since many cross between the core themes. If anything, this reflects the complexity of the volume's subject matter and the breadth of scope that is both available in this subject area and attempted in this volume. The range of opinion within the chapters also reflects the diversity and at times polarity of views that the relationship between archaeology to the media has stimulated. It is of course for readers to decide which of these suits them and archaeology most appropriately.

Acknowledgements

Archaeology's relationship with the media has deep historical roots, but rarely has it been critically approached with any depth. In bringing together these authors, we have found that their unerring enthusiasm – coupled with their creative treatment of the themes – have refined our thinking and broadened our media horizons. While we would like to thank the authors for their dedication and patience with the project, special appreciation is owed to all those who have offered their support and contributed to the volume's fruition.

We thank our colleagues at the University of Manchester, particularly Timothy Insoll, Siân Jones, Stephanie Koerner, and Julian Thomas. Furthermore, we are grateful to Cornelius Holtorf and Stephanie Moser for numerous conceptual and practical discussions that have undoubtedly enhanced the volume. Moreover the comments of Mick Aston, Amanda Chadburn, Jonathan Cole, Sarah Colley, Vicky Cummings, Iain Davidson, Kathryn Denning, Don Henson, Mike Heyworth, Mark Horton, Anra Kennedy, John Prag, Julian Richards, Tim Schadla-Hall, Andrew Selkirk, Scott Simmons, Niall Sharples, Nancy White, Alasdair Whittle, and two anonymous reviewers are gratefully acknowledged. Paul Henley also offered invaluable direction in anthropology's media experience, and Georg Hartung was superb in translating the German text of Tom Stern's chapter. We are also indebted to our editors Mitch Allen, Richard Stoneman, Briar Tower, and Eliot Werner for their commitment to the volume and their forbearance and guidance. Furthermore, the fellows and students of St. Peter's College, University of Oxford, and St. Anselm Hall with Canterbury Court, University of Manchester, are thanked for allowing the editors both the time and facilities for the production of this work.

The beginnings of this volume were in many ways catalysed during the organisation of the 'Mis/Representation in Media' conference at the University of Manchester in summer 2004. The Faculty of Social Sciences and Law deserve our acknowledgement for its handsome funding of this event. The co-organisers and numerous delegates at that event should be mentioned as their input has continued to mould our interests. Particular thanks go to Ian Bent of the BBC, Jonathan Bignell, John Corner, Rajinder Dudrah, Anna Ford, Maxwell Jones, Peter Lawler, Conrad Leyser, the Rt. Hon. Tony Lloyd MP, Phil Manning, Gareth Palmer, Oxana Poberejnaia, Jasem Tarawneh, and John Whitelegg.

Finally, our sensibilities are still intact largely through the tolerance and support of Lavinia Ferrante di Ruffano, Louise Selisny, and of course our respective families.

TC and MB

1

INTRODUCTION

Archaeology and the Media

Marcus Brittain and Timothy Clack

Media's Past

'What hath God wrought?' The first message transmitted by electric telegraph by Samuel Morse in the mid-nineteenth century whispered a sharpened edge of uncertainty that was soon to cut through the world, transforming it forever. Revolutions of media followed: prewar radio, postwar television, and the entry into a digital era in which we are now approaching. Archaeology has, like many other disciplines, featured prominently in each. 'Television once bought me the best meal I have ever had on British Rail', Glyn Daniel wrote having enjoyed first-class hospitality after being mistaken for Woodraw Wyatt on a train bound from Cambridge to York (Daniel 1986: 269). But he could just as easily have been recognised as Glyn Daniel, professor of archaeology and British Television Personality of the Year for 1955. Archaeology, it might be thought, had not just sung a note of celebrity, but a whole chorus.

A deeper look into the first figures for television ownership in private domestic households in Britain for 1956 might put this into a different context. These estimate that the total number of homes with a television tallied to just 36.5 per cent. The consumers of this relatively new media were predominantly well off, educated, middle-class citizens, and although the transmission of particular programmes became an event of communal viewing, their accessibility was limited. The perception that archaeology was reaching a mass public is in many respects correct, but an understanding of just how, who, or through which media is justifiably a little skewed. Even so, electronic media had begun its relationship with archaeology that is today of greater magnitude than ever before. But various chapters in this volume reveal how other forms of mass media – well established before TV – continued to be fascinated by new and amasing archaeological discoveries, as well as the conflicts, personalities, and imagination of a past that could be made less foreign with an expert touch. What is more uncertain is how archaeology should be equipped for the digital age of multiplicity in voice, choice and unparalleled speed, and scope of communication.

Media, in its most basic form, is a means to mass communication, or an agency by which that communication is transmitted, transferred, or conveyed. 'The media' may be viewed as an entity in itself, a body of journalism with broadcast values that intersect markets of commerce, audience profiles, the boundaries of discursive space, and disciplinary expertise. It may also be understood as a process of translation or engagement embedded in the materiality of the media form. Different media convey different messages in varying ways, impacting on the context of interpretation as well as framing and reframing contexts for consumption.

The circumstances that precipitated the amalgamation of the following chapters began their course in summer 2004 when, during the organisation of an interdisciplinary conference on misrepresentation in the media, we realized that many of the concerns stated to us about the transference of scholarly research to a wider audience through the media of various technological forms were congruent with many questions being raised by archaeologists. Few of these were in print, however, and the vast majority was being expressed in pubic debates and conference venues, while many more appeared in the everyday exchange of views and opinions. While the relationship between archaeology and the media has deep historical roots, it has largely been perceived as a direct or hierarchical passage of information from expert to audience, complexity of scholarly rigour to the excruciating simplicity of popular tone. It was our aim, therefore, to bring together contrasting perspectives on a diverse range of media and their impact on the way archaeological narratives are produced and presented, along with the successes, failures, ethics, and potentials of a relationship that is ultimately symbiotic. The ways in which these perspectives are conveyed are equally varied, representing a range of communicative and analytical styles. This volume is therefore not a manual on how to enter the media or a handbook for communicating with the media (for basic guides, see Danien 1997; Klesert 1998; Milanich 1999; Stoddart and Malone 2001).

Two primary aspects of archaeology's relationship with the media have been 'frozen' for a moment in this volume. First, engagement with the mass media has precluded a conglomeration of concerns regarding representation of archaeology and archaeologists, accuracy of information and reportage, the 'dumbing-down' of information, individual credibility within one's discipline, and the legitimisation of archaeological narratives as recognised by a mass audience. While archaeology is enjoying more media presence than ever before, television is unlikely to be financially damaged if archaeology was to disappear from the screen. The enormous benefit of media interest is precariously balanced against 'non-professional' archaeological narratives and the proliferation of 'other' narratives. While multiplicity is a key aim of postprocessual methodologies and arguments, the openness of truth claims beyond disciplinary walls – expounded by the media – has become a cause for concern from numerous archaeological corners.

While the authority of archaeological narratives may be under scrutiny, the political accountability of archaeology's relationship to the media is also distinctly apparent (e.g., Coleman and Dysart 2005; Daggett 1992; Gero and Root 1994; Rao and Reddy 2001; Seymour 2004; Spriggs 1994). Ian Hodder (2003: 166; 1998) has described how at Çatalhöyük, for example, press conference days organized by the excavation sponsors attract fifty or more local, national, and international media representatives. This coverage has meant that Çatalhöyük has become a stage for politicians – both local and European – to gain their own media coverage with their own political intentions. These range from attempts to raise an awareness of the local importance of the site and region in the past and the present, the difficult question of the genetic ancestry of the local population to the ancient inhabitants, and the relevance and potential of the European Union for Turkey. 'As a professional archaeologist and as a member of society,' reminds Hodder (2000: 11), 'one has to be responsive to the impact of one's work'. A critical analysis of archaeology's relationship to the media is an essential part of this pro-active awareness.

Second, the materiality of the media bears an impact upon the way archaeological data is collected, compacted, interpreted, and disseminated. It also bears direct relevance to the means by which the mass media engages with archaeology and vice-versa. Old media technologies are not simply succeeded by new and novel technologies. They blend and merge many aspects of the techniques required for their function as well as retaining, enhancing, or displacing technological components or designs and the issues that these critically raise for social analysis. Media impact on the world and life within. As Bolter and Grusin (1999: 15) state, 'No medium today, and certainly no single media event, seems to do its cultural work in isolation from other media, any more than it works in isolation from other social and economic forces'. How should archaeology even begin to reflect on its situation among such tumultuous and rapid transfers, let alone contemplate its next move for survival?

Inevitably, television receives much of the emphases within this volume, and with good cause. It accounts for 40 per cent of all leisure time in Britain (Roberts 2004), and almost every survey that has been carried out on the public reception of archaeology has found television to rest comfortably as the most popular means to information (Merriman 1991; Paynton 2002; Pokotylo and Guppy 1999; Pokotylo and Mason 1991; Ramos and Duganne 2000; Statistiska Centralbyrån 2002). With important bodies such as the Archaeological Institute of America working closely with the Learning Channel (Hammond 1992), for example, television's visual impact has been instrumental in presenting archaeology to an audience hungry for images of the past.

The wide range of media technologies discussed in this volume signifies the diversity of research that is available from the archives and stores of broadcasters and museums. In some cases, media may be regarded as untapped resources either for communication or critical analysis. For example, one particular area for future consideration is radio – which, as mentioned in numerous chapters throughout this volume, has been used successfully at least since the BBC broadcasts from the National Museum of Wales, Cardiff, by Cyril Fox and his staff in the 1930s, forties, and fifties, and John Irving's *The Archaeologist* series in the 1950s. It is often perceived that because radio usually goes unnoticed, it therefore has a minor role to play in the routine of everyday life (cf. Pertti 1997). However, sound may be regarded as an ordering presence in a domestic routine, filling empty space and time with a familiar texture in which everyday life takes place (Tacchi 1999). Radio's regular use maps memories of past experiences and moods within an encompassing soundscape. Although the experience of listening is difficult to put into words, radio sound may be opened to analysis as part of the material culture of the dwelling place or an agent in the formation of the social environment.

This introduction aims to open a critical analysis of archaeology's relationship with the media by providing a background to the themes presented throughout this volume, situating these arguments within the broader context of media analysis and the related concerns raised within other disciplines. The chapters that follow will not only be of interest to archaeologists working with the media, but for wider debates regarding issues of representation, identity formation, public communication, and the political accountability of archaeological interpretation. The chapters that have been brought together for this volume can add not only to archaeology's awareness of its location within a sociotechnic world and the effects that media may have upon the structure of archaeological practice, but may actively contribute in the broader discussions of the history and possibilities of an increasingly media-oriented society.

We cannot escape media; it is all around us, permeating the practices through which our intelligibility of the world transpires. We cannot stop this mediation: it has no off switch; it lives and feeds upon our own *necessity* to communicate; we cannot escape media.

Archaeology's Reception of the Media

The terms 'archaeology' and 'archaeologists' embody a myriad of images and meanings both inside and outside the discipline itself. It might seem strange, then, that concerns of misrepresentation often dominate the reaction to any mere mention of mass media forms, when in reality there is little common consensus both nationally and internationally as to what constitutes these terms in the first place. Whilst heterogeneity of opinion lies within the profession itself, a series of caricatures are repeatedly conjured up within media images of the archaeological profession. As Ascherson (2004: 145) notes, the foundations for many of these lie upon nineteenth century stereotypes, although various others have been added more recently by Hollywood cinema (Day 1997; Hall 2004). A variety of assumptions exist regarding archaeology and archaeologists (Holtorf 2005a; Merriman 1991). However, many of the most prevalent distinctions are historically those between the heroic masculine explorer (either male or female) and the absent-minded collector, antiquarian, or professor – or as Kidder (1949: xi) once wrote, 'the hairy-chested and the hairy-chinned'. These caricatures are often combined with the portrayal of the archaeologist as the expert, adventurer, digger, discoverer, and treasure hunter (Ascher 1960; Bray 1981: 225–227). The most valued archaeologies appear as those that hold the key to mysteries unsolved, unravelling the truth behind the oldest, grandest, or most splendid of ancient wonders.

Reactions to these portrayals in commercial cinema are invariably divided between those who believe that there is 'a legitimate cause for concern... [in that] these often erroneous and stereotyped images are a driving force in shaping popular perceptions of our discipline' (Baxter 2002b: 18), and those who believe that 'the profession should derive a measure of pleasure in seeing itself evolve in film, very much in command of the great, grand sweep of time and place, the setting for human cultural and biological evolution' (Day 1997: 44). Placed somewhere between the two, Hall (2004: 171) believes that a fluctuation between images such as 'the positive pursuit of hidden knowledge' and 'the negative rape of the sacred and indigenous' is 'healthy', reinforcing 'the reality of cinema as something made by diverse makers and audiences and reflecting wider political debates, not just what we might call the mechanics of the discipline'.

The concern with how archaeology and archaeologists are portrayed in the media signifies the importance of representation (e.g., Felder et al. 2003; Gale 2002). With regard to broadcast television, Cornelius Holtorf's chapter 'An Archaeological Fashion Show' identifies the way archaeologists present themselves through what they wear. It becomes clear that archaeologists may express a combination of their personality and ambitions, or their clothing may draw upon specific contexts of archaeological practice. Depending on what is being signified – the exotic, the (sexy) adventurer, the competent professional, the eccentric, the scholar – particular popular stereotypes may be emphasised to their own advantage, utilising the perception that you are what you wear. However, Holtorf warns, fashion styles may be ambiguous, open to unintended interpretation. Yet it is this ambiguity that may open discussion about what an appropriate image of archaeology and archaeologists might be, thus empowering archaeology to present its own image against the morass of traditional programming.

It is arguable that many of these images have been challenged through innovative programming in the last 15 years. This has not meant that series such as Channel 4's hugely successful *Time Team* (first broadcast in 1991) are closed to criticism (Fig. 1.1); in fact, the success of the series has instilled those two words 'Time Team' as a bye-word for British archaeology in the public consciousness, and has subsequently opened the programme to criticism as to what an appropriate media portrayal of archaeology and archaeologists should be. Cleere (2000: 91), for example, expressed his disappointment that the

Figure 1.1 The *Time Team* crew film Francis Pryor at the excavation of a
Neolithic causewayed enclosure at Northborough Fen,
Cambridgeshire, in 2004 for an episode in the programme's
twelfth series, broadcast 30 January 2005 (Marcus Brittain).

producers lacked, in his words, 'confidence in the appeal of the subject' by relying on a non-archaeologist as the link between specialist
knowledge and narrative communication (see also Stoddart and
Malone 2001: 461). Added to this, Cleere's criticism of the programme's format of a three-day excavation as 'presenting a somewhat distorted and oversimplified picture of what archaeology is all
about' (2000: 91–92) is unlikely to be alone. The media portrayal of
excavation and the ongoing process of interpretation are two of the
main topics of disapproval within the discipline. While Fowler (1981:
63) acknowledged that these may be 'flatly unphotogenic', Hudson
(1981: 119) – applauding the extent of archaeology's media attention
in previous decades – lamented that archaeologists had yet to present
to the 'great mass of the population in [Britain] the importance of a
disciplined and logical approach to our heritage'. Little difference
may be noted in today's criticism of archaeological excavation and
recording on television, reproducing an image of a practice that is
'simple and speedy' (Hills 2003: 207) or 'untidy, rushed and incomplete' (Schadla-Hall 2003: 56). As Finn (2001: 265) acknowledges,
'[I]mpatience, necessary to the process of journalism, rubs against the
pace of archaeological excavation'.

Finding a successful format in broadcast media, one that suitably
pulls in the audience ratings and satisfies the demand for appropriate

representation by the subjects of its content, are hard to come by (West 2004), but *Time Team* appears to have at least contented the former with viewing ratings in excess of 3.4 million, if not fully succeeding with the latter. Its 'sister' spin-off *Extreme Archaeology* was directed at a younger, fashionable viewing audience, attempting each week to enter a danger zone and investigate perilous sites often under potential threat. The reception to the all-bar-one female cast (a welcome blend in an otherwise male-dominated frontline role) was mixed despite a format otherwise not dissimilar to that of *Time Team*. One broadsheet commentator rather crudely described the programme's intention as 'a cross between Charlie's Angels and Tomb Raider' with a result nearer to 'a joke' (Hoggart 2004).

The content of a broadcast format is a measure of its time and its audience and may be tightly bound with changing ethical certainties. In an episode of the BBC's archaeological quiz show *Animal, Vegetable, Mineral?* in the 1950s, for example, a number of models characterising varying ethnic physical traits were paraded in front of the studio panel of distinguished academics, whose task was to name their country of origin. Despite the embarrassingly offensive comments by one member of the panel – a rather inebriated Margaret Mead – the episode was relatively acceptable over 50 years ago (see Daniel 1986: 253–254), yet the same format would be unthinkable today.

The popularity of *Animal, Vegetable, Mineral?* was due largely to the magical personalities of its contestants (Fig. 1.2), but its game show format in the 1950s and 1960s succeeded, as Mortimer Wheeler explained, because the viewer was 'interested in watching your process of thought' (quoted in Hawkes 1982: 299). Much more of the archaeological thought process is presented in *Time Team*, but as with many archaeological programmes, the product of that thought process is then left open to criticism. A lack of interpretation, and the mistrust of insight to the past beyond the material reality of the artefact (Holtorf 2003: 126), lies precariously balanced against the alternative that is an excess of interpretation. While the latter may grasp the heavy baggage of metanarrative, each could be tried and in many cases found guilty of lacking the wider context informed by previous research (Hills 2003: 208). When used, previous research may vary in quality and extent between media forms or individual reportage. The popularity of 'treasure hunting' and narratives of the past often labelled 'fringe,' 'fantastic', 'cult,' 'alternative', or 'independent' archaeologies are often framed within these formats considered to be media friendly (Cole 1980; Feder 1984; Fagan 2006; Williams 1991). This entails a proliferation of imagery, a lack of information on previous research, and high

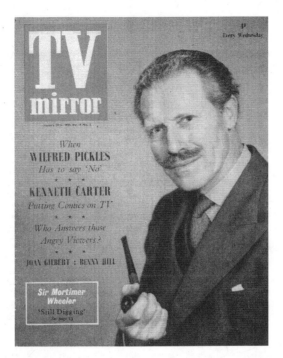

Figure 1.2 **Sir Mortimer Wheeler, British Television Personality of the Year for 1954, as featured on the front cover of *TV Mirror* magazine, 29 January 1955, promoting his book *Still Digging*. Copyright © IPC Media, Ltd.**

entertainment value, all in contrast to the seriousness of scientific endeavour. 'Alternative' and serious archaeology subsequently have become perceived as two separate cultures competing for the same audience. It is no coincidence that the French word for static or interference in media transmission is *parasite*. Silence is a hindrance to the transmission of news, and archaeological dead air or gaps within the media market are regarded as an empty space to be filled, and a parasite to be removed before it is fed by 'erroneous belief' or irresponsible 'treasure hunting' (Eve and Harrold 1987; Gregory 1983).

A different view has been that 'alternative' and serious archaeology can be merged together in a programming format that, by combining the interests of each party, would ultimately rationalise mistaken belief into responsible practice. However, with a title reminiscent of a 1950s BBC television series *Buried Treasure*, a recent attempt to merge these two 'cultures' within a BBC series entitled *Hidden Treasure* (first broadcast in autumn 2003) proved less than successful in satisfying vexed opinion (see, for example, Fowler, this volume). Described as 'absurdly irresponsible' by Tony Robinson (2003), the celebrity presenter of Channel 4's *Time Team*, the format of *Hidden Treasure* was straightforward enough: recent finds, usually via an independent metal detector enthusiast, are analysed, recorded, and conserved before the findspot is subjected to a small excavation comprised of modest evaluation trenches to recover any other associated artefacts and place the original find in a context of interpretation. However, the main criticism directed towards the programme was its keen emphasis on the artefacts' present-day monetary value – declaring in the opening sequence that there is 'serious money to be made' – and the attraction that this inevitably had with regular viewing figures in the region of 2.6 million (Selkirk 2003: 390). These concerns are directed towards the effects that these messages may have against the hard work of finds liaison officers and others in the UK to present the ethic of the Portable Antiquities Scheme and the Treasure Act, under which any finds of gold, silver, coin hoards, or prehistoric metalwork are reserved by the crown. Equal disdain has been noted against the British Museum's cooperation with the programme as part of an outreach agenda and related exhibition, *The Buried Treasure: Finding our Past*[1].

As Merriman (1991) has shown through a series of revealing surveys, a particular level of heterogeneity of public opinion with regard to the usefulness and purpose of archaeology suggests that attitudes to alternative archaeological narratives and techniques are open for consumption through the media. Rather than equating this appeal with a dangerous opening in the 'media market', the response has been to suggest a complex alignment with multiple individual attractions to the past based on personal value and social background. Irwin and Wynn (1996) have revealed that the public understanding of science depends upon the social context in which knowledge was an issue. It has been suggested that this is an area in which archaeology lacks research and an understanding into the 'psychology and culture of professional antiquity looters' (Fagan 1996: 241) and, as Holtorf suggests, 'the specific contexts from which, in each case, the fascination for a particular approach to archaeology and the resulting interpretations of the past emerge… [and the] social and cultural needs to which they respond' (2005b: 549). As Cooter and Pumfrey (1994: 249–250) acknowledge, if a distinction exists between the 'popular' and the 'learned', it is 'not because the latter is poorly understood, but because it is developed by its recipients for different purposes'. Without disregarding the ethical accountability of both archaeology and the media (see Fagan and Rose 2003), it is maybe within this space that a mutual benefit for different archaeologies may lie – not, as illustrated in the example above, by merging the two perceived 'cultures' together.

Education or Entertainment?

In its earliest days, public service broadcasting (PSB) began with the recognition that the new media of television and radio would have a significant and beneficial impact on society. In the pursuit of healthy citizenship, it was imaged that PSB would play a leading role by providing particular genres of impartial programming with a series of definable qualities that served particular audiences and moral cultural codes. This tradition of PSB began with the ethos that the expert knew more than the viewer and that detached from the reality of their content, programmes could observe social life at a much deeper level than the common person confined to its experience (Murdock 1999: 14). Today, PSB has been relaxed in wake of a competitive multi-channel commercial market. According to Ofcom, the UK's independent broadcast communications regulator, the purpose of public service broadcasters is to provide a wide range of subjects through high-quality programming with the view to inform, educate, and entertain the widest possible range of audiences (Ofcom 2003, 2005a, 2005b). As Tim Gardam of the BBC explains, this is no easy exercise in which 'modern television' relies on innovative formats to 'find new ways to bring an area of experience to an audience' (3WE 2000: 164).

The line perceived between education and entertainment sometimes mistakenly draws a distinction between learning and leisure, or when one is either active or passive in engagement. Although the mass media is widely acknowledged as a potential educational medium for archaeology to offer informed views of the past, television in particular has accredited debate as to what an appropriate format for presentation should be in an accessible yet informative way. Norman (1983) acknowledged that for archaeology to have some educational basis, its presentation should be in an entertaining format. But there is no clear-cut set of rules as to what this format would be. 'What is entertainment?' ask Curran and Seaton (1988: 236). 'All media industries compete to create it.' The regular grumble against the presentation of 'alternative' archaeologies, the caricature of archaeologists and archaeology in general, or the 'dumbing-down' and exaggeration of serious archaeological issues is a familiar tactic when claiming legitimacy to matters of fact, but it as also precluded by a mediatisation of that archaeological desire – the pursuit of a viewing public and audience ratings.

In reality, the broadest range of credible programming will include both education and entertainment in a blend that is messily termed *infotainment*. But it is important to remember that the television or radio programme is not an end in itself. Hunt (2004: 94), for example, perceives history on television as a process in which history is only the beginning. The viewer is an engaged participant who is drawn into a subject as a result of his or her initial contact with a programme. This is a 'learning journey' in which the inspired viewer is gradually given the opportunity to 'travel' to a series website from which he or she will be guided to further reading (probably an accompanying book to the series), after which the viewer may then travel to a historic attraction, heritage centre, or museum. The final destination in this journey, according to Hunt, is higher education where the more specialized learning is nurtured. History on television is therefore not regarded by Hunt to be the same as academic research, and he maintains that they should not be compared with the same goals. 'Television's purpose', Hunt (2004: 95) claims, 'is to excite and inform a broad public, not push the boundaries of scholarship in the same way as a monograph or journal article'. In this view, television is the bridge between an increasingly specialized academic language and an accessible popular narrative. This is discussed further below, but if Hunt's views are valid, then there is a pressing concern that archaeologists must consider.

An important point noted by Hills (2003: 207) is that the increase in media interest in archaeology corresponds with an emerging threat to the place of archaeology in the English national curriculum and archaeology's uncertain status within the university system. The number of people completing the journey to archaeological courses in higher education is also decreasing in the UK. According to the Universities and Colleges Admissions Service statistics, a high of 3,543 admissions to undergraduate level in 2000 dropped to a low of 2,603 in 2003 – a decrease by almost 27 per cent – with only a marginal rise again in 2004. This is partly a reflection of the dramatic rise in the 1990s of university places in expectation of a boom in applications resulting from media interest, only for many of these new seats to remain empty resulting in a considerable over-supply of undergraduate places. Consequently, departments have been forced to recruit from a much wider social spectrum, which has been possible because of the subject's accessibility through television, leading to some of the best widening participation figures in higher education (Mark Horton

2004: personal communication). Reasons for this decline in admissions are likely to be multi-faceted. One likely cause is reflected in a recent survey of graduate's starting salaries from British universities[2]. Archaeology ranked last out of 61 different subjects. This is matched with overall low profit margins and low rates of pay (Aitchison 1999: 30–49; Aitchison and Edwards 2003: 38–52), a condition mirrored in the United States (Wilson 2001: 37–38). While the media presentation of the reality of archaeological practice is favourable in principle, should we really be asking where the distortion truly lies?

Trust and Mistrust of the Media

'Unchecked fantasy about the past,' Fowler wrote in the early 1990s, 'splurges forth daily without blush' (1992: 36), yet accuracy is regarded as one of five key journalistic values. The susceptibility to inaccuracy or blatant misrepresentation remains a common matter of anxiety and mistrust towards media journalism. This is a concern that archaeology shares with many other disciplines (e.g., McCleneghan 1994; Moore and Singletary 1985; O'Keefe 1970; Tankard and Ryan 1974). But the prevalence of inaccuracy is debatable. Recent analysis of television reports of the Rwandan refugee crisis of 1994 and the conflict in Angola, for example, concluded that a significant degree of the information was misleading and sometimes inaccurate, presented as facts with little social or political explanation and context, and that gaps in coverage were filled in with images based on neocolonial beliefs. Different media presented parts of the larger picture, reporting broken narratives and a piecemeal view of reality (Philo 2002: 175). Elsewhere, a survey for the coverage of science news in reporting found that almost 60 per cent of the scientists interviewed felt that it was generally accurate (Tichenor et al. 1970), although another survey reported that only 29 per cent of the stories reviewed were free of errors (Pulford 1976). Inaccuracy may be due to journalists not taking into account the expertise of their source, opting instead for individuals less qualified for comment on a particular subject (Dunwoody and Ryan 1987). Even for stories where it might appear more appropriate to consult multiple sources, 'a sizeable proportion of journalists may use very few' (Stocking 1999: 25).

Most archaeologists who have had contact with journalists will have a tale to recount of an occasion of inaccurate reportage to varying degrees. But how prevalent are the worst cases? A survey of Cultural Resource Management (CRM) reports in New York State newspapers published between 1995 and 2000 found that over 10 per cent of the articles contained overt inaccuracies (Kuhn 2002). This is marginally higher than other survey results of scientific accuracy (e.g., Borman 1978), but is still marginal in the broader context of archaeological communication. Why then might mistrust in the media still remain?

Mistrust of the media has historical bases in 1930s sceptical visions of technological futures, particularly in reactions from the so-called Frankfurt School to early visions in the opening decades that drew upon the Enlightenment promise that utopia would be realized through reason. In 1932, Aldous Huxley's *Brave New World* antici- pated a future of social and biological conditioning centres run by an efficient totalitarian state of docile human clones blissful in their servitude to an overbearing political executive. 'To make them love it,' Huxley wrote in the foreword to the 1946 edition (reprinted in 1994), 'is the task assigned, in present-day totalitarian states, to min- istries of propaganda, newspaper editors and school-teachers'. An iron curtain silencing the truth had been wedged between knowledge and reality. This would be echoed later in the century in the simulacra of Baudrillard (1988) in which individuals, duped by the mass media, would choose spectacle over reality.

While Huxley prophesised, Adorno and Horkheimer (1972) simi- larly claimed that contemporary capitalist society would divert the route of reason away from utopia into a route towards chaos. Instead of enriching human life towards emancipated consciousness, they saw a progress of knowledge that had amounted to a reason of tech- nical expertise, instrumental in the violent domination of nature, the subjugation of people equated with 'the primitive', and the fortifica- tion of powerful and dominating systems of belief. Replacing the term 'mass communication' with 'culture industry', they argued that culture had become industrialised and commoditised, and that the reproductive capabilities of technological media had transformed the free human spirit – embodied within the creative possibilities of art – into an alienated subject obedient only to its dominant political mas- ter. Although television was still in its relative infancy, Adorno (2005), writing in 1951, could see the immediacy of its future triumph while lamenting the concealed realities of the Second World War in the manipulation of public opinion through 'information, propaganda, commentary, the film crews in the leading tanks and the heroic death of war reporters'. He feared for the future of media when already 'the identity of film interests' lay side by side with 'weapons interests'.

By the 1980s, Marxist analyses demonstrated with clear empirical data the tensions between political ideologies and the media's potential as an ordering mechanism in the construction and maintenance of citizenship. In a classic example, Curran and Seaton (1988: 5–113) described how a radical press in Britain during the first half of the nineteenth century was fervently consumed by a working-class audience. Standing independent from the vagaries of commercial or political pressure, vital issues of social interest were addressed, challenging not only the managers of policy and political trust, but also the editors of mainstream journalism for fuelling rather than questioning the policies that had led to a redundant and impoverished culture. Curran and Seaton revealed that in order to suppress anti-government fervour, Parliament attempted to restrict the readership of the press to the affluent, more 'respectable' levels of society by raising stamp duties and introducing press taxes. Moves were then set in motion to transfer ownership of the presses to 'responsible' entrepreneurial 'reformers' who cared more about profit and self-gain than they did about free speech. The result was that industrial commercialisation flourished once the press taxes had been repealed, enabling cheap popular newspapers supported with commercial advertisements to out-circulate the radical press, emphasising views that would sustain subservient citizenship and social order.

In recent years, exposé journalism has continued to attract a popular following revealing the bowdlerisation of political 'spin', corporate agendas, and military blunders among others. With accessible and persuasive writing, Noam Chomsky, for instance, has infiltrated the common consensus of the educated politically aware on the media portrayal of current affairs. His criticism of the American mass media presupposes that since media productions are now owned by large corporations, they work within the constraints of state and private power and under the same pressures of competition and profit as other corporations (Herman and Chomsky 1988). This, according to Herman and Chomsky, is to the detriment of the quality and freedom of reporting, particularly since the main source of news is the government – thus necessitating a favourable relationship with its source and by implication a favourable, perhaps less accurate, report of political issues. Furthermore, Chomsky (1989) has argued that citizen participation in political expression may lead to an 'excess of democracy' that threatens the authority of the elected government, hence necessitating a 'necessary illusion' of a democratically free and inclusive society propagated by the media that in turn may be regulated and restrained by the powers that be.

Cynicism towards the media in the last two decades has continued to be framed with scepticism towards political institutions in general.

In the UK, the turnout of the electorate for the general election fell from 72 per cent in 1972 to 59 per cent in 2001 (MORI 2001). In the United States, more people voted for the final of the *American Idol* singing contest than in the presidential election. At the same time, surveys have indicated that only one-third of Americans trust the accuracy of news broadcasts (Pew Research Centre 2002). One explanation for increasing scepticism of media news reporting is that the reportage of political issues through a cynical media lens inverts that cynicism back to the bearer of information (Cappella and Jamieson 1996).

With these external influences, archaeological scepticism lies partly within the degree of journalist accuracy, but also in the ongoing reiteration of the representations that have already been outlined, fuelled by fiction, cinema, and caricature. But if these perceptions are currently being questioned and reframed, then a space is also being opened in which the political accountability of the media to archaeology can also be re-addressed. In the United States, for example, many CRM schemes are supported by both state and federal taxpayer money and projects can have an enormous impact on local communities. Through local and national press, public opinion may have a significant influence on the government stance in a particular issue (it is, after all, public favour that wins votes), and these decisions quickly flow in the direction of agency decision makers (Kuhn 2002). In this context, accurate press coverage is deeply relevant for the long-term survival of thorough archaeological investigation.

Translating Archaeological Narratives

Archaeology's use of the media for securing archaeological futures is by no means new. Mortimer Wheeler found in the 1920s that media interest could be fostered as an aid in securing donations and additional funds for excavation. Why then has such little attention recently been paid to the relationship with the media? Is mistrust to blame?

This is a difficult question, particularly in light of Karol Kulik's 'A Short History of Archaeological Communication'. Kulik traces a long and mutually beneficial relationship between archaeology and various forms of contemporary media, noting the earliest mass communication of archaeological issues at least as far back as the 1840s. A flourish of media interest between the 1920s and the 1950s coincided with the developing technologies of electric media. However, Kulik identifies the period between the 1960s and 1980s in

Britain as a 'schizophrenic time', during which a split between a 'digging' and a 'thinking' profession overlaps with an ambivalent period of archaeological communication despite a public and mass media still hungry for the past. The media subsequently became attached precariously to the 'digging' side of the profession, while the thinkers slipped into hibernation from public view. Kulik explores why, despite such a varied and historically symbiotic relationship, there has been 'amnesia' about the relevance of archaeological communication and the changing forms that this has developed through time.

The era of changing attitudes to media identified by Kulik coincided with an era of significant transition in archaeological thinking – what Clarke (1973) called the 'loss of innocence'. This characterised one of a series of archaeological crises of interpretation, and in many ways paved the epistemological way for the so-called post-processual archaeology, chewing the heart out of disciplinary foundations and then spitting them back out, fragment by fragment.

During the 1980s and early 1990s, post-structuralism had become a burgeoning theoretical pursuit for archaeological 'readings' of material remains. This was a violent deconstruction process of the traditional (or modernist) foundations of archaeological thinking, looking to break away from author-centred interpretation and instead explore the potentials of a multiplicity of interpretation, reflexivity, and intertextuality. Eventually, the effects of these transformations would be felt in almost all aspects of archaeological thinking. However, the principles that were embodied within the media offered little for the revisions of post-processual archaeology. Perceptions were that the mass media remained locked within in an age of positivist certitude. Why might this be?

The distinct presence of archaeology in the media between the 1920s and the 1960s coincided with the emergence of two new information technologies: prewar radio, and postwar television. As an analogue media, the television – like the press – produced a linear sequential output of information, passed from one recipient to the next. This was a hierarchical exchange of information from expert to witness, scientist to layperson, from a centralized source akin to the laboratory. In this positivist sequence, the *press* may have been likened to an empowered individual body that was ahistorical, autonomous, and rational, lacking context through a perceived objectivity (Christians et al. 1993: 27). Similarly, analogue *television* displayed what Gripsrud (1999: 35) describes as an orderly barrage of 'free-floating signifiers and addictive entertainment that eludes serious contemplation'. This was clearly the antithesis of archaeological post-structural theories of the text. Instead, the media was better suited to a passing era in which archaeologists and journalists were of the same breed: neutral observers and the collectors of value-free empirical data. This notion of diegesis left little room for multiplicity or reflexivity. In a very broad sense, this fostered scepticism and mistrust of a mass media that was thought to be dualist, balancing singular narratives of truth and falsehood, right and wrong.

It is no mere coincidence that the resurgence of media presence by the early 1990s corresponded with an increasing accessibility and speed of digital technologies. 'It was inevitable,' writes Julian Richards (2004: 48), archaeologist presenter of Channel 4's *Meet the Ancestors*, 'that the relationship between archaeology and broadcast media would change'. In the final section of this chapter, the parallel associations between globalised digital technologies and archaeological goals are discussed in more detail, but what is pertinent here is to acknowledge that the nonlinear, hyper-mediated digital information flows of this new technology correspond with the multi-vocal objectives of contemporary archaeology.

Storytelling the Past

Today, through a series of external and internal pressures, it has become accepted that an integral part of archaeological management is that people should benefit from archaeological research in some way. One of the difficulties has been communicating the complex results of the theory building that is identified with post-processual narratives of the past. Added to the jargon bursting of much archaeological analysis, the often complicated language of theory and science is ill equipped for the direct transfer of information to a consuming public. Again, these are issues that have been voiced within the wider academic field. Since the 1960s, creative styles of writing that are fluent and comprehensible have been something that science editors have increasingly preferred to publish (Hollander 1987; Ramsey 1986). Yet it is still necessary for Wynne to restate that scientists 'need to communicate more clearly and entertainingly in lay terms' (1992: 38).

This is just one of the issues that Brian Fagan and Francis Pryor discuss in this volume, maintaining their dissatisfaction that increasing specialization and a 'publish or perish' mentality has little time for generalized narratives in a language that is accessible to lay audiences. Holtorf (2005b: 547) even notes a disciplinary air of resentment towards the storytelling of 'alternative' archaeologists, whose capacity for popular narrative has proved to be successful for connecting to mass audiences. But popular writing, Hills (1997: 222) has suggested, is thought to be simplistic in both content and practice – a natural ability that, unlike academic authorship, does not necessitate training or rigour. In reality, the most successful and receptive forms of mass communication writing are from a craft that has been moulded, rehearsed, and refined. However, 'contrary to received opinion,' Pryor (1996) has retorted elsewhere, 'it is beyond (and not beneath) the training and perhaps even the ability of many archaeologists.' Few university courses include creative 'popular' writing as a taught requirement, yet at least one consensus states that, '[t]he best archaeologists are invariably the most skilful storytellers' (Young 2002: 241), while another acknowledges storytelling as a form of archaeological analysis (Gibb 2000). Writing the scientific and the poetic may not be that far removed from each other. As Locke (1992: 203) cogently argues, 'Life itself is inaccessible, incomprehensible, meaningless, but the metaphors of science and the metonymies of literature, of all art, help to make it accessible, comprehensible, meaningful.'

Archaeology has been drawn upon as both metaphor and inspiration in the fictional and poetic literary traditions (e.g., Evans 1989; Finn 2004a; Garcia i Quera 2004; Girdwood 1984; Korte 2000; Russell 2002a, 2002b). The idea of the past and archaeological remains have been sources of imagination in creative writing for centuries, and friendships between the men and women of letters and archaeological pioneers have inspired some of the most popular classic works. The current fashions of popular culture are thus that an extensive readership exists for works that combine an in-depth archaeological setting with a fluid storyline – 'a very good example,' writes Evans (1983: 70) regarding fictional works, 'of archaeology serving the present.'

These themes are amalgamated together in Christine Finn's chapter 'Darkness Disseminated', in which she explores the emotive sensation that quietly weeps from the photographic images of P.V.Glob's 1965 classic text *The Bog People*. This insight retraces the interweaving connections between journalist reports, editors' use of Lennet Larsen's photographs, a group of English schoolgirls' inspiration and innocent fascination, audiences, artists, translators, and writers, all of which conceal a collective influence in the merger of science and wonder in Glob's work. But the interplay of Heaney/Larsen/Glob (poet/artist/archaeologist) ultimately results in a powerful form of storytelling. Finn recalls the immediate captivation awakened by her first experience of the book and her surprise that 'no longer part of common parlance', the work had become omitted from 'popular cultural currency'. However, Finn's chapter describes the recent stirring of Larsen's photographs and Glob's work from the dormancy of memory. Never tired of expression, it is a healthy reminder that good storytelling – unlike many academic texts – is a curious phenomenon that never dies.

Communication as a Continuum

Clearly, this form of authorship reaches an audience well beyond most academic textbooks. Its currency lies in the responsiveness of the audience. An alert, intrigued, and returning audience is invaluable. As novelist Jean Auel asserts, 'Romance the public. They'll love you for it' (1991: 128). However, the translation of academic texts by the media for a mass audience is more often berated either for dumbing-down intricate and detailed research, or for a shortage of accurate dissemination. In many ways, this perceives two realms of authorship that work on different levels of authority completely separated from one another. In one corner is academia and science, in the other popularisation and non-science, competing against one another for overall recognition by the public mass and legitimacy to claims of 'matters of fact'. In this conflict of narratives, the flow of information is one way, from the top of 'high' culture to the bottom of 'low' culture: academic to popular (Hilgartner 1990). The popular is then regarded as a sacrifice of authority and scholarship, and hence irrelevant to its forward progress. Yet while various media may rightly be criticised for sensationalism or misinformation in specific cases, mistrust in the filtering process of translation for the public consumption of archaeology has been less critically discussed. The reality may in fact be a complex circularity of recursive ideas rather than a simple top-down linear passage of information.

The public communication of archaeology requires the art of storytelling, but the formal language of academic writing also tells a type of story, one that serves professional needs within the archaeological community. By no means homogenous, these have a purpose in addition to the communication of ideas: they are the product of research and a measure of individual or team diligence and aptitude; they 'define communities and hierarchies in their author bylines and citations'; and they are an author's claim for their small place in archaeological history (Gregory and Miller 1998: 115). This is a multi-layered form of storytelling in a particular language grounded in context and tradition. The surface layer is the transmission of the idea. But when that idea is being transmitted as a story to the public, it is not necessarily a different *kind* of story to the one presented in the professional text, where it differs is the *degree* to which that story is told. The *way* a story is told will have a significant impact on the outcome that is the production of knowledge (Curtis 1994).

Popularised knowledge therefore actively filters back into scholarly research, feeding the process of knowledge production (Whitley 1985). There is an extensive body of literature on the communication and public understanding of science that has tried to come to terms with this issue (see, for example, Weigold 2001). A classic argument by Cloître and Shinn (1985) is a useful introduction to the applicability of these works to an archaeological context. Rather than defining a stern distinction between narratives of science and narratives of popularisation, they identify four types of scientific text placed along a flowing continuum (Fig. 1.3)

- *Intraspecialist* – typified by the specialised academic publication with empirical data, supporting expert theory, and references to other key works.
- *Interspecialist* – including those texts and presented papers that bridge between related academic specialisms.
- *Pedagogical* – or the textbook stage of communication, in which the completed theory and paradigm is presented and set within a historical perspective of disciplinary progression.
- *Popular* – in which characteristic images and analogical metaphors are presented in the popular press and broadcast documentary.

These gradual differences in the styles and contexts of communication and reception emerge along a continuum as the transmission of ideas flows between the intermediate stages of communication. Moving along an continuum of archaeological communication, one might expect to see decreasing reference to the methodologies for the collection of data, or detailed discussion such as empirical phenomena (statistics, spatial analyses, etc.) and typological distinctions, or soil composition and matrixes, but increasing reference to the historical significance of the work in comparison to other work. Also, devices such as graphs, tables, and detailed plans give way to montages, cutaway diagrams or plans, and a reliance on metaphor and icons. Similarly, specific or quantitative arguments shift to broad and qualitative narratives.

The flow of information along the stages of the continuum is not necessarily smooth or without difficulty. Cloître and Shinn (1985) describe how a series of barriers may hinder this flow in a process that they describe as 'crystallisation'. Here some theories or detailed

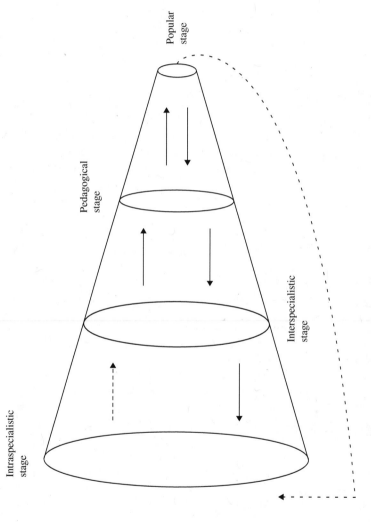

Figure 1.3   Science communication as a continuum (after Bucchi 1998: 10).

aspects of knowledge may be less suited than others for the media, while some may not be suitable at all. In other cases, the specific constraints of a medium's format may mean that information may be suited to one medium over another (radio rather than the press or TV).

The continuum of Cloître and Shinn exposes the recursive nature of popularisation back into the scholarly field, but through a way in which the movement of *knowledge production* stops along the continuum at the point of popularisation. This is a model that has largely been implicit within archaeological conceptions of media communication. The production of knowledge at the level of the specialist is presumed to be distanced from popularisation. Popularised knowledge therefore becomes regarded as a justification of archaeological practice in which, as Cloître and Shinn (1985: 47) suggest, it is 'more crucial to know that something has occurred than to know the minutiae of the occurrence itself'. By distancing the production of knowledge from the sphere of popularisation, archaeological practice is thought to be legitimised as certain and authoritative (Bucchi 1998: 11). It is no wonder, then, that parody and guffawing sometimes accompany television programmes such as *Time Team* when inflated details in reconstructions arise from the minutiae of data with partial or no explanation of archaeological inference.

But to what degree is this a problem? Could this in fact be regarded as an opportunity for creative dialogue in a space in which some ideas may skip a stage of the continuum altogether in a process that Cloître and Shinn (1985) call 'deviation'? Indeed, it is here that Massimiano Bucchi (1998) has argued for a positive tension between academia and the media, breaking from the traditional top-down hierarchy of knowledge transferal by relocating it within a site of plurality rather than a 'celebratory discourse'.

The implications of these arguments for communication as a continuum open various avenues of discussion from which to approach archaeology's relationship with the media. First, this is a means through which the Popperian demarcation problems between what constitutes a science and non-science are avoided. Second, the boundaries between disciplinary fields are allocated fluidity for intersection between multiple considerations and approaches to specific issues. Third, the recursive nature of archaeological communication is open for both analysis and consumption. The production of knowledge can be seen to begin not just at the top level of a hierarchy of communicative stages, but could be conceived at any of the stages through which numerous forms of knowledge are transferred at any given time. Clearly, this is related closely to the social studies of scientific knowledge in which, for example, the early works of Bruno Latour (1987) and Joseph Rouse (1987) demonstrated how academic knowledge is produced within a network of external and internal power relations, multiple competing dialogues of narrative, and the accountability of expert knowledge systems to historically situated sociopolitical contexts. The media seeps between the levels of the continuum, not as a facilitator of icons of truth between two opposite realms separate from the practice of knowledge construction, but as a part of the practice of archaeology itself.

Has the Media Changed Archaeology?

Archaeology's relationship with the mass media remains contentious. However, apprehension is not confined to archaeology. Unease is reflected throughout the wider academia field.

Describing the tension between the media and academia in general, Gripsrud (1999) and Peters (1995) suggest that different forms of cultural production are being shaped within each. The journalist is located in a media world constrained by a time and space of sharp deadlines and frames for presentation that are alien to academia. Academic publications, by comparison, are often the result of a lengthy research project and are written for a relatively small and closed group of specialists. Both, however, inhabit a common ground with a professional ethos historically rooted in the Enlightenment, where through 'critical examination of available information', the forms of knowledge about the world in which we are placed could be distributed with 'some responsibility for the nature of public discourse' (Gripsrud 1999: 39–40). Journalism and academia are brought together in a complex endeavour in which both strive to maintain legitimation and recognition within their own professional field, as well as the field adjudged by the anonymous 'mass' public. At present, this is a field in which the mediation of information to the public is more suited to the everyday practice of the journalist rather than the academic. This may necessitate a particular level of media literacy on behalf of the academy in order to successfully report on a particular relevant issue.

As Marion Benz and Anna Katrien Liedmeir demonstrate in their chapter 'Archaeology and the German Press', knowing when or how information should be exposed to journalists is no easy matter, and timing is key as to whether or not an archaeological story may take precedence over other news when media interest is searching for a theme most relevant to a specific social context. They note that variations in editorial interest may result in competing styles and frames for presenting the news to which they are held responsible, and that the *desired* knowledge of a readership may be closely aligned with the amount of space that will be allocated for certain types of news. Local news reports stress different aspects of a story to that of the national news, and may be the first stage in the dissemination of news between sources that rapidly expands reportage and readership. The novelty of Benz and Liedmeir's work lies in their perspective on 'the press' with the view to understanding the dynamics of the decision-making processes from the perspective of news marketability. Knowing where, how, and when to publish a press release can be the difference between a successful report and one that goes unnoticed.

The field in which the media and academia make contact may be tipped in favour of the former not just as a result of media literacy. As Gripsrud (1999) outlines, the mediatisation of scholarly information and the strive for a heterogeneity of popular recognition – as opposed to homogenous recognition within one's disciplinary field of expertise – may even be deemed academically damaging. There could be many reasons for this, but one in particular is what Gregory and Miller (1998: 108) describe as 'the traditional rules of science popularization'. This entails the professional taboo of disseminating information about data prior to its publication in academic journals. A recent example of this conflicting interest in Australia is recounted by Colley (2002: 154–161), when in 1996 an article was submitted to *Antiquity* journal in Cambridge claiming that thermoluminescence dating of flaked-stone artefacts from the Jinmium rock shelter in the Northern Territory could establish a human presence in Australia as far back as 116,000 BP, doubling all previously authenticated dates. The implications of new claims for human evolution are significant for origin theses on a global scale, and there was an inevitable scientific debate thrown between articles in various peer-reviewed publications. New dates offered for indigenous settlement in Australia have additional political sensitivity with the interest of descendent communities, requiring the greatest of care to ensure media accuracy when reporting new information. Having agreed to pass the story to a journalist in the *Sydney Morning Herald*, the Jinmium findings were to be made public simultaneously with the journal publications. However, for reasons that remain unclear, the news broke several weeks early, quickly spreading to media outlets worldwide. What followed were a series of articles published in the *Australian* national newspaper rebuking the dates and criticising the release of the story to a single newspaper, while also criticising the political stance (in this case pro-Indigenous) that the *Herald* had adopted. 'The Jinmium researchers', Colley concludes, 'fell foul of rivalry between two Australian newspapers owned by competing media interests'.

While the consequences of a media profile may be perceived by some parties as a hindrance to the progression of one's own career, another perspective views the entirety of contemporary academia as a practice completely transformed by the media. According to Pierre Bourdieu (1984, 1998), journalistic values and commercial criteria – including a dependence on viewing figures as a judgement of success and quality – have infiltrated the academic field and transformed the nature and standard of scholarly output. This is illustrated by the replacement of long-term research projects with modest or uncertain outcomes by projects designed with the intent of rapid social recognition, necessitating short-term production and a clearer result in sight. Even more alarming for Bourdieu is that traditional assets of scholarly value become replaced by the cogs of the publicity machine, not just through public monitoring systems such as the Research Assessment Exercises or University League Tables in the press, but the whole principle of research in general.

These concerns have been echoed throughout archaeology particularly where inappropriate ethical practice or the transgression of professional values have been explained by the desire for recognition within the media. A recent example is the Shinichi scandal in Japan in which the exposure of forged discoveries, redolent of the Piltdown and Moulin-Quignon experiences of the nineteenth and twentieth centuries, contested the confidence in Japanese prehistoric chronology. The scene centred upon Japanese archaeologist Fujimura Shinichi, whose uncanny ability to find rare Palaeolithic artefacts in the unlikeliest of locations had raised doubts about their authenticity. Nicknamed "God's Hands", Shinichi's finds had pushed back the earliest presence of humans in Japan by almost 600,000 years. But on 5 November 2000, after Shinichi announced his latest discovery, the daily newspaper *Mainichi Shimbun* printed a series of stills from a video recorded by journalists the previous night that captured Shinichi planting the artefacts. With the revelation in headline print, Shinichi's reputation was destroyed and the authenticity of 180 prehistoric sites came into question. An article in the British journal *Science* entitled 'Japanese Fraud Highlights Media-Driven Research Ethic' blamed the infiltration of Japanese media in archaeology for the failure to spot the fakes sooner (Normile 2001). It stated that the Shinichi case exposed 'a sloppy side of Japanese archaeology in which press conferences take precedence over publication' (2001: 34) and that impressive discoveries and press conferences are deemed more important than accurate scientific debate about the respective claims.

The Shinichi case is an extreme example and it is as yet unclear as to the degree with which the media's relationship with Japanese archaeology may be held accountable for an individual's duplicity. Three logics of blame have been cited in the Schinichi scandal that indicate a polarity of opinion.

- The media was not directly accountable. Academic pressure to produce spectacular results was to blame (Normile 2001).
- The increasing mediatisation of the broader archaeological field is guilty for the rise of fakes in general, of which Shinichi is but a part (Bahn, cited in Stoddart and Malone 2001).
- Japanese nationalism turns a blind eye to possible false claims because of its dedication to document the primacy of the Japanese race (French 2000).

However, other suggestions as to the media's influence upon the course of research within Japanese archaeology would indicate that an answer is far from simple. Within the climate of postwar Japan, a new vision of Japanese identity sought to rebuild from a prewar nationalist ideology based on emperor worship (Fawcett 1995). High-profile media attention began in the early 1970s to the mixed reaction of archaeologists, who sensed that political meddling was misrepresenting their interpretations in order to reinforce new pride in the past and present image of Japanese nationhood (1995: 243).

Habu and Fawcett (1999) critique the use of archaeological evidence for substantiating an ethnic homogeneity between past and present Japanese worlds in which the Yayoi period (ca. 300 BC–AD 300) had been a model for society and the main object of media focus. They describe a case in 1994 when new discoveries from an excavation at Sannai Maruyama – a site of the Jomon period (ca. 10,000–300 BC) – drew considerable media attention, and with the view to preserve the site, educational tours were encouraged attracting thousands of visitors. As a result, thousands of letters written to local newspapers lobbying for government funding to save Sannai Maruyama produced the desired result. Newspaper articles, television specials, lectures, and symposia about the site resulted in its designation as a National Historic Site to which by 1997 more than one million people had visited. In a transformation of values, the Jomon period has become a significant aspect of Japanese identity, regarded as the origin of many aspects of Japanese culture. This wave of thinking in the public consciousness was not new to scholars who had long engaged in the appreciation of the specificity of the Jomon period to modern Japanese identity. Previously, the main barrier for the communication of such ideas was an 'image of the Jomon people as impoverished and primitive nomads [that had] been perpetuated by the media'. With the relinquishing of such an idea by the mass media came new opportunities for the funding and exploration of a period that already had a presence in the academic consciousness, but on a scale that without popular support could never have been realised.

Each of the two cases outlined above contain an archaeologist's or archaeological use of the media to forward a programme of research. One, of course, is distinctly negative; the other, though still open to critique, is more positive in contrast. In any event, they each represent (a) skilful steerage of media coverage to their advantage, and (b) the infiltration of the media into archaeological discourse. The first of these, as Kulik explains in this volume, has been prevalent throughout archaeological history at least since the 1870s. The potential of, for example, future funding through media coverage is ever anticipated with welcoming delight. The second point, however, is more often regarded with an uneasy anxiety or pessimism. It would be unsurprising if there were not discomfort in the realisation that the course of academic scrutiny has been influenced in some way by media interest. But new and significant discoveries can inevitably lead to a lifetime's work, and the media, after all, *is* driven by revelation. There are positive and negative sides to this impact on the discipline, two sides that are inherently ethical in nature.

In light of this, the media's impact on the blossoming of archaeological research on battlefields of the First World War is the subject of Jon Price's chapter 'Great War, Great Story'. This contribution follows personal experiences on the Western Front of France in a modern-day attrition of belief that has transformed a negative media perception of the disturbance of twentieth century unmarked war graves into a positive statement of mutual gain. Innumerable bereaved families received letters or telegrams with the words 'Regret – No Trace', receiving a year later by a Red Cross decree the chilling confirmation 'presumed dead'. In an anonymous poem 'To My Unknown Warrior', written in 1920, the painful thought of an unmarked grave has been powerfully articulated.

> The most terrible words in all writing used to be 'There they crucified Him', But there is a sadder sentence now – 'I know not where they laid Him'…Surely 'missing' is the cruellest word in the language.
> *(quoted in Bourke 1995: 41).*

It should bear little surprise that the empathy of events still moist in recent memory should attract a high level of public interest. Price elucidates how this media and public interest awakened conflicts between professional and amateur as to who should be excavating this past. His account demonstrates how the media, in the right context, is both willing and wanting to finance projects that in turn can offer a visual journey with a strong story, particularly one that bears direct relevance to present-day memories. As Price's case unfolds it becomes clear that the support of the media in Great War archaeology also stimulated a course of academic interest and pursuit that was largely absent before.

A Visual Archaeology

Decline of Television Anthropology

Throughout this introduction, we have maintained that archaeology is among a range of disciplines that share many distinct concerns regarding public communication and their location within a world informed through the mass media. Arguably, one of the most significant similarities with archaeology's fluctuating presence and role within the media is the changing reception of anthropology within popular culture.

Self-reflective critical analysis of anthropology's relationship with the media is far more established than that of archaeology, principally through the lens of what has been called 'visual anthropology'. Three core perspectives on the remit of visual anthropology have emerged. The first concentrates on the production of ethnographic film and its application in pedagogical communication. The second is the study of pictorial media, in particular the historical and indigenous visual record (Scherer 1990). The third addresses visual communication in its widest sense and encompasses all forms of visual culture in the human world, ranging from gesture, ritual, and performance to architecture, artefact, and landscape (Banks and Morphy 1997).

For two decades from the late 1960s until the late 1980s, ethnographic film had a distinctly high profile on British television. It is estimated that over 100 hour-long television documentaries were made during this period that were based directly on the fieldwork of consulting anthropologists (Henley 2005). Exploring a range of styles and formats, the most notable programme during this period was *Disappearing World* produced by Granada Television. Broadcast from 1970 with peak-time transmission, its success was recognised by a British Academy for Film and Television Arts award in 1974, and it was voted by the public as the best commercial television series of the year in 1978 (Henley 1985: 9).

After the early 1990s, funding for ethnographic film dramatically decreased, and between 1989 and 1999 the number of broadcast hours of ethnographic documentaries placed within the category 'international documentary' declined by 42 per cent while those filmed specifically in developing countries reduced by 50 per cent (Ruby 2005: 160; Stone 2000: 4). *Disappearing World* disappeared from the television screen in 1993, and programmes that attempted to follow the series were scheduled outside of peak-time viewing and were heavily criticised for resorting to sensationalism (Singer 2002). Despite suggestions that recent geopolitical events could benefit from a revival in programming that directly sought to educate and bring about understandings through cosmopolitanism or relativism, no such trends have been identified within the programming mix, leaving the once prevalent anthropological presence on television screens distinctly absent today (3WE 2001). This decrease in broadcaster's and audience interest in anthropology lies in distinct contrast to the rapid increase of archaeological output on television screens and media outlets in general. Exploring some possible reasons for this may be informative as to the status of archaeology's currency in the media.

In the late 1960s, Margaret Mead (1967: 169) had heralded electronic communication media as a 'quantum leap' in the development of human society, while others in the 1970s attested to its integrative capabilities for dispersed communities of individuals by 'participation in social and political events, a common perception of the world, and a reinforcement of public opinion' (Eiselein and Topper 1976a: 111). But it was also regarded as an imperfect tool, evident in the 'violence, tension, alienation, personal anxiety, [and] bewilderment' that ensued in everyday life. The rate of social change was deemed too fast for the individual to cope with. Hence, with its 'holistic, cross-cultural, and objective viewpoint of man,' anthropology, it was argued, 'could provide insight into the nature of our society, [which] if communicated to the masses, could serve to further integrate our mass society with a common understanding of ourselves'. Academic texts were inadequate for passing this message, but a mutual gain of social change could be gained from a relationship between anthropology and the media. By expressing their research findings to a mass audience through the media, it was thought that it might be possible to draw a positive reaction from policymakers and legislators, therefore fulfilling anthropologists' responsibility as a citizens and legitimising their academic place in society (Eiseline and Topper 1976b: 119). However, a series of events had already tarnished the authority of these ideological romanticisms.

In 1971, a controversy emerged upon the declaration of the discovery of a lost, primitive tribe removed from modern civilising processes and living in caves deep in the forests of the Philippine island of Mindanao. The Tasaday tribe caught the imagination of the world with early media reports claiming the tribe had no words for 'war', 'weapons', 'conflict', or 'violence' and had been living 'a quiet, unobtrusive life outside the boundaries of the civilized world and its problems' (Palmer 2000: 226). Doubts as to the tribe's authenticity described the discovery as a case of misinformation or propaganda devised and dramatised by the government of President Ferdinand Marcos to quell the anti-war and environmental protests of the 1970s. Arguments over the tribe's authenticity regarded claims of its primitiveness as exaggerations or overt errors of fact, resulting in a blend of uncertainty and 'scholarly ambivalence' – the consequence of which was a loss of public confidence (2000: 225).

Developing the filming techniques of Robert Flaherty's ethnographic films from the 1920s, Margaret Mead and Gregory Bateson shot a series of silent films in 1930s Bali with the intent to observe the unfolding of everyday events, devising hypotheses of the culture as a whole. By the 1960s, the tradition of cinema verite (or 'truth film') became the favoured model for recording the actualité of the world by immersing the camera within the reality of the social – thus setting the film outside its context as a neutral, detached observer of events. But only later was it realised that this neutrality was an illusion, when in fact the situation itself was being transformed by the presence of the camera (Sherman 1998: 21). In a distinctly archaeological manner, the object of study was destroyed in the process of recording.

Rosaldo (1993) has argued that claims of primitivity, such as that with the Tasaday controversy, are connected with those tenets of colonialism that display nostalgia for the cultures that it has destroyed. The transformation from a bygone, exotic, traditional, and ideal society to one tarnished by the touch and modernising effects of the Western gaze is experienced as if it were a personal loss. This empathetic nostalgia is set within its own historical and cultural specificity (1993: 71), one in which '[m]ourning the passing of traditional society and imperialist nostalgia cannot neatly be separated from one another' (1993: 86). This has been a difficult issue for a discipline whose legitimacy for describing social reality has been questioned through a 'crisis of representation' (Marcus and Fischer 1986). And it appears that ethnographic film in the broadcast media has as yet been unable to resolve its imperial legacy (Fischer 2003: 371–392; Jenssen 2005). Palmer (2000: 230–231) summarised these concerns by stating that '[d]isciplinary consciousness and even embarrassment over "primitivity,"... suggested to some observers that anthropology might not be able to sustain itself without it.... Eliminating primitivity as a working category leaves anthropologists with few, and some might say impoverished, options to describe indigenous people'. This was further compounded by the indigenous use of the media to seek political goals by deliberately presenting and emphasising dominant popular images from the Western gaze to attract further media attention for the authentication of their own ethnicity (Conklin 1997; Ramos 1987; [Fig. 1.4]). In addition, 'Indigenous Media' has also become recognised as an important voice for the drive towards self-determination and resistance, even if maybe reinforcing aspects of an 'Us' and 'Them' distinction (Ginsburg 1991, 1994; Hartley 2004; Meadows and Molnar 2002).

These are important issues for an archaeology located within a postcolonial world of globalisation and multiculturalism, and an archaeology that is bringing into dialogue and reflection the ontological baggage of its modern origins. Yet these remain issues that have yet to transgress any discussion of archaeology's accountability to

Figure 1.4   Eytan Kapon and Andre Iteanu filming in Papua New Guinea for their documentary *Letter to the Dead* (Andre Iteanu).

social life through the media. Recalling for a moment Rosaldo's culturally situated sense of nostalgia, '"We" (who believe in progress) valorize innovation, and then yearn for more stable worlds, whether these reside in our past, in other cultures, or in the conflation of the two' (Rosaldo 1993: 70). It is therefore informative to consider for a moment – beyond pragmatic pedagogies, self-representation, and commerce – what archaeology's role within the media is thought to be if anthropology and the 'primitive' had not been overlooked by broadcasters so much as replaced by archaeology. What would be the implication of this statement?

To open the discussion in its most basic form, one might say that whereas media executives once looked to anthropology as the voice and image for legitimising Western otherness and claims as to what it is to be human (stimulating a distinction between 'Us' and 'Them', 'Modern' and 'Pre-Modern'), archaeology through advanced visual technologies now serves to either reinforce this traditional ethic in a more cautionary way, or to openly challenge it. Alex Holmes, a BBC executive producer, has commented, 'We need human stories, reflecting the world back to people, with strong narrative' (3WE 2000, 159).

This forms a significant theme in Tim Taylor's 'Screening Biases' in which it is argued that by 'reflecting our own prejudices' through the medium of television, it may be possible to undermine and 'screen them out' from archaeological inference 'by presenting a broader view of what it is to be human'. This, Taylor argues, necessitates an open mind and a distinction between 'sensationalism' and the 'sensational'. Though a matter of perspective, the sensational is among the common aspects of human life that we share – if not by experience then by common knowledge of its existence, such as sex and violence. If deemed 'sensationalism' they would be unworthy of inquisitive scrutiny. The distinction is an important preservative for, in this case, aspects of prehistory that could lose interpretative grounding when a distinction is not in place. The discomfort that Taylor describes towards evidence of cannibalism, for instance, lies in the desire to view the past in light of the present to view ourselves.

Always a controversial topic (see Salmon 2000), discomfort with the archaeology of anthropophagy lies within a perceived universality of humanness. Cannibalism is therefore a focal taboo – an act of self-consumption (Morris 1996: 144), simultaneously unsettling and intriguing. This is personal. And it is the personal, the human, aspect of the past that archaeological programming has succeeded from anthropology. The personal is expounded in narratives such as Howard Carter's ongoing search for King Tutankhamun's tomb in the

BBC's recent *Egypt* series (broadcast in 2005); the retracing of the fate of Ötzi in NOVA's 'Return of the Iceman' (broadcast in 1998); and the uncertain final years of life before the eruption of Vesuvius in Channel 4's 'The Private Lives of Pompeii' (broadcast in 2002). Indeed, the pinnacle moment in each episode of the BBC's *Meet the Ancestors* series is when the viewer is confronted with the bust of a three-dimensional facial reconstruction from the cranial remains of an individual. Since the nineteenth century, the face has been presented in such a way as to signify the nature of the inner human state (Tagg 1988: 37). Presented as an artefact in a darkened room or a specimen in a laboratory, the reconstructed faces hold a plain expression of peaceful, timeless neutrality, a reminder that whatever gruesome events may have led to this person's death, the victim of history is born inherently good (Fig. 1.5). Literally putting flesh onto the past, it is the metaphorical epitome of the journalistic translation of archaeological narrative.

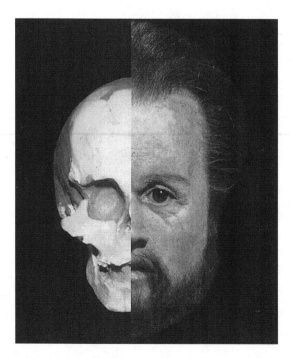

Figure 1.5   A facial reconstruction by Richard Neave from the skull of Philip of Macedonia (John Prag, Manchester Museum and British Museum Press).

There is a broad context in which the changes in fortune of archaeology and anthropology in the media may be understood since a whole pool of serious documentary programming on television in particular has disappeared from the schedules. Third World development and political issues have virtually disappeared, along with global environmental matters (although this latter is now emerging again as a topical issue within the media). Yet archaeology proliferates. Why might this be? First, much of archaeology programming could be regarded as light entertainment rather than serious documentary on serious issues. This may not be desirable, or indeed justifiable in many cases, but may often be the perception. Second, archaeology must be tapping into what programmers generally regard as the dominant collective sentiment. Though it will differ from nation to nation, the reaction to a global present – if reflected in the majority of the most detailed and most successful British archaeological programmes – is one of a distinctly 'local' feel. The archaeological context for these programmes lies predominantly within the British Isles. When these formats, such as *Time Team*, have expanded to 'exotic' international locations, the viewing figures have been notably lower than the domestic stage. Indeed, the appeal of the 'local' to the distinct disadvantage of the 'global' is a marketable product, acknowledged by television executives (3WE 2000: 152, 159):

> I know from past experience that films from the developing world don't bring in the audiences. They're not about us, and they're not usually about things we can do anything about.
> (*Steve Hewlett, director of programmes, Carlton Television*)
> People want domestic stories.
> (*Peter Salmon, former controller, BBC One*)
> Ratings indicate there is a more limited interest in international programmes.
> (*Tim Gardam, former director of programmes, Channel 4*)
> The developing world is not of general interest unless there's a very British angle.
> (*Chris Shaw, senior programme controller, Channel 5*)

Archaeology's presence in the media is clearly not detached from the history of programming, sociopolitical perceptions, market trends, or credibility of other broadcast genres. If archaeology's relation with the media and archaeology's place in a particular historical context are to be fully appreciated, then a comparative analysis and step into media discourse is required. This may prove instructive in future research to provide a clearer understanding as to why some narratives and programme formats are preferred above others, or why archaeology is better suited to be received and favoured by a viewing audience in one particular way rather than another.

Film as an Artefact of Visual Archaeology

A recent document issued by Tessa Jowell, secretary of the British government's Department for Culture, Media, and Sport, argued for the cultural benefits that are gained from government funding of the arts. Reference to film was notable only by its omission from the discussion, despite the citation of museums, music, drama, painting, and opera (Jowell 2004). The reasons for this absence may lie in a distinct opposition between 'entertainment' and 'cultural engagement', reminiscent of the dualism between 'high' and 'low' culture, grouping film as some all-encompassing term for the entertainment of large audiences (Hill 2004). In this view, the visual qualities of film become located within the peculiarities of cultural taste conceived through the inner workings of Bourdieu's 'cultural capital'. The heterogeneity of film is disclosed within Bourdieu's (1984: 271) distinction between '"ambitious" works that demand a large cultural investment' and works 'overtly designed to entertain'. Within this model, film as an expressive form becomes ambiguously situated in a position relative to the other arts, with the potential to become recognised as legitimate art (Bourdieu et al. 1990: 96–97; cf. Hill 2004: 30). However, a hierarchy between different styles of film – industry, entertainment, and art – ultimately creates an uncertainty about its position in relation to other art forms in a hierarchical order of cultural ranking. In spite of this, film has mass appeal whatever its position, and in whatever form is produced, a double status may at once be apparent: that of educator and tool of social improvement, and that of threat to appropriate social norms and requiring censorship and regulation.

It is unsurprising, then, that much of the analysis of archaeological film has been set within this popular distinction, favouring critiques of archaeological representation within cinematic film-as-industry as a result of its popular appeal and excess of repetitive imagery. The importance of these analyses has already been alluded to, but their emphasis has created an imbalance against the consideration of pedagogical films, the novel use of film as cultural commentary and political expression, and film as a document of archaeological practice. If in place of categories of distinction, these film forms were merged together along with the practices of filmmaking and the trajectories of engaged viewing, then their totality would redefine these works as material documents or *sites* for deliberating historiographies of archaeological discourse. Commercial broadcast television is also pulled into this single frame. Traditionally, archaeology is presented within a programming format that embodies many of the conventional strategies of documentary film and the cultural and technical tensions inherent in the presentation of authentic reality.

In a similar way, many of the technological traits and skills associated with photography became embodied by its cinematic successor (Carlson and Gorman 1990) – a sense of the medium within the medium, or what Bolter and Grusin (1999) call *remediation*. This, in conjunction with traditional notions of reality, gives photography a dominant place in the representational field of archaeology and warrants discussion here as a visual form open to be 'read'. Collected together, these elements of film are artefacts of visual archaeology, similar to the principles of what Sherman (1998) calls 'folklore documentary'. This approaches film as a surface reflection or trace of something produced in a specific time and place, 'a reflective process of interpreting ourselves and culture' (1998: 1). Through focus and frame – action and interaction – both on and off the screen, something is revealed about the filmmaker, the object of the work, the audience, and the context of the work's production and reception, each within their own historical situation.

This places five media artefacts of visual archaeology (to which others may be included) within an equal space for reflection, from which layers of meaning may be extracted. These media artefacts offer new insights into past and present archaeological practice, the situation of archaeology in contemporary popular culture, and the currency of novel and traditional documentation media.

Film as Cultural Commentary with Political Expression

In Tom Stern's '"Worldwonders" and "Wonderworlds"', film is explored from the standpoint of 'cultural investment' as a counterbalance to dominant industrial cinematic forms. First, he identifies a number of changing trends in the portrayal and use of archaeology in twentieth century German film, placing these shifts in their historical social context. He then explores an alternative style of film, one that could transcend the dominant categories of representation that have been constructed through 'the repetition of stereotypical imagery', and 'the excessive usage of superlatives, and media-friendly sound-bites'. Stern elucidates a tradition of archaeological filmmaking that since the 1980s has been developed in a series of annual European film festivals, providing 'a link between science, education, museum, film production, and the public' and uniting 'archaeologists and filmmakers, historians and physicians, museum directors, editors and students, interested lay persons and journalists' (Denzer 2004: 39). In recent years, these have proliferated, with at least seven festivals of archaeological film in Europe and the United States in 2005 and the inclusion of a session for material culture and archaeology in the Royal Anthropological Institute International Festival of Ethnographic Film. Stern is looking to identify a mode of filmmaking that does not just represent or portray an idealised world, authenticated through classical forms of cinema and documentary, but one that asks questions of archaeology itself and the practice of investigating the past.

Pedagogical Films

Films used as teaching aids for archaeology students have been in use in institutions at least since Jacquetta Hawkes was commissioned during the Second World War by the British government to make an educational film about prehistoric life in Britain (Hawkes 1946). Pedagogical films, particularly in the 1960s and 1970s (see Allen and Lazio 1983), have been commissioned to provide accessible introductions and guides to all forms of methodological practice and thematic interpretation. When documentary films such as *Archaeology in the Laboratory*, *Advance into the Past: Modern Archaeological Methods* (see Bricker 1973 for a review), *The Survey* (see Clewlow and Cowan 1975 for a review), *The Artefact*, and *The Dig* (see Beale 1975 for a review) are considered along with contemporary introductory texts and practical manuals, the methods of filming, the reasons for their commission, and the methodologies objectified within the films offer an alternative historiography of the changing discursive location of these principles of practice.

In many cases, the sociopolitical relevance of a film may offer alternative views on the accountability of archaeology to its historical context, questioning the received view. For example, while filming *The Beginnings of History*, Hawkes pondered the necessity of its commission, writing that 'it is remarkable that in the middle of a war two Government departments... should undertake a work so apparently unpractical and so little urgent' (quoted in Finn 2000a: 127). With heavy references to invasion and a cleanly 'charm more usually seen in war-time romances' (2000a: 128), it is tempting to hypothesise that when glossed up, the 1940s archaeological narratives could potentially provide a propaganda device for social cohesion in a time of crisis, reflecting concerns of invasion, but simultaneously reassuring with an enduring image of time-honoured British origins.

Searching for Reality in Commercial Broadcast Television

As an artefact of visual archaeology, broadcast television commercially aimed for a mass audience betrays the measure of what may be regarded as an appropriately authentic image of the past. The degrees of reality that are considered stable enough as a stage for the past appear to hold no fixed position. But where lies the reality? Richard Leakey (1983: 162) humorously recounted the choreography for a film shoot of the moment when an Australopithecus skull was first uncovered, whereas on the ninth or tenth 'discovery' of the skull, he finally 'no longer cared if it remained lost for ever'. The question of the 'real' is one that lies deeply at the heart of discontent regarding archaeology's relationship with the media. Is it possible to balance a level of uncertainty with claims of legitimacy for narratives of the past?

Different genres of film have both aspired and alluded to different levels of reality (Corner 2000). To reveal the visible world, the classical realist film of cinema verite relied on an invisibility of form and style, a camera that is forgotten by the viewer, and a narrative to expose the reality to the viewer. The documentary form that many archaeological programmes utilise draws from these conventions, presenting a fiction through an unsteady camera, a crouching trench level shot, the scraping of the trowel. As Caughie (1980) has previously established, these 'apparently unpremeditated' fictions serve to create an impression of 'unproblematic fact' and guaranteed authenticity. The real world is not therefore revealed directly through the mirror of a documentary form, but is presented by reference to other established conventions associated with its reflection.

The conventional procedures of documentary production have become enriched and expanded by computing technology generating the experience of reality with an ever increasing minute exactitude. But even the simulation of realities with the impressive digital technologies of Computer Graphic Imagery (CGI) resort to the 'cinematographic deceits' of film to satisfy the expectation of a viewing audience familiar with film animation (Earl 2005: 214). When 15 million people tuned in to watch the first episode of the BBC's CGI spectacular *Walking with Dinosaurs*, the hyper-realism of cynodonts and Leaellynasaura was viewed with the same 'shortcomings and flaws associated with traditional media,' such as grainy monochrome night footage or the presence of the camera when 'the hot breath of a meat-eating utahraptor steams up the lens' and T-Rex showers the camera with a roar of saliva (Scott and White 2003: 322–323). In each case, a simulated reality bears its presence through the screen.

The assertion of truth and authenticity through the choreography of the real in forms of archaeological documentary is the subject of Angela Piccini's chapter 'Faking It'. Piccini observes the rhythmic landscapes of light, movement, and sound utilised to instil an aura of immediacy in archaeological documentary. Despite the performative tweaks and pulls that are utilised in the documentary strategies for authenticating truth claims, the audience appears to place its faith in dramatised simulated reconstructions – the past in costume. This, Piccini deduces, is due to a 'visual and sonic richness' of slow-motion film, allowing 'the eye to linger on detailed materiality' and 'dramatic sound design'. This is the texture of experience. The presence of immediacy becomes authenticated through the familiarity of the 'grainy visual texture and low lighting and/or sepia tones'. This is the materiality of memory. Simon Schama justifies his preference for traditional film as opposed to digital video by explaining a mode of engagement for the viewer in which 'digital video is not the same.... [T]he plasticity of film... does better approximate the cognitive writing we use when we summon up memories, both public and private' (2004: 29). He is referring to a dream-like state in which recollection is abstract, piecemeal, lacking clarity and focus; tape achieves something 'other than the passive recording of reality' (2004: 30).

Elsewhere, the step towards authentic levels of reality for archaeological truth claims in film has taken a different path towards the broadening genre of 'reality television'. In the 1970s, a BBC production called 'Living the Past' housed a group of people of different social backgrounds in a reconstructed Iron Age village as an experiment to see if the modern citizen could cope with a prehistoric way of life (Percival 1980). The programme was recast in 2001 with a fly-on-the-wattle-wall reality format under the name 'Surviving the Iron Age'[3]. For the purposes of authenticity, the 17 participants were inhibited from carrying out research into Iron Age life before they were filmed spending seven weeks in an alien prehistoric world. As either a social or archaeological experiment, the programme was doomed from the start. After one week – with no background research, only three days of food provisions, and concessions of medication, contraception, and clean water miraculously beamed into the Iron Age – food poisoning, contestation, and foul weather started to take its toll. Subsequently, private medical care and rubber boots were also beamed into the Iron Age. The choice of participant was also questionable. Having entered the Iron Age fiasco, one participant pondered that 'I don't think you can live an Iron Age life-style anymore because there is too much legislation these days'.

Grimacing aside, there is a serious point here in questioning the quality of such programming and its validity to archaeology's relationship with the media. Juliet Gardner, historical consultant for the first recent-history reality programme on British television, *The 1900 House* (first broadcast on Channel 4, 1999), claims that viewers are likely to imagine themselves in the 'particular historical circumstance' in which the participants have been placed, asking, 'What would it have been like for me?' (Gardner, cited in Nelson 2004: 4). This creates a picture of the physical conditions of the past through a passage of empathy and an attachment to the participant's own situation, returning again to what Merriman (1991: 28–29) describes as a means for 'orienting themselves in the present'. However, while the blend of the modern and the past in this particular format holds the potential for a viewer's engagement with the past through distinctly archaeological means – excavating a surface reality and projecting one's background knowledge upon the depth to reveal the contours of the past and the present – the result in this case is that archaeology is resigned to the status of a production prop, the stage for social observation.

It is inevitable that successful television themes become merged together, but *Big Brother* and archaeology have been an unlikely and unsuccessful partnership. At first glance, these genres specifically design 'abnormal terms of living within surveillance space' to study contemporary social interaction by dispensing with the difficulties of separating the personal from the social by creating its own form of the social to extract a particular form of the personal (Corner 2002). Yet the opportunity to observe the 'real' behaviour of people remains illusive since the conditions of such behaviour have been manufactured, creating a new microsocial in which living space becomes performance space. 'Surviving the Iron Age' lacked authenticity because it was never intended to be 'real'. Instead, as Palmer (2003: 23–24) acknowledges, it belonged to a 'product-commodity aimed at consumers,' seeking not diversity or plurality but to 'engage our appetite for the titillating and exploitative' by bringing together 'contestants' that stereotypically represent various opposing communities (e.g., homosexuals and homophobes, Pagan druids and Roman Catholics) with the anticipation of social breakdown, trauma, and conflict. This represents the cautionary tale of an archaeology, albeit a cursory one, entering a media frame that is the direct inverse of contemporary archaeological discourse. Archaeology's relationship with the media is a continual learning process, but examples such as these must be highlighted for both their strengths and their failings and critically analysed to continue an understanding of archaeology's reception within the media and popular culture.

Photographs: Readings and Realities

At least since the seminal works of Berger (1980) and Barthes (1981), the certitude of photographic representation has been put into question. No longer is a photograph merely the consequence or passive document of a combination of mechanical shifts and chemical reactions, but a physical, material artefact resounding with meaning and open to be 'read' and scrutinised as a product of discourse. In order to connect with a form of reality, photographs require a temporal context (Baines 2005; Shanks 1997: 79). The photographic reality is a discursive idea through image. Both the visual primacy of an idea and the quality of imitation or semblance are etymologically linked with the Greek verb 'to see' (Mitchell 1986: 5). The representational power of the image may therefore invoke a tumult of emotion through passion, hatred, fear, and love, transforming the image into a gesture to act. It is no wonder that anxiety often amounts from images that support truth claims to reality.

In Layla Renshaw's 'The Iconography of Exhumation', the emotive quality of images is exposed within the context of Spain's contemporary political economy and the social memory of a crushing civil war. Renshaw delicately pieces together a conflict of images within the threads of a society still in anguish with its own history. As the Spanish Civil War gained notoriety after the 1930s as a testing ground for European ideologies and new weapons under the conditions of war, so too did the press coverage receive an onslaught of critique empowered with hindsight (Aldgate 1979; Bennett 1982; Large 1990: 223–266). In a retrospective essay on Spain's civil war, George Orwell wrote, 'I saw newspaper reports which did not bear any relation to the facts, not even the relationship which is implied in an ordinary lie' (1974 [1938]: 233).

However, Renshaw outlines a current conflict of images between two competing forensic groups in Spain, each exhuming the skeletal remains of its forebears. One is strategically moving away from the objects of Orwell's criticism, emphasising the personal identity of the deceased and the human rights of their living descendents without explicitly expressing political utterance; the other, more overt in its ideological message, emphasises the political affiliation of the deceased. Within the exhumations, the tender bodies bear trauma marks, a 'silent witness' to their own horror. The silent gesture of these images is framed within the media's photographic representations of the graves, removing all trace of 'archaeological, forensic, or even historical methodology', valuing the act of exhumation rather than the process. Then, by deliberately choreographing the juxtaposition of flesh and bone, the living and the dead, the power of the image transcends time by drawing on familiar icons to carefully critique successive governments while maintaining its own historical frame through the secure reality of archaeological science. While Latour (2005: 14) laments that '[t]he beautiful word "reality" has been damned by the too many crimes committed in its name', here at least – in the exhumation of the Spanish Civil War graves – it is striving for forgiveness.

Documents of Archaeological Practice

Considering the contemporaneous invention of photography with the earliest forms of archaeology, it is unsurprising that the photograph has sustained its primacy within archaeological documentation (Bohrer 2005: 189). However, as Miller (1972) has acknowledged, the early documentary capabilities of the photographic medium for archaeology were restricted first by traditional interpretations of reality drawn from eighteenth and nineteenth century notions of truth and the precisions of fine art, and second by the limitations of the medium itself to capture the detail of the feature being presented. Embodying the photographic medium and enhancing it with the properties of motion, the purposeful use of film as an interpretive aid in archaeology has been proposed and utilised numerous times since the 1960s. Varied uses of film include an efficient time-saving recording device for excavations working within limited time frames (Girouard et al. 1973; Hanson and Rahtz 1988; King et al. 1970); the recording of underwater shipwrecks (Gifford 1974); and in ethno-archaeology to penetrate and interpret the world of the 'other' (Pratap 1988). However, film has remained fairly limited in use largely due to cost, varying quality of resolution, and issues of storage, accessibility, and presentation of the films.

Despite these shortcomings, there are a range of interpretive possibilities that are embodied within the stores and catalogues of museum basements and television archives. Many newsreel archives contain a wealth of unique short footage recorded around the world since 1910. Some of this is already available on line and is open for use in the classroom or lecture theatre (see Grant n.d. for appropriate hyperlinks).

In addition to the hours of footage filmed for 10–60 minute broadcast documentary programmes, numerous motion picture films, often high-quality home movies, were recorded during early excavations throughout the world. Sometimes 'limited in scope and context by their silence,' they still remain of 'considerable historical interest today as visual ethnographies of the archaeology of a bygone era' (Beale and Healy 1975: 890). Tarabulski (1989), for example, describes the experience of piecing together film from the 1925–1930 excavations by Alonzo Pond in Algeria for a documentary production 'Reliving the Past: Alonzo Pond and the 1930 Logan African Expedition'. The black-and-white silent films on 16 mm and 35 mm nitrate stock had originally been produced as a visual supplement to the collection of photographs from the excavation. Subsequent interviews with Alonzo Pond re-inscribed contextual meaning to the films, making a historical artefact come alive as an interpretable document of the excavations as well as an historiography of archaeological practice in Africa during the 1920s. In a similar vein, films recorded on excavations by Agatha Christie in Syria during the 1930s and at Nimrud in Iraq during the 1950s are more than interesting artefacts of individual voyeurism. They reveal unknown insights into the everyday life on the excavations, the connections and interactions of excavators and onlookers, unuttered aesthetic interests of the cameraperson, and a record of early archaeological investigations in changing countries (Trümpler 2001).

The archival material for past television broadcasts also offers similar insights, but recent uses of such material point to an additional potential. This became apparent during recent research at Sillbury Hill in Avebury's World Heritage landscape. From 1968 to 1970, four seasons of excavation at Europe's tallest Neolithic man-made mound were broadcast as part of the popular BBC series *Chronicle*. For centuries, local folklore had claimed that the mound concealed a burial with great treasures of a chieftain king, thus attracting a number of audacious excavations in the eighteenth century – the largest being the first, when in 1776 Colonel Drax, the duke of Northumberland, sunk a vertical shaft directly through the centre of the monument, recovering little sign of any burial or magnificent treasures. Following the line of a horizontal tunnel dug at the base of the mound in the nineteenth century, the BBC footage of miners cleaving their way through soil and stone (under the archaeological supervision of Richard Atkinson) was set to make 'television history', with the pinnacle moment being the opening of a central chamber. In an anticlimactic finale, neither chamber, body, nor treasure were found. The shafts were backfilled and Silbury Hill retained its mystery.

More recently, the ethic behind the television sponsorship of this glorified treasure hunt has been firmly placed in question (Smith 2004; Wainwright, in Whittle 1997). There are two key reasons for this, each of which has benefited from a return to the BBC film footage. First, apart from a small popular chapter in the BBC's accompanying book of the *Chronicle* series (Atkinson 1978), a report of the excavation was never published until the difficult task was accepted by Alasdair Whittle (1997) 30 years later. However, most of the original plans and drawings had been lost and many of the photographs and slides were without context or index. But many hours of uncut black-and-white film footage did survive and proved useful in piecing together the unnamed fragments of the archive. According to Whittle (1997: 13; 2005: personal communication), a three-dimensional perspective in the film was hindered due to the cramped conditions of the excavation tunnel, but in conjunction with the site diaries, a clearer context could be salvaged from the audio records of the workers' discussions, individual views, and Atkinson's interviews while inside the tunnel.

The second critique of the excavations appeared after a torrential storm in 2000, when the 1776 shaft reopened as the material covering its entrance twice collapsed into a deep, seemingly bottomless cavern. Investigation by English Heritage concluded that the rainwater had seeped through voids in Atkinson's shaft, possibly a result of poor backfilling in 1970, and a number of large cavities threatened the structural integrity of the whole monument (McAvoy 2005). After alien hunters caused further damage by abseiling into the open shaft in 2001, English Heritage used the film footage in conjunction with seismic technology to assess the changing condition of the 1968–1970 excavation shaft. The results were later broadcast in a documentary on BBC2 called 'The Hill with the Hole'. For Amanda Chadburn (2006: personal communication) who led the investigation, combining the films with the original project design for the *Chronicle* programmes provided a familiarity with the biography of Sillbury's previous investigations and formed a 'reality' of past events, offering an environment for understanding the current instability within the structure. The films now provide a pathway to addressing the lack of detail in the archive by providing a context and subsequent index for the surviving material in Avebury's Alexander Kieller Museum. The Silbury Hill film footage, although maybe not directly intended as an archaeological document, has breathed life and soul into an otherwise fading event. While this may have been an unimagined resource for the construction of future memories, its monochrome tint has become a substitute body for an otherwise silent record.

Archaeology, the Media, and the Digital Future

Writing about the glitzy streets of Paris in 1935, Walter Benjamin mused upon the enticement of the consumer by the display of commodity fetishes: 'Look at everything, touch nothing' (Benjamin 1999 [1935]: 805). Consumers, Benjamin believed, had become epitomised by the mass-flâneur taking delight in the conditions of detachment that provided their frame for spectatorship of the sights laid before them. Capitalism had induced a dangerous 'dream-filled sleep' over Europe, facilitating, among other things, the rise of fascism (1999 [1935]: 391). Society needed to be awakened. In 1936, while the Frankfurt School despised the oppressive forces of media for its legitimisation of fascist claims and prophesised subsequent chaos out of the 'phantasmagoria of false consciousness', Benjamin argued for the positive use of image reproduction technologies to 'shock' and 'illuminate' the collect of mass culture into democratic revolution (Benjamin 1992 [1936]; cf. Buck-Morss 1989: 253). Motion picture film, according to Benjamin, was not only an object for criticism but the medium through which the present state of mass culture could be criticised (Hansen 1987: 182). 'Any man today,' he wrote, 'can lay claim to being filmed' (Benjamin 1992 [1936]: 231), hence upsetting the authoritative chain of hierarchy between the author and the viewer/reader.

Benjamin's important essay of 1936, 'The Work of Art in the Age of Mechanical Reproduction', was not translated into English until 1969, over 30 years after its original German publication. Benjamin's vision of a democratic revolution through technology has only recently enjoyed serious reflection owing to the development of digital technologies of 'image (re-)production' and the globalising effects of communications media. This digital future is here, 'proliferating faster than our cultural, legal, or educational institutions can keep up with them' (Bolter and Grusin 1996: 314). In this final section, we look to how archaeology is equipping itself for the new media world and the effects that this may have on future disciplinary discourse.

Digitising Archaeological Practice

Previously, we outlined how the old medium of film could be brought into a serious analytical frame for archaeological reflection. More recently, new digital audiovisual media have become recognised as an archaeological medium to enhance interpretive capabilities during and after excavation. This is largely due to a combination of discursive trends and the increasing accessibility and affordability of digital technologies. With the view to plurality through a 'reflexive' excavation method, Ian Hodder (1997, 1999, 2000, 2003; also Berggren and Hodder 2003) has consistently argued for 'social engagement' both on and off site in a continual interpretive process that highlights multivocality, interactivity, and contextuality. The methodology incorporates a range of multimedia as integrative devices for tracing this process, attaining what John Cole anticipated film could achieve in the early 1970s if archaeologists turned the camera on both 'their sites and their actions upon them' in the realisation that how a site is dug is just as important as what is recovered (1972: 12). In each case, the goals are similar. Film, according to Cole, can provide 'a fluid, continuous record of excavation progress and process' (1972: 12); digital video, Brill (2000: 229) suggests, can provide a record of 'the daily evolution of the dig as well as the accompanying processes of interpretation and decision-making'.

Digital video is now used as a pedagogical tool for the dissemination of a range of flexible ideas, as well as an integral element in the realisation of the multi-vocal challenge that a reflexive methodology entails (Brill 2000; Nixon 2001; Stevanovic 2000; Witmore 2004). This experimentation with digital technology may appear similar to that of film, but digital technology has many advantages over the old medium. The footage can be edited into manageable chunks and uploaded with ease for either public consumption or professional deliberation. The footage can also be viewed immediately on or off site, allowing the replay of conversations and ideas to be shown between team members in different parts of the site at different times or simultaneously. The expense of reproduction is greatly reduced and a computerised database permits search capabilities and direct access to the archive, as well as its storage in a manageable way.

Through the remediation of old technologies into new, many of the challenges, difficulties, and epistemologies associated with the older medium become reframed and realigned rather than replaced. It takes time for cultural practices to catch up with novel technologies. Virtual reality, for example, has the means to involve the viewer in a participatory experience of architecture reconstructed from material remains (Fig. 1.6), but instead reconstructions invariably reproduce the underlying cartographic principles of traditional excavation photographs, sterilized of human life (Earl 2005: 214–215). Digital ink scanning is replacing hand-drawn diagrams, but more often than not, these are still printed on paper for traditional bound copies of reports. The conditions of onsite practice continues to be altered by the presence of the digital video camera, although – as Brill (2000: 232)

Figure 1.6   Virtual reconstruction within the uncovered remains of a Neolithic settlement at Banpo Museum, Xi'an, China (Timothy Clack).

acknowledges – this is a matter of acclimatisation, alleviated with time as the new medium becomes a familiar or naturalised presence during practice. The question of reality, however, may be entirely reconfigured by the digital medium. Whereas the reproduction of the mise-en-scéne may be choreographed for photographs and film (cleaned, scaled, emphasised, dehumanised), the frail innocence of the photograph is jeopardised when digital images are manipulated with relative ease, constructing an entirely new reality and authorship. Owing to the sheer abundance of imagery that can be produced in digital form, the ambiguity of these themes may be overlooked. The image itself may even be lost or forgotten altogether.

Alternatively, the addition of other metadata – such as a signature or hyperlink to an original – may enhance the authenticity of the image, combining durability, usage, and memory (Tringham forthcoming).

The key issue here is that new forms of media pervade every facet of our everyday lives. Whether it was the analogue technologies of prewar radio or postwar television or today's digital technologies, each has changed the way we perceive and act in the world around us. Different forms of media affect different situations in different ways, but in each case a new opportunity for revealing meaning and creating narratives is brought to light.

One of the classic attempts to understand these associations is in the work and foresight of Marshal McLuhan (1964), whose ideas argued against linear narratives of explanation. Prior to the electronic media, the output of information through media technologies necessitated a mechanised sequential structure with interlinked parts of a whole laid out in a series, one following the other in a linear form. McLuhan's dissatisfaction with this sequential exchange stemmed from its inability to provide explanation with any principle of causality. One mechanical event in the sequence simply resulted in change – a relayed passage of motion from one component to the next. Instead, McLuhan argued that an explanation of causality would emerge when this sequence was broken by the flow of the instant in the 'nuclear age' of electronic media. This form of media could handle many operations at the same time, producing a synchronised, non-sequential information flow moving at such a speed that cultural practices would have to adapt to cope with novel situations.

Crucially, it was not until the advent of a new medium that 'the lineaments and assumptions' of the old medium could be revealed (McLuhan 1960: 567). Indeed, McLuhan notes that 'our practice can be years ahead of our thoughts' (1960: 574), and it is practice that is infiltrated by electronic media with 'personal, political, economic, aesthetic, psychological, moral, ethical, and social consequences... [leaving] no part of us untouched, unaffected, unaltered' (McLuhan 1967: 26). Analysis based on a linear sequence of change was unsuitable for the explanation of these associations. A nonlinear sequence could provide self-understanding of mediation by looking at the manifestation of the process itself. By 'probing' the technologies, their interconnections could be revealed. This was a deconstruction designed not, as Gordon (1997: 302) points out, to 'finish' the hole that the drill makes, but to understand what it 'churns up'. With every new medium, institutional organisation would be transformed, along with 'new patterns of awareness of human association' (McLuhan 1960: 572). Informational studies that looked for understanding in the content of media transmissions were therefore missing *the* key point: that the content of the medium was another medium. The message that was carried by a medium or technology was the particular 'scale or pace or pattern' of change that it brought to human affairs. McLuhan's famous line that 'the medium is the message' emphasised the necessity to understand the medium itself because it is that which 'shapes and controls the scale and form of human association and action', not the information or message that it relays (1964: 9).

McLuhan's work preempted the age of digital media, an age in which Giddens, echoing McLuhan, has recently commented that '[i]nstantaneous electronic communication… alters the very texture of our lives' (1999: 11). As was previously noted, a parallel between the increasing presence of digital technologies in our lives and the presence of archaeology in the media is unlikely to be a coincidence. Setting aside the market forces and audience desire implicit in the resurgence of archaeology in the media, the parallels between the conceptual apparatus of digital systems and the values of postprocessual archaeology are compelling. Hodder (1999: 178–187) identifies no less than nine direct convergences between the goals of 'archaeological theories based on the metaphor of the text' and the framework of these new technologies. These directly concern archaeological practice in a globalised world through the use of multimedia technologies for processing and critically interpreting archaeological data. Deciding upon which intersection of text to follow in hypertext, space blurs the distinctions of authorship of data, empowering the reader as part of the interpretive decision-making process. Similarly, placing data on the Internet makes it accessible and open for contestation and adjustment to multiple viewpoints in a narrative that is collaborative and radial or rhizoidal.

These digital encounters have already been recognised for their potential in archaeological pedagogy. At the grass roots, archaeological teaching has been criticised for remaining in a methodology of linear information exchange even though the technologies of teaching have changed significantly in the last 30 years (Fagan 2000). With this hierarchical form of preaching, the lecture hall creates 'an intellectual chasm between student and teacher', whereas a future pedagogical philosophy would place the student at the centre of a net of resources (including the instructor) interacting with materials and ideas in a nonlinear flow of information and multimedia (Clarke 2003; Michaels and Fagan 1998). This appears an appropriate model for a new generation of students already relatively media savvy and taking responsibility for their own learning. As Pickering (1997: 56) remarks, 'When a difficulty arises adults are likely to say "where's the manual?" Children are more inclined to say "let's ask the computer"'.

Elsewhere, broadband technologies have generated an added incentive for prospective benefactors to invest in archaeological work, creating a mutually beneficial relationship between recipients. For example, the Archaeology Channel, an online information resource, obtained underwriting support through commercial companies by designing video productions of the funded work that may be marketed as a presentation of public outreach. One of these films is *A Journey Through Time: Archaeology at St. Johns*, a 15-minute documentary about a late prehistoric Chinookan village near Portland, Oregon. This film was produced for CH2M Hill, which provided partial funding for the excavations – the financing of which allows a level of self-sustainability for the Archaeology Channel, while projecting an archaeological story to a wider public (Prouty 2005)[4].

So much data: input, output, upload, download, link, hyperlink, file, transmit, transmute, troubleshoot, search, save, send, receive. Where does one begin? In 'Digital Media, Agile Design, and Politics of Archaeological Authorship', Michael Shanks looks at the materiality and interconnectivity of media during the decision-making processes in the creative design of cybersystems for data consumption. The material qualities of media technologies, Shanks explains, are deeply embedded in the course of processing information. Changes in technology extend a new world of engagement with information. As Lupton (1995: 99) suggests, our own bodies even become inscribed with particular forms of media (a PC, for example) to the degree that media forms from previous engagement (pens, for instance) become awkward and unfamiliar, or inadequate extensions of the self. Rather than defining a process of collection or presentation of data, Shanks argues for an interactive process of translation. Through this engagement, assumptions and preconditions that lie historically embedded within the categories of data may be freed from the constraints of essentialism in a creative experience of democratic pluralism.

A Digital Democratic Discourse?

Many of the visions for a future digital world resonate of the contrasting arguments during the early twentieth century. On one side is a democratic utopia, an openness of free speech and transparency of information – a unity through diversity. On the other side are alienation, privatisation, and overpowering surveillance. Somewhere in between lies contextualisation of the cultural situation of democracy and multi-vocality of opinion – what Giddens (1999) calls the democratisation of democracy.

In the 1960s, Habermas (1989 [1962]) lamented the transformation of rational public discourse from a forum of enlightening discussion into the marketing of legitimating discourses by exercising public relations upon the stage of commercialised entertainment. At the same time, however, the technology of Informatics was moving towards a new field of communication and social relations. In 1969, the first commercial satellite was launched into the earth's hemisphere. More than 200 now link people and their machines – a network of interconnected political, technological, and cultural practice – i.e., globalisation (cf. Giddens 1999: 11). The impacts of the associations between the media that we create and the mediations that create our social framework are transforming the way we live our lives and the course of archaeological futures. If this entails a democratised democracy of narrative and archaeological practice, which indeed it should, then the media's relation to this process will be a driving force.

In one of the most radical document statements by a public service broadcaster in 80 years, the BBC recently outlined its perspective on the future of digital broadcast technologies (BBC 2004). It was predicted that the two phases of a digital revolution will have taken place by 2012 when the switch from analogue to digital in the UK will be complete (2004: 54). The first phase took place during the early to mid-1990s, when improvements in the distribution and mobility of digital technology provided a wider level of consumer choice. The second phase – characterised by an increasing number of the population adopting the technologies of the first phase, and more importantly the rapid growth of high-speed broadband opening access to a 'potentially limitless range of programmes, services and content on demand' – has only just begun. The BBC's (2004: 8–9) foresight is exciting and dynamic, arguing that

> [i]nteractivity, effortless communication and sophisticated consumer content creation will all become ubiquitous in digitally-enabled homes.... [This] will include new ways to involve people in civic processes and institutions, personalised learning tools, access to previously closed archives, new ways of connecting communities, more convenient ways to watch and listen to programmes, more localised content, tailored services for minority groups.

Soon digital TV and radio will offer the same flexibility as the Internet, empowering users with the choice of where and when they wish to watch any particular programme (2004: 51). The BBC expects that by 2016, seven in ten homes will be able to set their own viewing or listening schedules (Fig. 1.7). Audio-video downloads and fileshares, and the increasing portability of the Internet and on-demand video – such as personal video recorders, mobile phones, and podcasts – opens an unprecedented level of choice to an engaged audience. In addition, interactive TV brings the nonlinear logic of hypertext into the viewing experience, enabling non-teleological encounters with archaeological narrative.

At present, more than half the population in the UK has digital TV and Internet in its homes, four million of which have broadband access (Ofcom 2004). However, engaging future generations with traditional television programming will become much harder with a fragmented audience showered with choice. Declining viewing figures may be expected for individual archaeology programmes, but with a simultaneous increase in the number of people watching archaeology programmes in general. The future of viewing fashions poses a challenge for archaeology in the digital age. News media may resort to commercial strategies of 'partisan news' to entice audiences, while archaeological programmes that represent the frontispiece to a viewing journey may become even less concerned with quality and content. This is a risk justified by surveys indicating that homes with digital media tend to watch less serious or 'high ground' programmes than homes with traditional analogue (BBC 2004: 54–58). The challenge is for archaeological programming to continue to innovate in style and content, building on its already substantial market and popular interest in order to maintain its appeal in a multi-choice broadcast environment.

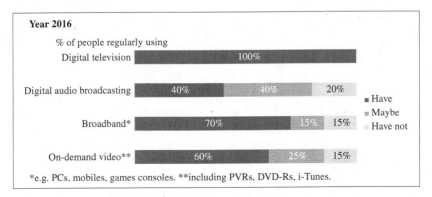

Figure 1.7   Estimated use of digital media by 2016 (BBC 2004: 51).

It might be that the future of interactive archaeological experience lies beyond traditional television programming formats. Indeed, television itself appears to have declining relevance in the lives of many young people. In research carried out by the BBC in 2004, over the space of a decade, children between the ages of 10 and 15 consumed over 20 per cent less television per week (BBC 2004: 91). One probable reason for this, the research concluded, may be the wider range of media technologies that many children now have in their bedrooms in comparison to their parents' living room (BBC 2004: 53). Video games are one such media device. In another BBC survey, 59 per cent of 6–65 year olds play computer games of one sort or another, with a total of 26.5 million 'gamers' in the UK (Pratchett 2005: 5).

In 'The Past As Playground', Andrew Gardner describes how images of the past that have been propagated from archaeological pursuits have infiltrated the passivity of video game leisure time. Yet in many cases these images are an array of curiosities and disturbances of the past. Gardner suggests that this use of the past and archaeological situations by gaming industries indicates not only an embedded interest, but also an opportunity for new narratives of the past to be explored among the 'gamer', console and screen. 'Diverse and challenging visions of past societies' may be opened to and through the gamer in a learning experience, particularly where anticipation in simulations results in a different ending to the past upon every visit.

Uncertain Futures

Digital broadband technologies may soon be the media norm for viewing patterns and the rapid dissemination of information at all levels of society. These have been described as a citizens' medium, or what Žižek (2004) has called a 'netocracy'. Indeed, with 32 million Americans publishing and reading Internet 'weblogs' and one-third of Americans below the age of 40 using the Internet as their main source of news, these are unsurprising claims (Himmelsbach 2005; Pew Research Centre 2005; Shanks, this volume). In many cases, these developments will restructure not only the way archaeological information is presented and consumed, but also the way it is created. The power of this medium is reflected in the growing number of reported 'cyber dissidents' who express views or write news reports news 'deviate from the government line' in countries regarded by Reporters Without Borders as 'enemies of the Internet'. At least 1,006 cases of censorship were reported, in 2005, while on the first day of January 2006, 70 cyber dissidents were in jail around the world (Reporters Without Borders 2006: 6–7). It is no surprise that demon and *demos* have the same etymology (cf. Latour 2005).

Digital cyberspace simulates realities and miracles; it does not spontaneously manifest them. In many regards, the future is uncertain. The expertise necessary to design and function digital technologies, and dominant programming systems required for their function in addition to their cost, could prove to marginalise rather than empower multiple communities around the globe. Similarly, the shrinking of public space through centralisation by large, unelected multinational media corporations leaves the visions of a future 'democratising medium' in the balance. Assessing the future importance of public service broadcasters, for instance, the BBC estimates that by 2010 'substantial parts of UK broadcasting will be owned by large global companies (BBC 2004: 58).

Giddens forewarns that a digital world brings with it new responsibilities to avoid a future parallel between the 'Global Village' and 'Global Pillage' (1999: 16). Already deeply accountable to globalising processes (Olsen 2001), archaeology's role with the media will change in tandem with media technologies of global communication. So too will the way that archaeology is practiced, produced, and presented. It is essential that archaeology broaden and extend its understanding of its location to such transfers in the future.

Notes

1. http://www.thebritishmuseum.ac.uk/buriedtreasure/ (accessed Sept 2005).
2. http://www.timesonline.co.uk/pdfs/graduates.pdf (accessed Sept 2005).
3. http://www.bbc.co.uk/history/programmes/surviving_ironage/ (accessed June 2006).
4. The film may be viewed online at http://www.archaeologychannel.org/content/video/stjohns.html (accessed June 2006).

PART I

ARCHAEOLOGY'S RECEPTION
OF THE MEDIA

2

AN ARCHAEOLOGICAL
FASHION SHOW

How Archaeologists Dress and
How they are Portrayed in the Media

Cornelius Holtorf

Introduction

This chapter is about the portrayal of archaeologists on TV and in
newspapers, with a particular emphasis on their clothing styles
(for a broader discussion, see Holtorf forthcoming). The distinctive archaeological wears shown in the media reflect different perceptions of what an archaeologist does. Archaeological fashion
evokes particular themes governing the image of archaeologists
both in the media and in other realms of society. Intriguingly,
much the same dress styles can also be found in the way archaeologists dress in real life, and that too will be discussed in his
paper.

Throughout society, statements made through fashion contain
significant social and personal messages. As the widespread popularity of formal and informal uniforms shows, clothes are a key
aspect of peoples' identities. Often they are indicative for the self-
perceptions and aspirations of those wearing them. At the same
time, the clothes of others are perceived and interpreted in ways
that may be unintended but can be highly informative. In many

situations, people choose their own way of dressing, yet what they wear is at the same time closely related to collective perceptions and social conventions. If we really live in an emerging *Experience Economy*, as has been argued (Pine and Gilmore 1999: 55–56), the integrity of the customer experience depends in parts on role-appropriate clothing.

Archaeologists do not wear formal uniforms and make choices of what they want to wear each day. Despite this apparent freedom, there is no endless variety in how they dress. Archaeological clothing expresses how archaeologists see themselves and which role they wish to play in society. This paper is only a first attempt at coming to terms with archaeological fashion. I am fully aware that both theoretically and empirically there is a lot more research to be done in this field. At this point though, I enjoy the privilege of sketching out a topic in some of its most interesting dimensions, while still being somewhat naive about the true variety and complexity of archaeological fashion, its full social significance, and the body of secondary literature about fashion and clothing in various professions – and in society generally – that no doubt already exists.

Schlampiges Räuberzivil or *Uniformierte Krawattenheinis*?

How significant archaeological fashion and the image it conveys is to the archaeologists themselves can be demonstrated by the attention it has already received in several previously published papers as well as on electronic discussion forums. Heated discussions can emerge among professionals concerning the question how one should (or should not) dress as an archaeologist. For example, when David Webb published some of his images in *The Archaeologist* – the newsletter of the British Institute of Field Archaeology (IFA) – in 1996, they created an animated discussion (see Fig. 2.1)[1]. Whereas some felt that they ring particularly true, others argued that the numerous breaches of health and safety regulations and poor living conditions reflected badly on the IFA and the 'good practice' and professionalism the organisation was trying to promote (Swain 1997). Martin Biddle and Birthe Kjøbye-Biddle (1997), for example, wrote a letter in which they argued:

> This is precisely the kind of image which damages our profession. It reinforces stereotypes about archaeologists in the eyes of the general public and of other professionals, not least in the development and construction industries from which over 90 per cent of archaeology's funding now comes.

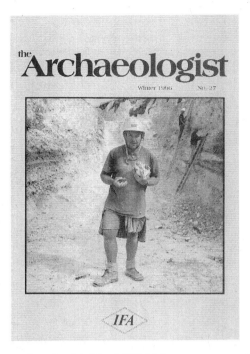

Figure 2.1   The archaeologist (David Webb).

Similar issues surfaced again more recently in a discussion on the German electronic discussion forum *arch-de* in February 2003. The arguments raged between those advocating a professional image of an archaeologist wearing appropriately 'neat' clothes like 'insurance reps or doctors', and others who were not prepared to give up their beloved army wear with many 'practical', large pockets and other useful features (cf. Russell 2002a: 50). What some considered as 'scruffy old stuff' (*schlampiges Räuberzivil*) – signifying a desperate desire to be different from the rest of society – was described as 'comfortable' clothes in line with public expectations by others, who in turn mocked those in suits as 'tie idiots in uniform' (*uniformierte Krawattenheinis*). The latter responded by insisting that only neat packaging in 'middle-class outfits' can express the credibility of a respectable profession and thus lead to success in tough financial negotiations.

A very similar, and similarly heated, debate took place on the *British Archaeological Jobs Resource* discussion forum about one year later (in

February 2004)[2]. Some snippets from that discussion are extremely revealing for the issues that are at stake here (all spelling as in original).

> [W]e are treated with a degree of amusement and even contempt by many developers and developer contractors. In fact anyone who's worked in this game long enough will have encountered such prejudice towards us. One of the reasons for this, is that they see many archaeologists dressing and behaving like a bunch of twats.... I have been rather embarrassed at times by the way my colleagues have been dressed like a bunch of ******* crusties in the presence of the people who pay their wages. Ive seen them roll on to sites tattooed, pierced, smelly, and with a certain style of dress that labels them as having had a privileged upbringing.... Theyll take us all a lot more seriously if you stop looking like drug-addled, shambolic idiots.

> Pay me the 40,000 a year the developers are on then come back and talk to me about dressing like them. I wear combats, knackered t-shirts etc because they are cheap and hard wearing. I also work **** hard and know my stuff and can say without a shadow of a doubt that some of the hardest working, knoweldgable and able archaeologists I have worked with have piercings, tattoos etc, in addition I have met some really useless wastes of space who look nice and tidy and shave every day.

> I didn't intend to suggest that people who dress in a certain way are lazy, because that's clearly not true. It's more that I often get the feeling that they share an unspoken attitude that those who have dreads are the guardians of some mystical flame of archaeological authenticity, while anyone who doesn't is in some way a part-timer who is not fully immersed in the 'real' archaeological lifestyle.

> On many occassions people have said to me things like: 'My god your not wearing sandals'. 'You haven't got a beard'. 'Your the only archaeologist I have met who looks comfortable in a suit'. With my first fee cheque as a consultant gues what I bought – a Jaeger suit.

> For too long, archaeology has suffered at the hands of beardy tree hugging types who only care about the new Levellers album and where their next pint of cider is coming from. Since PPG16, archaeology has been forced to work within the planning process to get any money at all for sites at risk. The developers (the people who pay for all the archaeology that gets done) have this image of the old school hippy archaeologist. To them, we are little more than a joke profession to be largely ignored or trivialised.... The best way to get more digging done properly is to at least look like we know what we are doing. This doesnt mean turning up on site looking like you've come straight from a four day rave. You can still be a crusty, goth, or dress up as a balrog in the evenings and at the weekend. Its a job like any other, not a lifestyle.

Whereas all archaeologists agree that the suit is not appropriate while working in the field, there is no agreement whether or not it is the appropriate fashion statement in more formal contexts either. Behind this are assumptions about the significance and meaning of two major archaeological fashion styles: suit-and-tie *manager wear* on the one hand and scruffy but practical *field wear* on the other. Through the clothes the archaeologist wears, important messages are conveyed that all relate to one central question that is as of now unresolved, both among the professionals themselves and in the media: is archaeology a job for professionals (Fig. 2.2) or a life-style for dedicated individuals (Fig. 2.3)? If the latter, one might expect archaeologists to wear similar clothes when they are not in the field. This is a hypothesis that can be tested. An admittedly small survey of 29 archaeologists revealed that more than half admitted to looking always (4) or often (13) like they are in the field even when they are not. A substantial minority (12), on the other hand, agreed with the statement 'I might be an archaeologist but I don't want to look like one'[3]. This test has thus proven less than conclusive.

Many archaeologists are very aware of archaeology's fashion conflicts. Some will openly speak about their particular strategies – among them John Walker, chief executive of the York Archaeological Trust. Although he wore a suit and tie when I met him in 2003, according to his own testimony, he comes from an archaeological subculture that he calls 'the drunks' and which is distinct from another such subculture that he calls the 'young managers'. His maxim is that as archaeologists we need to use the widely held image(s) of archaeology to our advantage. When meeting politicians, for example, it is not necessarily the best strategy to wear suit and tie in order to state that 'I am one of you', since they are far better at dressing in this style anyway. In such circumstances, Walker therefore prefers to wear what he calls 'normal' clothes, since it gives him the advantage of coming across as 'a little peculiar' and as 'the eccentric archaeologist', incorporating some of the stereotypes of archaeologists that abound in popular culture. For the same reason, he says, to have a beard is an asset for any male archaeologist (see Fig. 2.4).

'We're Complete Scruffbags'

For the business of archaeology, as for other businesses, TV coverage is the single most significant way in which messages about its character are being conveyed to very wide sections of the population. In 2001–2002, two adventures of the film archaeologist Indiana Jones were each watched by an audience of more than 10 million British

Figure 2.2   Professional archaeologist wearing manager style (David Webb).

Figure 2.3   Digging archaeologist wearing field wear (David Webb).

Figure 2.4   Bearded archaeologist wearing normal clothes (David Webb).

people, resulting in rankings among the top ten programmes shown on BBC1 during that year. In addition, in 2001 alone the five terrestrial British TV channels taken together broadcast 31 series and 19 single documentaries with archaeological content (Council for British Archaeology 2006: personal communication). According to another study, between 1998 and 2002, a stunning 651 archaeological documentary programmes (including repeats and episodes within series) were scheduled on the four British channels BBC1, BBC2, Channel 4, and ITV. The most popular ones attracted more than five million viewers (Kulik 2003). Probably even higher figures could be cited for some historical documentaries. In this light, it is hardly surprising that in 2001 the First World Congress of History TV Producers celebrated historical documentaries as 'the new rock "n" roll', being one of the few thriving sectors of the media (Willis 2001). Film historian Karol Kulik (2005) argued accordingly that the period roughly from 1995 to 2001 should be considered a 'golden age' of archaeology in the British mass media.

The TV documentary series *Time Team*, which Tim Taylor has been producing for Channel 4 since 1993, arguably revolutionised the portrayal of archaeology in the British media[4]. More than 100 episodes have been filmed of this ordinarily 50-minute programme. According to data supplied by Channel 4, episodes broadcast in spring 2003 still attracted regularly around 3.4 million viewers and a very impressive 15–20 per cent total market share (on average, 51 per cent of the viewers were male and 56 per cent were between 16 and 54 years old). These are astonishing figures, especially if you take into account that Channel 4's *Big Brother* series, then promising real sex on camera (broadcast after 10:00 PM), attracted in May 2004 a very similar figure of 3.3 million viewers, or a 15 per cent audience share!

During the 1990s, *Time Team* has brought archaeology to the people in a way that had previously been unthinkable. Through *Time Team*, archaeology has become a part of British everyday culture, says Peter Addyman (whom I met in York in 2003). In the past, local farmers may not have been all that interested in archaeology on their land and onlookers of an excavation project may have asked questions like 'Have you found any gold yet?' Since the success of *Time Team*, Addyman explained, archaeologists are welcomed with the question 'Will you do a geophys?' The normal *Time Team* format is a one-hour programme documenting a three-day archaeological excavation at a chosen site in the UK, but there have also been episodes filmed abroad and *Time Team Specials* with live reporting over the course of several days or showing what goes on 'behind the scenes'. The special characteristic of the *Time Team* format is that, on each site, a fairly down-to-earth, local historical question is being investigated by excavating in front of the cameras. The regular team featured in the series consists of presenter Tony Robinson and professional archaeologists Mick Aston, Carenza Lewis, and Phil Harding (see Fig. 2.8 below), all of whom have become minor (if not major) British celebrities. In addition, there is a large team of support staff and a pool of experts that are consulted when evidence in their area of expertise comes to light. Besides excavations, the programmes also involve experiments and demonstrations with re-created techniques and reconstructed artefacts.

The enormous popularity of the series has a lot to do with two factors in particular. First, *Time Team* thrives on the notion of archaeologists discovering a series of material clues and gradually solving a hidden mystery, usually with the help of science. Second, *Time Team*'s appeal also relies on some very special personalities involved – particularly Tony Robinson, who gets so reliably excited whenever new discoveries are made and has a very down-to-earth attitude, mediating between the viewers and the archaeological experts. The archaeologists are colourful personalities and interesting to watch, not the least because of what they wear. *Time Team* celebrates the dirt and the mud as well as the gradual process of learning about local history by investigating material clues. The field archaeologists shown in this series, as in many other documentary series, are characterised by clothes that are not very trendy and often deliberately unfashionable. In other words: varieties of field wear (see Fig. 2.8 below).

Time Team presenter Tony Robinson once said that you could distinguish archaeologists by their poor dress and terrible haircuts. Mick Aston, one of the *Time Team* heroes and famously sporting hand-knitted sweaters (Fig. 2.5), admitted that 'we're complete scruffbags'. Significantly, as many other archaeologists too could have said, he added, '[B]ut I don't care. I'm not remotely interested in appearances, life's too short for that'[5]. As John Walker knows, even when archaeologists do wear suits, they can appear looking odd and somewhat out of place in an environment of professional suit wearers like managers and politicians.

Figure 2.5   Mick Aston (right) in one of his trademark sweaters (Teresa Hall).

Timeless Medieval Peasants?

Not seldom, field archaeologists find themselves in situations that are seemingly closer to 'nature' and more 'primitive' than how we normally live today. In this sense, too, the archaeologist can appear to be 'out of this world' (Stern and Tode 2002: 77). Intriguingly, field wear can be taken to show how properties (or stereotypes) of the period being investigated are transferred onto the archaeologist. Colourful Vikings who once experienced adventures and made discoveries, having had to cope with the many challenges of their lives and wearing Thor hammers around their necks, are being excavated by colourful archaeologists who are engaged in adventurous fieldwork and make discoveries, having to cope with the many challenges of their projects and wearing Thor hammers around their necks (Petersson 1994: 61, 70–71). For some, these convergences may even imply a privileged understanding of the past being investigated. On the other hand, as recently stated on the *British Archaeological Jobs Resource* discussion group, '[J]ust because I don't choose to dress as a medieval peasant doesn't mean I can't understand the archaeology of a medieval site'[6]. However that may be, archaeologists in the field certainly tend to look odd and maybe even exotic in their all-weather gear or combat clothes, unshaven or only half-dressed (Petersson 1994: 39) and occasionally sporting ancient designs tattooed on their bodies.

The actual look of archaeological diggers in the field has been well documented in David Webb's photograph series *Diggers* showing real archaeologists on excavations (see Figs 2.1–2.4, 2.6, 2.8 below)[7]. Interestingly, archaeological field wear does not appear to be subject to the same kind of fast fashions to which the rest of clothing tends to be subjected. British archaeologist Francis Pryor (2001: 28) has been looking back and stated about the experience of excavating three decades ago:

> Most of us wore heavy boots, tattered shorts made from cut-off jeans, and old T-shirts that might once have been coloured. Nowadays, when I look at photos of the team, I'm surprised by how little our appearance has dated, when compared with the images in the flossy magazines of the time, which invariably appear extreme and ridiculous. A 1970s field archaeologist could readily slip unnoticed into a twenty first-century team.

There is one major exception to this continuity though, for recently an altogether new kind of clothes has come to be associated with field archaeology. In Sweden and beyond, archaeologists in the field are increasingly wearing protective gear in very bright luminous colours that are designed akin to the clothes of workers employed on road construction or building sites (Fig. 2.6). This fashion style can also be reduced to a bright vest or helmet combined with either manager or field wear (see Fig. 2.1). Such *health-and-safety wear* signifies the competent professional operating in a professionally managed working environment; it also makes archaeologists highly visible in their role as the 'Heritage Police' on building sites. Depictions in newspapers and TV documentary series like *Time Team* are increasingly showing the archaeologist at work wearing this kind of protective clothing. However, that particular appearance has not yet made it prominently onto the big screen. The cinema (and video/DVD) screen is still mostly the realm of a rather different set of archaeological clothing.

Figure 2.6   Professional archaeologist wearing health-and-safety wear (David Webb).

The Great Outdoors

Without much doubt, Indiana Jones's famous fedora is the single most significant dress element of the quintessential movie adventurer and archaeologist. In the wake of Indy's cinematic popularity, authentic fedoras are also available commercially.

The Holy Grail of Indy hats...THE HERBERT JOHNSON FEDORA! Imported from England from the hatters of the royal family, the Herbert Johnson has been difficult to obtain and highly sought after by Indy fans. It is well known that the Herbert Johnson Hat Shop in London was the source for the original film-used hats.... I will be glad to style your hat for you.... Here are the distinct Fedora Styles you can choose from:

- 'ROTLA Dress': This means Raiders of the Lost Ark style, but nice and neat and straight. The crown is pinched tightly in the front.
- 'ROTLA Raven Bar': This means styled like the hat used in the Raven Bar scene and the Peru scenes in the opening of the movie. The brim is lop-sided but the crown is fairly neat.
- 'ROTLA Cairo': This means styled like the hat used in the Cairo street scenes, and the truck chase. The brim is lop-sided, and the crown is very beat-up and dishevelled-looking[8].

The fedora characterises the archaeologist in a way very different than that discussed in the first section of this paper. The adventure hero dresses in colonial style, often resembling exploration, safari, or indeed camping gear. Besides Indiana Jones, Lara Croft has been prominently modelling such *adventure wear*. As Michael French (n.d.) put it, '[I]f Indiana Jones's khaki and leather outfit is in line with the outdoors wear of the 1930s, which it is, then Lara's khaki shorts, boots, and spandex are the very definition of 1990s adventure wear'. Key elements of that look are the sun protection on the head – preferably fedora or pith helmet, the 'practical' shirt and trousers with many pockets, the solid boots, and the earthen khaki-colours that all pieces have in common. Colonial-style clothing is so closely linked to archaeology that German photographer Wilfried Beege 'naturally' chose an actual excavation in Egypt as a backdrop for his fashion shoots (Fig. 2.7).

The traditional archaeological adventure wear not only evokes colonial times, but also the great time of travelling at the turn of the last century and of course the more recent image of the Camel man (Stern and Tode 2002: 72). Today, the adventurous look has often

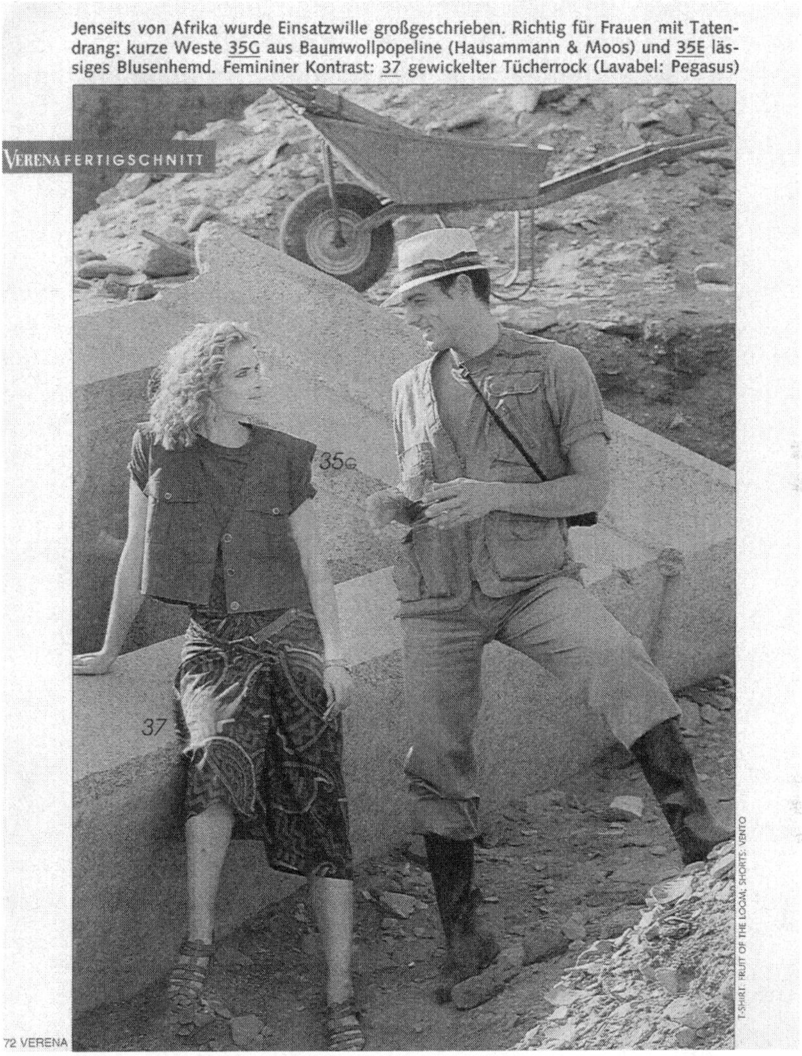
Jenseits von Afrika wurde Einsatzwille großgeschrieben. Richtig für Frauen mit Tatendrang: kurze Weste 35G aus Baumwollpopeline (Hausammann & Moos) und 35E lässiges Blusenhemd. Femininer Kontrast: 37 gewickelter Tücherrock (Lavabel: Pegasus)
VERENA FERTIGSCHNITT
35G
37
T-SHIRT: FRUIT OF THE LOOM; SHORTS: VENTO
72 VERENA

Figure 2.7 Colonial-style fashion depicted against the backdrop of an actual excavation site in Egypt (from *Verena* magazine, May 1990 [W. Beege]).

strong sexual connotations. Whereas Indiana Jones represents female fantasies about strong, good-looking, and resourceful male heroes, Lara Croft is the female adventurer featuring a body corresponding with the desires of many males. Even in an explicit pornographic context, photographers and web designers have been known to give their girls the image and outfit of an archaeologist. An example is Kyla, the intern archaeologist: 'Archaeology has never been so hot!'[9]

Today, if you want to create an archaeologist recognisable at first glance, adventure wear is the look you choose – as so many caricatures demonstrate (DeBoer 1999; Russell 2002a: 49-50). Even archaeologists themselves can find the adventure look irresistible. For example, between the mid-1980s and early 1990s, Swedish archaeologist Göran Burenhult produced a series of beautiful coffee-table books and TV documentaries about his research that combined archaeological fieldwork in Sweden with ethnoarchaeological explorations on various islands in the Pacific, especially Papua New Guinea and the Trobriand Islands. His investigations tended to involve Land Rover and helicopter rides as well as cruises on his yacht. Often being seen to wear variations of adventure wear, Burenhult is now the best-known professional archaeologist on Swedish TV. With his special interest in the inhabitants of paradise-like islands of the Pacific, Burenhult took the archaeology/exotic adventure connection further than most of his colleagues.

In Germany, too, the adventurer image of the archaeologist is very prominent. On German TV, archaeology is often portrayed within the mindscape of exotic place – exciting adventure – spectacular discovery. The image of the archaeologist in Germany is often a mixture of Heinrich Schliemann, Howard Carter, and Indiana Jones: they are 'exotic beings' carrying out exotic work (Schmidt 2000: 241; see also Stern and Tode 2002). This is particularly true for several very successful TV series associated with writer Gisela Graichen, among them *C14 – Advances into the Past: Archaeological Discoveries in Germany* (several series, broadcast since 1992) and *Schliemann's Heirs* (several series, broadcast since 1996).

C14 was the first ever TV series dedicated to archaeology in Germany. Up to 1.7 million viewers turned on their television sets for each episode, corresponding to around 10 per cent of the adult market (14-49 years old). In each 30-minute episode, several short reports about different archaeological projects were presented. The *C14* series effectively married professional archaeology in Germany and its scientific methodologies with popular stereotypes of archaeology, emphasising exciting quests for historical treasures and revelations by scientists about secrets of the past. Graichen (1999: 17, my translation) explained once that 'today, the adventure of archaeology consists not – only – in finding gold treasures. The treasure consists of the insights which high-tech methods can deliver about our past'.

This approach was continued in *Schliemann's Heirs*, where already the title referred to the best-known stereotypical archaeologist in Germany. The name of Heinrich Schliemann still evokes a range of colourful associations about digs in foreign places, rediscovering lost empires, hidden golden treasures – and the eventual rewards of persisting with a controversial quest against much scholarly opposition and many practical obstacles. It was hardly surprising then that this series managed to attract regularly an even larger audience of around five million viewers, or around 15 per cent overall market share (again, 10 per cent of the adult market). *Schliemann's Heirs* broadened out from archaeology in Germany and embraced German projects carried out abroad. After all, Graichen (1993: 14, my translation) knew that 'the search for the traces of the past is more likely to be touched by a sense of adventure when history is more distant from us – both in time and space'.

The approach towards archaeology taken in all these films is well illustrated by some book and chapter titles of the accompanying publications: *Treasure Hunters in Germany*; *Schliemann's Heirs and the Message of the Lost Cities*; *Angkor, the Atlantis in the Jungle*. Graichen makes frequently explicit references to the Indiana Jones archaeological stereotype. For example, two chapter titles in one of the accompanying books (Graichen and Hillrichs 1999) refer to the German title of *Raiders of the Lost Ark* (in German: *Jäger des verlorenen Schatzes*): 'Der Jäger des vergrabenen Schatzes' and 'Das Tal des verlorenen Baches'. Graichen's TV programmes and associated book publications have grown out of a long tradition of depicting the life and work of scientist/adventurers on their foreign explorations. That tradition is not restricted to Germany but it has been particularly popular there, even over recent decades (Stern 2002, this volume). Immediately after World War II, C.W. Ceram (1980) wrote his 'fact-based archaeological novel' in this broad genre, as did later followers such as Philipp Vandenberg and Rudolf Drößler.

I remember, throughout my childhood, watching numerous episodes of a TV series entitled *Countries, Humans, Adventures* (*Länder, Menschen, Abenteuer*) reporting about people in exotic places around the world, their cultures and ancient monuments, and attempts by anthropologists, archaeologists, and others to find out more about them. Amazingly, after more than 400 episodes since 1975, this series is still running. Since 1982, the rival public TV station (ZDF) in Germany has produced a series called *Terra X*, adopting a similar general format. It likewise became very popular, attracting similar viewer numbers as *Schliemann's Heirs*, and is still running. Various sorts of documentaries such as *Terra X* are currently shown under the label *ZDF Expedition*[10]. The ZDF homepage for archaeology can be found following the online tree *Knowing & Discovering > History & Adventure > Archaeology*. The words used in all these titles are of course not coincidental but characteristic for the theme of adventure. No wonder, then, that archaeologists on German TV often look like adventurers on camping safaris.

Clearly, such marvellous celebrations of exotic adventures are a far cry from *Time Team*. Nothing, it seems, could be further from the scruffbag image of the archaeologist than the neatly dressed Western professor exploring exotic worlds. However, fashion styles depicted in the media are not pure but often ambiguous. The same clothes can occasionally be interpreted in different ways. For example, Stephanie Moser (2006: personal communication), an archaeologist specialising in representations, described even *Time Team* star excavator Phil Harding as an explorer and adventurer (Fig. 2.8).

> With his long hair, leather jacket, jeans, hat and strong regional accent, this fieldworker lives up to the popular conception of what it means to be an archaeologist. The cowboy type hat that he wears is of particular significance as a symbol of adventure and exploration.

When adventurers return from the field (after the summer or after their youth), they tend to be pure scholars. The scholar wears a jacket and tie or, better, a bow tie – *scholar wear* (Fig. 2.9). Not infrequently, glasses and a beard adorn this character too, as in the case of Indiana's father Professor Henry Jones. With increasing age, archaeologists are generally more likely to dress as scholars and less as diggers or adventurers.

Several decades ago, both Mortimer Wheeler (1890–1976) and Glyn Daniel (1914–1986) were popular archaeologists in their programme *Animal, Vegetable, Mineral?* Wheeler's and Daniel's appeal was precisely that of the intellectual and lovable professor who told stories about strange artefacts from long dead civilizations, discovered on adventurous expeditions (Jordan 1981; Russell 2002a: 43). Tom Stern and Thomas Tode (2002: 72) observed about contemporary TV documentaries that when name, title, and institution are blended in just above the waist of archaeologists wearing scholar wear, this does not clash with the rest of the image at all. Instead, it accentuates the appearance of the scholar by emphasising the charisma of authority that is already implied by the clothes anyway.

Figure 2.8 The quintessential field archaeologist? Phil Harding of *Time Team* fame (David Webb).

Figure 2.9 Archaeologist Professor Glyn Daniel modelling scholar wear (Antiquity Publications, Ltd.).

Conclusion

Interestingly, there is a historical development in how archaeologists have chosen to dress over time. American historical archaeologist Adrian Praetzellis (2000) once depicted the history of archaeology through changing styles of headgear (Fig. 2.10). In each age, archaeologists have been depicted with characteristic hats. Whereas antiquarians and archaeologists of the nineteenth century wore toppers, pith helmets, or bonnets, the first half of the twentieth century saw the development of archaeology both as fieldwork and as an academic discipline, as represented in the mortarboard, fedora, and cowboy hat. Since then, archaeologists in the field have been wearing ball caps, headbands, and – with the advent of commercial archaeology – increasingly hard hats. By choosing what to wear, archaeologists have always been making fashion statements about who they are as archaeologists. They may emphasise higher abilities as scholars, exhibit dreams to be adventurers, express their personality as field archaeologists, conform to health and safety rules at work, or signify particular professionalism as archaeological managers.

It is interesting that in each case, archaeologists are portrayed – or portray themselves – in terms of a particular take on the process of doing archaeology, rather than in terms of any specific results of their research. Verbs tend to be more significant in media descriptions of archaeology and archaeologists than nouns. As much as scholar wear is about reaching sound knowledge through careful reasoning, adventure wear emphasises exploring and discovering treasures in exotic locations. Similarly, field wear is considered to be practical while working in the field, whereas health-and-safety wear is about taking the risk of accidents at work seriously. Finally, manager wear signifies that a project is professionally carried out.

It is generally true that in popular culture, the research process – archaeologists in action – is more significant than the actual research results themselves (Holtorf forthcoming). That is immediately evident in TV series like *Time Team* or *Schliemann's Heirs* where archaeologists are constantly seen energetically doing something (whether that is digging with a trowel, running to a trench or driving a Land Rover) and the actual findings are almost always pretty coincidental. Newspaper images, too, depict archaeologists working on site, digging up things. That tendency was also born out by Bodil Petersson's (1994) study of newspaper articles about the famous Swedish site of Birka. In terms of illustrations, approximately one-third of the associated images showed archaeologists at work in the field and one-quarter depicted individual finds.

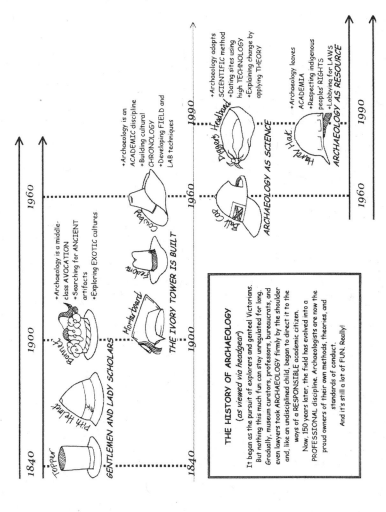

Figure 2.10 History of archaeology as viewed via changing styles of headgear (from Praetzellis 2000).

Newspaper stories about archaeology thus confirm the emphasis in TV programmes on the process of *doing* archaeology in the present. They all focus on archaeologists digging, discovering, revealing, managing, and studying things. How you dress as an archaeologist will immediately be read as a statement about what kind of archaeology you (want to) do. Archaeological fashion statements can lead to animated discussions and may in fact cause considerable controversy as to what kind of archaeology may be evoked and how appropriate any particular image of archaeology might be. The mass media have been fuelling the heat of these debates by supplying readily identifiable model archaeologists. Yet it is also the archaeologists themselves who have to make up their minds about how they wish to dress and what image they prefer to convey.

Acknowledgements

Thanks to Peter Addyman, Antiquity Publications Ltd., Mick Aston, Wilfried Beege, Göran Burenhult, Karol Kulik, Stephanie Moser, Adrian Praetzellis, Catrin Sandberg, Emily Smyth. Tom Stern, Hedley Swain, and John Walker for support and assistance in various ways. I am particularly grateful to David Webb for supplying some of his evocative images.

Notes

1. Galleries of his images are available on line at http://www.archphotodw.co.uk/DW/frameset.htm (accessed 28 June 2005) and http://www.archdiggers.co.uk/diggers (accessed 1 November 2005).
2. The BAJR Message Board is at http://www.bajr.org/BAJRForum/default.asp. However, this particular discussion has since then been deleted from the message board and was made available to me by David Webb.
3. http://www.archaeologyfieldwork.com/cgi-bin/yabb/YaBB.cgi?board=survey;action=display;num=1091428512 (accessed 29 June 2005).
4. http://www.channel4.com/history/timeteam/ (accessed 28 June 2005).
5. http://www.building-history.pwp.blueyonder.co.uk/Mick/Mick.htm (accessed 28 June 2005).
6. See Note 2.
7. http://www.archdiggers.co.uk/diggers (accessed 1 November 2005). See also Note 1.
8. From http://www.toddscostumes.com/indy/herbert_johnson_fedora.htm (accessed 29 June 2005).
9. http://girls.twistys.net/preview/019/pic10.jpg (accessed 29 June 2005).
10. http://zdfexpedition.zdf.de (accessed 29 June 2005).

3

NOT ARCHAEOLOGY AND THE MEDIA

Peter Fowler

Introduction

'Archaeology' and 'the media' are each worth considering as entities, as concepts even, before we discuss their relationship. Each is bedded in its own culture, each exists in its own matrix, and both would happily exist without the other. The media, however, are far more important to archaeology than archaeology is to them. Indeed, despite some contemporary indicators to the contrary, the past is of relatively little interest to current media (or politicians) as a whole. On the other hand, if we extend our initial rather limited definition of the media (below) into the more abstract concept of 'communication', communication is the lifeblood of archaeology. Conferences, meetings, and lectures are crucial, archaeology's lifeblood, because we are communicating about shared interests, ideas, knowledge, and experiences – about 'worthwhilenesses'. We are signalling to each other and perhaps to a wider audience that we think it worthwhile to support the existence of learned archaeological societies that publish regularly, and that it is worth our while to spend our time in reasonably earnest public consideration of matters of more than specialist interest.

I first touch on a range of facets of the media/archaeology relationship in terms of 'communication', beginning with a brief look at what we generally understand to be 'the media' – TV, radio, newspapers, magazines, and websites. Among other ways of communicating that I am consciously omitting, however sadly, are demonstration ancient farms (e.g., Butser Iron Age Farm, Hampshire, and Bede's World, South Tyneside [Fig. 3.1]) and novels, despite a range of fiction from the late Glyn Daniel's 'whodunnits' to Peter Ackroyd's creative account of life and death on a long barrow excavation. I then comment on a few aspects of 'social archaeology' – treasure hunting, education, and museums – before a short passage on art involving film, photography, and painting. I end with one or two thoughts on archaeology in its social, economic, political, and intellectual matrix around the concept of communication – archaeology communicating with its various audiences and those audiences communicating with archaeology.

The Media

There is lots of archaeology on TV nowadays. Hurray! It is what many in my generation always hoped for, indeed worked towards as we experienced the embryonic stages of television as a popular medium. We saw it as a means of projecting our wonderful subject to our fellow human beings and educating the populace to its benefit – or so we believed in our ethos of the 1950s and early 1960s that so markedly became anachronistic in the 1970s and 1980s. One of the things to which we can point in historical perspective as having gone wrong is that, after Mortimer Wheeler and Daniel, each a Television Personality

Figure 3.1 Bede's World Anglo-Saxon Farm (Peter Fowler).

of the Year, archaeology did not produce a David Attenborough. Brian Hope-Taylor – perhaps the most influential of early TV archaeologists – Gordon Childe, Stuart Piggott, Richard Atkinson, Hugh Shortt, and Charles and Nicholas Thomas were among those whom I recall seeing on flickering black and-white-screens in the 1950s and 1960s in series such as *Chronicle* and *Animal Vegetable, Mineral?*

Following them came the scholar-presenter Magnus Magnusson (not an archaeologist but someone who well understood it and in many ways became the face of archaeology) and academic archaeologists such as Colin Renfrew, Barry Cunliffe, and me in the 1960s, 1970s, and even 1980s. By then – in much altered broadcasting circumstances – new faces appeared from the next half-generation led by the likes of Tony Gregory, Christopher Chippindale, and Mike Pitts. But none of us grabbed the plentiful opportunities to become nationally recognised TV personalities, as distinct from being quite good archaeologists making, sometimes, quite good TV archaeology programmes. Indeed, I remember personally eschewing such a role and even feeling rather ashamed at finding myself once cast as a potential 'personality' rather than an academically correct but boring archaeologist on a TV panel game (which was, perhaps not surprisingly and certainly fortunately, cancelled after the first installment).

Personal failures apart, the basic trouble was of course that we attracted the cameras on site but we continued doing our archaeology in our anachronistic ethos, broadly top down from we who know to you who do not, while television – now serving several millions instead of hundreds of thousands –became mass entertainment. This meant that archaeology had to serve it, instead of it just showing our beautiful game as a worthwhile pursuit for its own sake: if you want to play the TV game, you have to play it by TV's rules, as other professions (notably medicine and law) have learnt to their cost and our merriment. Meanwhile, by grasping that challenge under a gifted front man who knew, like Wheeler, how to 'sell' his subject, natural history became central to TV. It proved visually 'fascinating', though Attenborough eschewed the word: he did not need it. As a result, my children's generation grew up in febrile televisual awareness of everything from Australian wombats to wombles on Wimbledon Common but with little recognition of the past around them. At worst, that past was nonexistent or inconsequential; at best, it was all too often just rather quaint. Even now, we have not successfully lined ourselves up in public with environmental concern or even heritage conservation; the big public issues tend to escape the archaeology that is presented in public.

Meanwhile, in the early years of the new century, poor old Attenborough was savagely attacked for what the new breed of nature conservationist charges was his deliberate turning of his eye away from the many threats to wildlife and habitat while pursuing over decades his biased coverage of a rather cosy and endearing Mother Nature. Personally, I agree with that point of view but would argue that it is his popular and scientifically acceptable treatment of nature over those decades that helped sensitise us to receive the environmental messages of justifiable doom and gloom in more recent times. And Attenborough himself drove that message home in 2006 by making his professional conviction that climate change and global warming were humanly driven a very public TV affair. You can shout such messages till you are blue in the face but you are wasting your time unless people are interested, and he had made them interested while building up their trust.

The recent, great opportunity – with an interested audience laid on to begin with – to engage with big cultural and environmental issues, to enlarge and even change peoples' perception, was blown on BBC2 in 2004 by an all-too-often apparently bewildered Dan Cruikshank on his treasure-seeking trudge around the world: wonderful places, pity about the commentary, whispered or otherwise. Without adequate cultural knowledge and certainly without an archaeological background, he inarticulately repeated 'fascinating' as both description and explanation of many of the 80 monuments and objects he visited.

Fortunately, British archaeology now has a real celebrity TV archaeologist again: Mick Aston, though not yet in the Attenborough class, is not just a pretty face or self-important poseur but an excellent archaeologist highly respected in the trade. He has emerged at a time when, far from an archaeological TV programme being an infrequent event, there is so much archaeology on TV that television critics are now complaining of a surfeit and indeed bad-mouthing archaeology itself. One advantage of so much nowadays is that everyone can see that there is good and bad archaeology, good and bad TV archaeology, and good and bad TV programmes using archaeology. Fitting the epithet to the programme is largely a matter of personal choice. For example, *Salon*, the electronic newsletter of the London-based Fellows of the Society of Antiquaries, opined in 2004 that 'one does tend to make the automatic assumption that all good archaeology programmes on TV emanate from the BBC – whereas the recent *Hidden Treasure* programme has proven that that assumption is a mistake, and that, in reality, it is Channel 4 that deserves the credit for intelligent TV programmes about archaeology' (see below). But TV archaeology can be bad for reasons other than ethics and methodology: over any month these days, for example, Channel 5 seems to specialise in submarine banalities and over-hyped truisms or speculation. Egypt, the Etruscans, and any sort of mummy provide fertile scenarios. We have too recently seen other attempts to use archaeology not for its own sake, but primarily as entertainment by inventing themes and situations to attract attention and fill a half-hour of screen time. 'Two in a Trench Go Trivialising' might be one suitably Blytonesque title, 'Extremely Silly and Unnecessary Archaeology' another.

BBC2's *Meet the Ancestors* series, despite its titular preoccupation with skulls, find a nice balance between the archaeologically acceptable and popular interest. It also broadcasts *Horizons* in which, from time to time, you can have the privilege of viewing classic, serious treatments of archaeology in Paul Johnstone mode – treatments with integrity in which gimmicks are at a premium and in any case serve an explanatory purpose, not themselves. They are, in other words, rather like current programmes that attempt seriously to explain quite complex subjects such as the workings of our brain. Lord Winston, like David Attenborough, doesn't need an animated garden gnome or shapely female bum obtrusively bouncing around between him and the viewer, though he uses effectively what used to be called 'visual aids' in order to make his points. Nor do archaeologists themselves need to demean themselves and our subject by behaving oddly: if we cannot make our subject interesting to lay people without wearing kinky apparel, affecting funny accents, or behaving quirkily, then we probably shouldn't be doing it in front of any audience, let alone televisual millions. Yes, use little tricks of delivery and presentation, some of them particular to TV technique, to gain and maintain interest – ask any good TV presenter, schoolteacher, or university lecturer – but there is no need to behave like an excitable weirdo even if the main objective of a programme is to entertain rather than educate.

Time Team, Channel 4's highly successful series, began by emphasising the peripheral, cultivating the idiosyncrasic, and shouting too loudly, all indications of lack of confidence (one suspects in the subject as much as in itself). It has now matured into successful presentation in another sense as it has realised that the meat of archaeology – its intellectual challenge and its range of techniques, for example – can be as televisually interesting as a more obvious 'treasure'. It can therefore address issues, not just finds and persons of a 'gosh-golly!' disposition. To my pleasure and interest, for example, I recently happened on its excellent treatment of an unexpected Neolithic mortuary structure in which the story line became the process of interpretation itself, not the finds or a presenter's infantile antics. That would not have happened some years ago, and that this should happen on and to *Time Team* is very encouraging for archaeology and its media. The series continues to pioneer, and Channel 4 continues to give us other seriously interesting archaeology programmes.

When I started doing regular TV in the mid-1960s, it was still – despite *Animal, Vegetable, Mineral?* and A.J.P. Taylor's history monologues – not the done thing for proper academics to be seen performing on television. I was very much looked down on by some extramural university colleagues at Bristol, to whom my short answer was 'Listen, I talk to more people in one half hour programme than you do in the whole of your career'. Mick Aston recently amplified to me that glib answer: 'Yes, of course numbers are important but for me the important point is I am talking to different people' (Aston 2005: personal communication), by which he meant people who wouldn't go near an adult education class or archaeological society and who wouldn't begin to look if they thought the TV programme was an 'academic' or, worse, a 'cultural' one. So the message is being spread, but of course there is a price.

While archaeology of a sort has been popularised, archaeology as a serious intellectual discipline has been compromised: it is a relative lightweight in academic matters, though several current archaeologists are weighty academics. On the other hand, many young people have had their interest quickened by TV but – so I am also told – as the *Time Team* generation arrives at university to read archaeology, it has to undergo a crash course in archaeological reality. Part of that reality is acquiring an awareness of the 'conservation ethic', something unknown in the sort of media-archaeology characteristically purveyed to the public. This is understandable: what appeal to the minor *genre* of tele-archaeology centred on excavation is there in the acceptance by the archaeological profession that 'preservation in situ' (i.e., non-excavation) is the best strategy for the archaeological resource? There is a real dilemma there – the same issue, incidentally, that critics now see as the weakness in Attenborough's approach – that neither *Time Team* nor any other outlet has even begun to address. On television, archaeologists dig, full stop. One tactic to circumvent this is to pretend not to be an archaeologist or at least to downplay one's status, to avoid a producer's expectancy of how an archaeologist should behave; another is to gain a voice on non-archaeological programmes. Some of our colleagues are excellent at this – for example, in being authoritative about forensic and pathological evidence in matters military and criminal. A small personal example recently was a few minutes with John Craven on *Countryside File* on a Sunday morning, an opportunity to put over a wholly conservation message about wear and tear on the Hadrian's Wall National Trail.

Radio archaeology is, you might well think, nonexistent: there is no archaeology regularly on the BBC's Radios 1-5. Listeners to the wireless, as it was then called, will fondly recall how it used to be: the regular Sunday afternoon archaeological programmes of the 1960s–1970s on the Home Service (= Radio 4). They were broadcast from Bristol, presented first by different people as *The Archaeologist* and then, monopolistically, by this writer when the series was called *Origins*. We broadcast live and so were able to be up to date with archaeological stories and include guests in the studio. I recall interviewing Richard Atkinson in weekly reports live by landline from Silbury Hill. I was eased out to make way for Malcolm Billings, and the series eventually died; but the tradition continues (sotto voce and perhaps obscurely for British listeners) on the World Service, where the tones of the mellifluous Billings still massage the global airwaves with archaeological news and stories. A recent series, for example, explored world heritage and tourism. In Britain, also obscurely in its way, radio archaeology not only continues but blossoms in its relatively new niche of ubiquitous local radio. There, the three-minute item, the studio discussion, and the question and answer – all live of course – are useful outlets for what collectively must be a great deal of audio-archaeology; but while it is hardly noticed except locally, it is of course precisely in that local context that it can be so effective. Many an archaeologist nowadays makes sure it is.

Archaeological journalism is remarkably good in British newspapers. Of course, you see unexplained snippets weekly about Chinese archaeologists finding, yet again, the earliest/biggest/smallest footprints of the oldest/shortest/fattest dinosaur; and every week or so, the normal sensationalism of the *Daily Mail* and below tells us yet again of aliens from outer space making crop circles around Avebury that encode messages leading to the treasure-laden pyramids of Atlantis where the mummy of the Queen of Sheba lies with the headless skeletons of all the illegitimate royal babies stolen by Lord Lucan while excavating in the Valley of Kings with Indiana Jones. Yet Norman Hammond has been contributing authoritative reports from the front line of academic archaeology to the *Times* for years, and for over a decade now, the indomitable Maev Kennedy has been covering single-handedly a range across 'the heritage' – she is probably the most-quoted journalist in secondary sources like the afore-mentioned *Salon* and magazines. In the interests of balanced comment, I examined in detail a *Daily Star*. As it happened, the edition in question was celebrating the end of the paper's Hot Bots week (non-gender specific, but seemingly female only) so it may or may not have been a fair sample, but it was certainly not preoccupied with archaeology. In fact, to be honest, archaeology was not mentioned; but then neither was Iraq, Blair, Bush, the United Nations, or other matters of serious passing interest. It is important to keep these things in perspective.

The record in the magazine field is not distinguished. As one of the founders of the ill-named *Popular Archaeology*, I note it as one of several failed attempts in recent decades to create a popular archaeology magazine, trying to take out into non-archaeological circles the good news about our subject. Because it absorbed the hard core of potential archaeology magazine readership, one of the big blockages in this field has been the presence for nearly 40 years of the subscription-only *Current Archaeology*. It has, within its limits, done a fine job if you do not mind taking your archaeology with large gulps of idiosyncratic right-wing propaganda; but of course it has not succeeded in taking the word into the wider world, sticking instead to its journalistically cosy subscription readership largely in the archaeological community. Now, the rival and journalistically much superior *British Archaeology* from the stable of the Council for British Archaeology (CBA) has actually broken out of that community and been accepted on to the shelves of W H Smith's and other commercial outlets. And it's true: I never thought that I would see it happen, having tried to do likewise with *PopArch* in the 1980s, but there is *BritArch* on Smith's shelves at Paddington. Whether it is any longer – or even should be – the mouthpiece of the CBA is now, however, a moot point.

The CBA has also led the way on the web. This is not the place to explore e-archaeology in detail but we must note it in our consideration of 'communication': silently it must be having a major effect on workings within archaeology and perceptions of the subject if people bother to click their way through vast arenas of data and discussion, ranging from huge academic bibliographies, through chatrooms on both obvious and very obscure fields of scholarship, to today's breaking news as seen through CBA eyes at York. It is paralleled by the afore-mentioned *Salon*, a near-weekly compilation of news and views, though its technique of vacuuming through reams of newsprint to recycle archaeological items has several times led it to perpetuate inaccuracies.

Social

There is of course only a blurred line between TV and society, with archaeology sitting on the fuzzy interface. With it, in the present context, are treasure-hunting and a recent BBC2 series called *Hidden Treasure*. Come back *Time Team*, all is forgiven! *Hidden Treasure* was presumably the BBC's attempt to cash in on *Time Team*'s popularity, but is it the price we really have to pay for being successful in popularising archaeology and for archaeology proving to be, for the moment at least, a popular subject with TV programme planners? Personally, I can find no redeeming feature at all about the series. *Hidden Treasure* was truly a shocker, a public demonstration apparently backed by the British Museum seeming to show that professional, academic archaeology has given up, allowing itself to be superseded in the field by often well-meaning but ignorant hobbyists with a blissful unawareness of the principles of archaeological excavation developed over a century and more since Pitt-Rivers established the basics. More importantly, it will prove to have done long-term damage not so much to archaeology as such but to the common heritage we share. Who would have thought that the same publicly funded body (with a remit to educate as well as entertain) that brought us *Animal, Vegetable, Mineral?* and *Chronicle* also brought us a series glorifying greed, ignorance, and damage to a national resource, fronted by the inevitable breathless bimbo, here of invisible academic credentials and ethics?

There is of course nothing new about treasure hunting or the abuse of metal detectors to hunt for treasure among your and my heritage or about the apparently often quite sad people who do it. I remember inveighing against both 35 years ago when the 'get rich hobby' was introduced from the United States by commercial interests led by the American armed forces, notably in East Anglia. This was, incidentally, either side of 1970 – not 1980, as the CBA's authoritative survey of treasure hunting for English Heritage seems to think. 'Oh, he was just bored at weekends', said one innocent wife in *Hidden Treasure*, shooting their marriage in all four feet as she explained how hubby, expecting a huge payout for raping two upper-class Roman graves near St. Albans, came to start treasure hunting. No wonder he got his buzz by taking to the fields.

He only got £31,000 of your and my money for needlessly yanking two rare sets of grave goods out of Hertfordshire's tough clay. This is where we merge from TV into the ambivalent world of museums, but I limit myself to just two questions. The chairman of the payout panel was shown on TV opining that not too much should be paid to the treasure hunter because of the cost of conservation of the many delicate and multi-material objects. Good for him, but I thought that we already had a serious overload of objects needing conservation and that we already suffered from serious storage problems in museums. Museum basements are full of gently rotting materials; the point is made in political circles and in appeals for your and my money, yet in this case (and in hundreds if not thousands of others each year), stuff needlessly yanked out of the ground is adding to that overload and indeed often taking priority over material patiently awaiting conservation but unattended for years. Worse is that, on *Hidden Treasure* and other such programmes, museum persons are seen drooling over such finds – some give the impression of being collectors first and curators second – instead of castigating the perpetrators of the misdeeds and the bad archaeology, which all too often seem, in front of the all-seductive camera, to be justified first and foremost by the thrill such glittering prizes give to an 'expert'.

Furthermore, in a world of supposedly limited resources for archaeology, where we are in effect charging developers for archaeological mitigation of their proposals, public archaeologists – as we saw in that St. Albans case – are having to drop everything on a Saturday and mount an emergency salvage excavation on the Sunday morning, cost-free to the treasure hunter. The excavation appeared to go on for weeks. How much did that really cost? What was NOT done as a result? Was the treasure hunter sent a bill? Though such questions apparently take us away from archaeology and the media, the relationship between the two has ramifications, including financial and ethical ones.

Of course, my brief treatment of this topic here is biased and provocative. I am quite happy with that: I despise treasure hunting for antiquities because it denies all that I believe to be good about archaeology and those who practice it properly. And yes, I do know the politically correct answers to my questions, including the mantra that archaeologists have to grow to love and lie down with treasure hunters in making the Portable Antiquities scheme work. But I nevertheless ponder over answers to the above questions. Do we, or do we not, have an artefactual conservation crisis in our museums? Have we really worked out the full resource and equity implications for society, not just archaeology, of official encouragement to archaeologically unskilled operatives to find and dig up archaeological material that – whether or not it is scientifically interesting – is part of our communal heritage? Do we not owe it respect rather than the suspect attentions of ill-informed hobbyists and professional treasure hunters? Would we allow do-it-yourself enthusiasts to work on the fabric of Westminster Cathedral or the Bayeux Tapestry on their Saturday afternoons? Is it not rather odd that laws exist and are

strictly enforced for natural history (for example, to prevent oppor-
tunists taking rare birds' eggs and certain plants) while the same public purse encourages and rewards a similar sort of mindset active in
the field of cultural heritage? You know what the answers are. But
you see what can happen when a subject becomes popular, fashionable even, largely through its promotion in a particular way by some
of the media.

Museums are one of archaeology's principal means of communication. The transformation of many of them as media for communication over the last two decades is remarkable, notably in the field of
education and particularly in the education of children up to the age
of about 12 or 13. The national curricula provided a very specific
focus for what museums could do with their resources, and many
have responded very positively – and that was before 1997, after
which 'access' in all its myriad manifestations, intellectual as well as
visual, became politically obligatory, at least if you wanted public
funding. The reality out there was forcibly brought home to me one
day when I was 'shadowing' the Bede's World senior education offi-
cer for the day. We entered St. Paul's church, Jarrow, part of which is
the very building in which the Venerable Bede worshipped. The
priest met us, two adults and two dozen 7–8 year olds from a decay-
ing area in a nearby post-industrial city. The priest started describing
the church interior in the most basic terms: 'We are in a church; you
are sitting in the nave; that smaller room behind me is called the chancel'. Hold on, I thought, this is a bit Noddyish, even for kids. 'In the
chancel', he continued, 'you can see what looks like a large, covered
box with a cross on top of it. Do any of you know what that is called?'
The silence was dramatic: not one child spoke. The familiar trappings
of the Christian church – even its focal point, the altar – were a closed
book to these children, the first generation of pagans since Bede had
taught there 1,300 years ago.

Let us not underestimate the challenge implicit in that anecdote. It
is a challenge not just to our ability to communicate with our succes-
sors, but to the very premises (such as written and visual literacy)
from which our subject proceeds. To meet that challenge, we need our
museums in addition to our schools: we need the excellent educational programmes of the big institutions of English Heritage and the
National Trust, and we need every possible local occasion to bring
archaeology as an interesting and significant subject to each child in
person – and to the parents too. Archaeology can and must make a
significant contribution. It is in a strong position to do so: it produces
the material that good education and good communication requires,

and it finds, explores, and helps maintain the landscapes and sites within which our ancestors lived, worked, and died.

Above all, however, if it can rise above the triteness of much of its TV presentation, it can contribute ideas – not just about site interpretation but about big questions such as 'How did our environment develop'?, 'Who are the British?', and indeed 'Who are we full stop'? Nor are such questions mere idle conundrums: what, for example, is the point of identity cards if we do not know who we are? One basic problem is that archaeology has been stereotyped by the very media that uses it as either fun and trivial or clever and arcane; it is not seen, and therefore seldom portrayed, as intellectually and socially relevant. Our failure to promote this latter message has not been more starkly illustrated, *ex silentio*, than by the recent efforts of senior political figures to address such questions of identity and 'Britishness' without any reference to archaeological background. That the musings of David Blunkett et al. scarcely rose to the level of undergraduate essays on precisely such issues in my 'Heritage and Society' course some 20 years ago makes this sudden political imperative even more depressing.

Cheer, however, came when I saw two programmes in the series *Landscape Mysteries* on BBC2. Those of you who followed the series will not be surprised to hear me say it is my sort of television with a knowledgeable, unassuming, calm presenter of my age group – actually a former professor of geology at Edinburgh University – dealing not with repetitive Arthur at Avalon nor Merlin-tattle at Tintagel, but with up-to-date information about genuine scientific mysteries of the landscape. One was the interglacial environment at the time of the male 'Red Lady' of Paviland 29,000 years ago. The other was about chalk-cut hill figures, beloved of soft-focus, obfuscating treatments. In both, the programme convincingly deployed current research. In the latter, it removed both the Long Man of Wilmington and the Cerne Giant from ancient times and dated them to the seventeenth-eighteenth centuries AD. Clearly, archaeology is not going to be a whiz kid topic on the back of this sort of *Landscape Mysteries*; but surely there is a place for such, just as there is a place too for more populist treatments, albeit properly informed and properly motivated.

Art

Archaeology in art, and art as archaeology, are not usually considered in the present context, but there is an important dimension to our consideration of media for communication here. We can but note the importance of photography – from the profound influence of images from Carter's Egyptian explorations in the 1920s on the very creation of Art Deco, as the 2004 exhibition in London's Victoria & Albert Museum illustrated, to the evocative landscape studies of Mick Sharp. We can also do no more than note the two-way influence of cinema: just think, on the one hand, how the Hollywood 'historical epic' has left a so far indelible mark on the modern world's understanding of what happened in that ancient world centred on places like Rome and characters like Ben Hur (Fig. 3.2). In contrast, think how archaeology, mixed with a large chunk of myth, provided the basis for the Indiana Jones series and, in reverse, how those films coloured for a generation public perceptions of archaeologists.

Other relevant artistic endeavours to note in passing must include sculpture. This three-dimensional medium is exemplified above all in our context here by the massively elegant body of Barbara Hepworth's work as displayed on a hillside near Wakefield and by the sea at St. Ives

Figure 3.2　Ben Hur on Hadrian's Wall: Charlton Heston and wife at the Museum of Antiquities, University of Newcastle (University of Newcastle).

in 2003, the centenary year of her birth, and always between the reed beds and Snape Maltings, Suffolk (Fig. 3.3). Much of it is about exactly what archaeologists in more mundane ways are trying to understand, as Hepworth's writings paradoxically make clear. Similarly, read Andrew Goldsworthy as well as look at his works on and about the landscape. Painting is a field in which I am currently enjoying my own heightened awareness. It comes from several sources: first, Colin Renfrew's *Figuring it Out* (2003), an inspirational discussion of relationships between art and archaeology. I just wish I had held something like it in my hands as a young man – it would have made my conduct of archaeology very different from the fairly rigid and straight-laced process I have taken it to be. Read it, particularly if you are young and starting out in archaeology.

One of the major interrelationships Renfrew explores is obviously that of archaeology and 'landscape art', in particular the work of Richard Long. There is a whole body of work and thought here, now well established and much broader than Renfrew is able to discuss; see, for example, the discursive and authoritative *Land and Environmental Art* edited by Jeffrey Kastner and Brian Wallis (2005). Some such art in Britain is in part publicly funded – for example, the 'field terraces' built over the last 20 years along the Dorset coast and Goldsworthy's drystone walls and earthworks in Cumberland and Northumberland. Meanwhile, landscape painting, viewed at one

Figure 3.3   Barbara Hepworth's 'Family of Mana' before a concert at Snape Maltings (Peter Fowler).

level as the field of great artists, is a booming activity both professionally and recreationally. It is easy enough to remark that much of the result is not very good art, but the really interesting point for present purposes is that so few artists seem to see the landscapes that archaeologists know are there – and indeed have largely revealed. That dimension is understandably hardly present among the accepted classics of historical fine art, as *A Picture of Britain*, a major exhibition at Tate Britain in 2005, demonstrated (though Turner characteristically is an exception); but that revelation has not communicated itself to the world of modern art judging by much of the output of contemporary practitioners. After looking at thousands of landscape paintings in the last three years, I number the 'archaeologically sensitive' contemporary landscape artists on the fingers of one hand; the rest are painting scenery.

My third point is very personal. I have discovered in my dotage, to my complete surprise, that I can paint (in fact, most people can but I did not know that when I initially picked up a brush). While thereby contributing to the oeuvre of bad landscape art, I have nevertheless become acutely aware of art as a hitherto largely unexplored medium of communication – not only between art and archaeology, but between our present understanding and that of our predecessors. I am an innocent here, but of course this is well-known territory to some of our long-term artistic and art historical archaeological colleagues. From the other end of the perspective, it was a connection glimpsed artistically (but without academic knowledge) by Paul Nash, and with the knowledge of a good local historian, above all by Peter Lanyon from his glider in the middle decades of the twentieth century. In 2003, I spent a day in Tate Liverpool at the Paul Nash retrospective centenary exhibition. In particular, much of my afternoon was passed in the one large room where, under the title *Megaliths and Menhirs*, were collected all his Avebury paintings and similar works. Unconsciously aping the great man, I have now painted 11 Avebury landscapes myself. Amazingly, they seem to 'speak' to some people and, interestingly, of different things that clearly relate to their experiences, not mine. One viewer wanted to know why I had put a large lampshade in the centre of one canvas; it was, to my mind, an outline profile of Silbury Hill in a multi-layered example of abstract realism attempting to express time and conceptual relationships in one of my favourite landscapes (Fig. 7.4). Another saw a circus ring where I thought I had painted, albeit somewhat impressionistically, the henge monument. Academically, this is all old ground in several fields of '-ology'; but, as with so much in art, how wonderful to discover it for oneself.

Figure 3.4 'Avebury Landscape', oil on canvas, 750 x 600 mm, by Peter Fowler (from catalogue, February 2004).

Hundreds of thousands of people, millions over the years, see the works of the Turners and Lanyons of this world as originals and, more commonly, as reproductions. Archaeologists should not overlook their contribution to the archaeology and media debate. Painting is indeed a powerful medium of self-expression, though not necessarily of communication; but in the case of real artists, we as archaeologists should recognise that powerful messages about our material and our subject are beaming out daily through artistic media from artists to people. Hepworth and Nash understood something of matters of which we also enquire; we should try to understand their understanding and meanwhile recognise that, whether we do so or not, their messages are received by others.

Archaeology in a Context

We all know Wheeler's fiat that archaeology is about people and my conclusion merely glosses that. I think Wheeler meant 'people in the past' whereas in the early twenty-first century there is much common ground among archaeologists – if not among our various audiences – that our objective is also to contribute to our understanding of people today. We therefore recognise that the context in which archaeology is embedded is basically social rather than material. Archaeology and the media can helpfully be viewed in this way rather than just as two perhaps confrontational poles, facing each other in isolation.

That 'the past is the present is the people' is a hard-won precept now recognised throughout the work of UNESCO in world heritage matters. This work involves many archaeologists and others concerned with studying, conserving, and managing some of the world's great monuments and landscapes. Communication on the ground is the key to much of the work, and the media interest in it around the world is intense. One reason for this is local pride; another is local politics; a third is economic, the ideas of access to grant aid and tourism development. These are big issues for any locality, but you do not have to go to the northern Philippines or the Andes to find them or the media interest. It is exactly the same in any place, including virtually any locality in Britain.

Issues that seem to matter in this context go far beyond whether or not *Time Team* is good or bad TV archaeology or good or bad archaeology on TV. But while archaeologists should be engaged in such contemporary affairs, they should also be thinking about how archaeology can maintain its status as an academic discipline with research agendas capable of addressing 'big' questions in the face of specific threats, such as populist versions as represented by treasure hunting and *Hidden Treasure*. Further, we need to face more general trends in society that are tending towards impatience with (even disrespect for) activities that take a long time, like a piece of archaeological research, or matters to do with learning, judgement, and self-discipline – like becoming a proficient archaeologist working, part time or full time, to professional standards. Media, such as television and the web, can seem to reinforce such trends. This is not necessarily because they are 'bad' in themselves or 'bad' by intent. By and large, they are reflecting what is happening socially rather than causing them to happen. *Time Team* was inconceivable in the 1960s and 1970s but it came about because of what was in the air in the 1990s, though subsequently it has undoubtedly contributed to the present popularity of the subject, or at least one version of the subject. So the question is whether it is better to communicate a partial message to many who previously received no message than to continue to communicate within accepted norms with the culturally and educationally privileged who watched *Chronicle* and today scan *Horizon* and *Meet the Ancestors*.

Your answer becomes particularly important when we move on to recognise the relevance of another big issue - not race as such but the interesting challenges to a range of interests, including archaeology, presented differentially in a society changing rapidly in ethnic and demographic terms. My own perceptions here have been sharpened by living now in inner London where age and ethnic variety in the square mile round home are visible each day, as are extremes of wealth and poverty and associated ill-health. I am struck too, as a landscape archaeologist much involved in countryside matters, by living among a community within which for many 'the countryside' simply does not figure – either because they are so rich and metropolitan oriented that they wouldn't dream of leaving *urbanitas,* or so poor in so many respects that thinking about it (let alone visiting it) is simply not part of their lives. Conversely, when I visit other parts of Britain now, especially in 'Countryside Alliance-land', I often feel I am visiting a semi-foreign country where they do things differently; but perhaps it is London that is different. It always has been, of course. Now, we are constantly told that we must enhance 'townees'' understanding of the countryside to improve our society, but in truth the real challenge is to bring some understanding to rural communities of what is actually happening in cities and large towns. Archaeology in the later twentieth century brought so much to our modern understanding of rural landscape and urban history that it should surely be contributing significantly to that debate. Is it?

The sort of matters in mind in this essay are reflected, and ignored, in a myriad ways. Examples printed from 2004–2005 include a comment by one cultural commentator that 'TV history favours battles, kings and queens, military hardware and the secrets of the well-born laundry basket. TV archaeology prefers the "treasure hunting" imagination of amateur metal detectorists to the laborious methodologies of the professionals'. History sees itself as beset by the sort of media problems I have touched on and many historians bemoan the 'regal' sort of history referred to above (itself a not very subtle reference to the obsessionally regal programmes of professional TV historian David Starkey, though Simon Schama also uses material culture largely as decorative backdrop). The angst of this situation is reflected by one historian's comment: 'TV is undermining university study by encouraging students to believe that the subject is an exercise in story-telling rather than rigorous intellectual discipline.' A TV critic, bemoaning the loss of mystery because of all the myth-puncturing TV programmes, referred to 'pesky archaeologists... fiddling about in the mud and muck of northern Greece.' English Heritage recently came up with a new logo, the quite appalling 'English Heritage It's Mine'. A government minister, echoing some of her colleagues, characterised museums as still being 'too middle-class' and not reflecting Britain's multicultural society (like universities and guided walks in National Parks).

In the empirical, catholic spirit of that last paragraph, this essay has sought throughout to mention many aspects of a dynamic relationship, that between archaeology and the media. It is, of course, neither inclusive nor authoritative. Indeed, its consciously personal approach and amateur, anecdotal sociology deny it – like appearing on television in the old days – academic respectability but perhaps allow it a provocative role in contributing to discussion of that relationship. I just think that we have to ponder seriously how archaeology should communicate with whom about what at such a time of potentially divisive but exciting social change. After all, in a very basic sense, archaeology is actually not about the past but about the present and the future; its role is to mediate between all three. Only just try telling that to the media: you would quickly be told 'THAT'S not archaeology…'

Acknowledgements

This paper is based on an invited lecture that opened a conference entitled 'Archaeology and the Media', organised by the Devon and Cornwall Archaeological Societies at Saltash in October 2003. I am indebted to those societies and the editors for encouraging me to recycle for present purposes the rare phenomenon, in my case, of a prepared text significantly revised and updated during 2006.

PART II

TRANSLATING ARCHAEOLOGICAL NARRATIVES

4

A SHORT HISTORY OF ARCHAEOLOGICAL COMMUNICATION

Karol Kulik

Introduction

For a discipline concerned with interpreting the past, archaeology has been slow to investigate its own past and, in particular, the roles that archaeologists, the public, and the media have together played in the communication of archaeological information. Over the past 15 years, however, changes in the archaeological and media professions in Britain have led practitioners in both communities to prioritise their relationship to each other and to the public, creating an upsurge in public interest in archaeology and in archaeology's visibility in the media. In turn, the public communication of archaeology and the relationship among archaeologists, the media, and the public have become timely subjects for study and debate in archaeological circles, featuring in conference sessions, university courses, and publications. As Jameson (1997: 11) writes, 'It is likely that the waning years of the twentieth century will be identified in the history of archaeology as a time when the profession, as a whole, came to the realization that it could no longer afford to be detached from the mechanisms and programmes that attempt to communicate archaeological information to the lay public.'

These recent developments have, however, fostered an impression that the archaeologists' need to communicate with the public is a new phenomenon, as implied by Jameson and witnessed in statements like Ucko's (1994: xii, emphasis added) that 'modern archaeology must recognize and confront its *new* role, which is to address the wider community.' It appears new, I would suggest, for three reasons. First, the discipline has been emerging in these years out of a generation in which professionalisation of the field and the development of new theoretical approaches and discourses were privileged over external communication. Second, changes in archaeological funding since 1990 have seen commercial companies engaged in land or resource development overtake the state as archaeology's main paymasters. This has reestablished a more direct link between the profession and publicity, forcing archaeologists to be more attentive to public interest and communication than had been the case in the previous generation. Even state funders like English Heritage and the Heritage Lottery Fund expect archaeologists to communicate their work to the public, often making this a condition in their grants. And third, it appears new because of archaeologists' amnesia about the history of archaeological communication. After all, the origins of the public communication of archaeology in Britain are rooted in how antiquaries disseminated information from the sixteenth century, and British archaeologists' relationships with the mass media go back more than 150 years. If one is to understand the current relevancy of archaeological communication, one needs to address this amnesia by looking back at how the communication relationship among archaeologists, the media, and the public has evolved.

To do this requires a framework, and the one that is proposed and sketched out in this paper presents the history of archaeological communication as a chronology divided into five distinct 'ages'. This account charts the fluctuations in the interdependency among archaeologists, the public, and the media, pointing out how this has affected the public communication of archaeology. It also highlights the similarities and differences between the periods, a comparison that proves that the present phase is not unique and that archaeological communication has not always progressed in an upward direction. Although many media are implicated in the representation of archaeology, communicating messages about the profession and its practitioners, this history deals primarily with the nonfiction media like exhibitions, books, journals, educational courses, radio, newsreels, and the Internet and, especially in the later 'ages', with the press and television.

The Age of Antiquarian Communication: 1700s–1830s

During this first phase, archaeology was a private endeavour, an amateur hobby rather than a profession, pursued by (mostly) men with private incomes or in professions like the church or teaching who had the education, interest, time and means to indulge their curiosity and passion for knowledge about the antiquities of the past. Usually well travelled and well versed in the classics or theology, antiquaries sought to make their contribution to historical understanding by discovering, describing, and interpreting inscriptions, monuments, sites, and artefacts, and by (crudely) excavating sites, retrieving objects, and establishing personal collections. Eccentric and with a tendency to communicate in arcane discourse, antiquaries were often ridiculed (Bray 1981: 227–229; Daniel 1967: 224; Wheeler 1954: 6; Piggott 1989: 14–18). They sought refuge in, and measured their success by the judgments of, brother antiquaries with whom they formed societies (for example, the Society of Antiquaries [1718] and the Society of Dilettanti [1733]). Many antiquaries ably represent the breed (e.g., William Camden, John Aubrey, and William Stukeley) – as does, in a lighter vein, Jonathan Oldbuck, the hero of *The Antiquary* (1816), the novel by Sir Walter Scott, himself an antiquary.

From the point of view of archaeological communication, what was important about antiquaries was their Enlightenment-inspired commitment to communicating their ideas. They did this through the media deemed most relevant: lectures at their societies; letters and articles in select journals like the *Gentleman's Magazine* (from 1731); and limited-edition books that were usually privately published (financed either by themselves, their societies, or advance subscriptions) and expensive. As these choices indicate, the primary public for antiquaries was their peers. In the early 1800s, there were, however, some educational initiatives aimed at the lower middle classes that helped archaeological information reach a larger audience. These included, for instance, the Mechanics' Institutes, where lectures on the 'geological beginnings of archaeology' (among other subjects) were given (Daniel 1950: 55; 1964: 152), and the penny periodicals, in which information about archaeology, although not news per se, was for the first time offered to this readership (Phillips 2004). Yet antiquaries' basic insularity and society's main focus in the late eighteenth and early nineteenth centuries on present concerns – e.g., the effects of industrial growth and revolutions in Europe and America (Colley 2002: 313–314; Lowenthal 1985: 393–395) – meant that there was little demand or inclination for antiquaries to communicate beyond their own well-defined limits. This circumscribed notion of archaeological communication was to change dramatically in the next phase.

The Age of Print Communication: 1840s–1910s

It was in this age that archaeology began to engage the attention of the wider literate public through popular books, magazines, and newspapers. Although the 1840s are usually singled out as a turning point in archaeological history because they witnessed 'the foundation of the first of the county societies' (Clarke 1981: 115; see also Wheeler 1954: 5), they were also a turning point in archaeological communication. Publishers like John Murray began to encourage a broader readership by publishing abbreviated and therefore cheaper editions of archaeological books (Daniel 1964: 154–155). In 1848–1849, for instance, Austen Henry Layard's abridged account of his excavations at Nineveh became a bestseller – selling, Layard claimed, as well as a popular cookery book. Most significantly, it was in this decade that weeklies like the *Illustrated London News* and *Punch*, both of which generously covered archaeology, were founded (Bacon 1976; Bray 1981: 221; Daniel 1986: 232). As Moser (1998: 154) points out, 'Throughout the late 1800s and early 1900s the *Illustrated London News* played a leading role in introducing the subject of archaeology to the wider public and quickly became recognized as a major international forum for reporting archaeological news from home and abroad'. Bray (1981: 221–222) adds that '*Punch*, too, was doing its bit' with cartoons and parodies, many of which displayed both 'an insider's knowledge and a genuine affection for the subject'.

During this phase, antiquaries slowly transformed into archaeologists with a growing interest in developing a more scientific approach to their work, but without a recognisable profession or career structure to support them. As Wheeler (1955: 9) reminds us, 'During the years before the First World War archaeology was still an unorganized discipline, its techniques were largely un-evolved. Systematic training did not... exist, and archaeological posts were in any case nearly non-existent'. Not surprisingly, these first archaeologists still largely conformed to the antiquarian mould in terms of gender, class, and financial independence. Heinrich Schliemann and General A.H. Pitt-Rivers can be seen as the epitomes of this transitional age, but they interest us here because of their commitment to communication. Through their prolific writings, lectures, press articles, and site or museum exhibitions, they were to define what the public communication of archaeology would mean for their own and succeeding generations (see Deuel 1978; Thompson 1977).

In the public arena, many Victorians viewed the past as a 'potentially stabilizing influence' at a time of widespread social upheavals (Cunliffe 1981: 192). Furthermore, anxieties about the effects of unfettered development led to initiatives and legislation – like the Ancient Monuments Act (1882), the National Trust (1895), and the Royal Commission on the Historic Monuments of England (1907–1908) – to protect and preserve the country's archaeological and historical heritage (see Hunter 1981: 24–30). On a more personal level, it was also during this era that the leisure activity of visiting archaeological sites and excavations – what I call, after Wheeler (1954: 8), 'picnic archaeology' – became a favourite pastime of well-off Victorian families. A wider public, albeit still largely confined to the upper or upper middle classes (Hudson 1981: 47, cited in Merriman 1991: 102), was becoming sensitised to archaeology's attractions at a time when, due to educational reforms, public literacy was on the increase (as was the public's disposable incomes and leisure time) and when the size and composition of the lower middle classes was changing (LeMahieu 1988: 8–10). Mass circulation journals and daily newspapers were established to address this expanding readership and competed with each other for different segments of it – e.g., women, white-collar workers, etc. Only four years after its launch in 1896, the *Daily Mail* would lead the field with a circulation of one million (Price 1996: 325).

These new outlets and audiences provided archaeologists with a platform for disseminating the exciting discoveries that were being made during these years. The *Illustrated London News* and the national press became archaeologists' closest allies. They published archaeologists' own articles and communiques from the field and sent out correspondents and illustrators to cover the more auspicious sites (Daniel 1964: 154; Moser 1998: 154). Moreover, from at least as early as 1873, when the *Daily Telegraph* funded G.A. Smith's expedition to Nineveh in search of the missing tablets of the Epic of Gilgamesh (Anonymous 2000; Ceram 1980 [1951]: 313), newspapers began to sponsor archaeological work, usually in exchange for exclusive coverage. This partnership with the press continues to the present day, but it was to diminish in value during the twentieth century with the emergence of new media partners competing for an even larger audience.

The Age of Mass Communication: 1920s–1950s

This enlargement of media and public characterises archaeological communication's third phase, which was framed by two key public archaeology events and two remarkable archaeologists. Marking the start of this age, Howard Carter's discovery of Tutankhamun's tomb in 1922 – the single most significant media event in the discipline's history – produced worldwide newsreel and press coverage that ensured that archaeology, 'almost overnight, acquired a new market-value' (Wheeler 1955: 76). A second discovery, that of the remains of the Mithraeum uncovered during building work in London in 1954, caught the imagination of the postwar British public – 35,000 of whom daily visited the site (Barrett 1995: 5) – and 'demonstrated conclusively that archaeology had a role to play in the cultural life of the country and would no longer be the preserve of the professional' (Wainwright 2000: 910). That same year (and the next), archaeologists Mortimer Wheeler and then Glyn Daniel were named Television Personality of the Year due to their contributions to the BBC's first two archaeological TV series, *Animal, Vegetable, Mineral?* (1952–1958) and *Buried Treasure* (1954–1959). These two proselytisers of what Daniel called the *'haute vulgarisation'* of archaeology (quoted in Howard 1992: 8) published prolifically, acted as editors or advisers for archaeological magazines and book series, and double-handedly dragged their colleagues and the profession into the homes of the British public via radio and television. It is hard to imagine how twentieth century archaeological communication would have developed without these men and events.

This phase witnessed the appearance of the first full generation of academically trained archaeologists, coming from a broader socioeconomic constituency (Jordan 1981: 209), and the initial establishment of many of the profession's organisations, boundaries, and practices. Over these four decades, there was also a change in how British archaeology was funded – from personal resources, small institutional subsidies, and direct donations from the public before the war, to state funding by the Office (later Ministry) of Works during and after the war. This shift began a sea change in archaeologists' relationship with the public (from direct economic dependence to indirect accountability) that would affect their attitudes and commitments to public communication. The postwar redevelopment of Britain's bomb-scarred cities created a climate reminiscent of today: a climate where rescue digs would dominate fieldwork, where – as Wheeler (1966: 93) put it – 'Chance and salvage govern our labours', and where 'archaeologists were paid to dig, but not to publish the results' (Pitts 2001: 52). As late as 1955, it was still the case that the profession had few jobs to offer (Crawford 1955: 173) and that career advice to young archaeologists was 'to inherit or obtain a private income' (Wainwright 2000: 910). Despite the lead offered by Wheeler and Daniel, that their legacies were not exploited to the full in the next phase can be seen partly as a result of archaeologists' growing need to address and resolve the profession's shortcomings.

During the prewar years, the print media remained the prime outlet for archaeological communication, with a continuation of the pattern of popular book successes and newspaper competition for archaeological exclusives established in the previous phase. For example, Sir Leonard Woolley's *Ur of the Chaldees* went through eight printings in 1929 (McAdam 1999: 51) and the *London Times* outbid the *New York Times* for exclusive rights to cover the official opening of Tutankhamun's tomb in 1923 (Patzek et al. 2001: 400–401). Three years later, Wheeler and the *Daily Mail* agreed to a deal for the newspaper to sponsor excavations at Caerleon in exchange for exclusive coverage (Wheeler 1955: 75). A broader readership for archaeological magazines was encouraged when O.G.S. Crawford founded *Antiquity* in 1927, a journal that was more independent than the specialist journals of societies and institutions and that aimed at being 'more than provincial or professional' (Crawford 1955: 311).

The print media would, however, soon have to compete with newsreels, radio, and television as important sources of archaeological news and information for the British masses. From my research, for instance, British Movietone News alone produced 21 features on archaeology in the 1930s and 1950s, including items on Wheeler's excavations and the Mithraeum discovery. BBC radio, whose licence holders tripled to nine million during the 1930s (LeMahieu 1988: 229), was imbued with the educational ethos of John Reith, its first director general. This led to 'Talks' programmes becoming a major component in its schedule and to archaeology joining other scholarly disciplines as suitable subjects for radio programmes, like those given by Woolley in the late 1920s (Woolley 1965 [1930]: 4) or, indeed, whole series like *The Archaeologist*, which started in 1949 (Daniel 1986: 245).

The 1950s saw an expansion in book publishing with the launch of several long-running generalist series on archaeology like Thames and Hudson's Ancient Peoples and Places (Peters 1981: 196–197), but it was the advent of television that was to have the most effect on public communication. The quiz show format of *Animal, Vegetable, Mineral?*, in which a studio panel of archaeologists had to identify and discuss artefacts, and the charisma and enthusiasm of the panel-lists, drew an audience – so its moderator Glyn Daniel (1986: 256) claimed – of five million viewers (representing 10 per cent of Britain's population). Its huge success led the BBC to produce *Buried Treasure*, a series on various archaeological topics that, despite cumbersome technology, pioneered most of the TV formats used ever since. By the end of this phase, it would come as no surprise that Sir Ian Jacob, director general of the BBC, would claim that 'archaeology and show-jumping' were the two most popular things on British television (Daniel 1964: 150).

This age was therefore crucial in the history of archaeological communication for its high level of public and media interest in the subject, an interest that for the first time transcended class and educational boundaries. Democratisation of the profession, its public, and the media was synchronised to the benefit of all three partners. By the 1950s, British taxpayers had become the 'patrons' of archaeological work, and as such needed to be 'cultivated and suitably rewarded' (Wheeler 1954: 192; 1955: 104). At that time, Ceram (quoted in Daniel 1964: 150) would write that 'the British were, and are, fascinated by archaeological questions as are no other people in Europe.' It was, as Daniel (1964: 151) adds, the 'agencies of mass communication' that had 'widened the audience in quality and multiplied it enormously in size.'

The Age of Specialist Communication: 1960s–1980s

These 30 years were a schizophrenic time both for the discipline, as the profession became divided between – as Pitts (2001: 50) writes – 'diggers and thinkers' ('not just different cultures, but separate species'), and for archaeological communication, as the 'thinkers' retreated from and the 'diggers' pursued public and media attention. From the 1960s, the largely government-funded profession turned inward to focus on its infrastructures, to manage an expansion in academic education, employment, technologies, and specialisations, and to articulate and dispute archaeology's theoretical bases and vocabulary. The profession-alisation of a maturing discipline inevitably shifted archaeologists' attentions to internal communication, increasingly framed in a more rar-ified discourse. For instance, Jacquetta Hawkes wrote in 1968 (quoted in Shackel 2002: 158) that archaeological discussions of the time

> seemed to me so esoteric, so overwhelmed with unhelpful jargon, so grossly inflated in relation to the significance of the matter involved, that they might emanate from a secret society, an introverted group of

specialists enjoying their often rather squalid intellectual spells and rituals at the expense of an outside world to which they will contribute nothing that is enjoyable, generally interesting or of historical importance.

This shift away from public communication was exacerbated by
academic pressure to 'publish or perish': career advancement
depended on publishing specialist articles or books for one's peers, not
popular ones for the public. It was also in this period that the unoffi-
cial rules of 'proper' scientific communication became established (see
Kulik 2005). Seemingly only accountable to the public in an abstract
way (through the public 'purse') and privileging internal over external
communication, archaeologists were able to professionalise their discipline. As Baker and Morris (2001: 608) confirm, this was a time when
'economic irrelevance allowed the discipline to develop internal
philosophies, methodologies and practices which were largely uncon-
ditioned by either external paymasters or wider social obligations.
Perhaps no bad thing in itself, this had a downside in weak structural
and intellectual contact with the rest of humanity'. Archaeologists
were therefore defining themselves and their profession as irrelevant
to the public and the mass media, except when it came to mobilising
public opinion over threats to Britain's archaeological heritage.
    Signs of concern about the profession's disregard of public com-
munication arose in the 1970s (Thomas and Arnold 1974: 241, 246) out
of the public campaign (known as RESCUE) that archaeologists
organised against the destruction of archaeological sites by uncon-
trolled land development (see Jones 1984; Rahtz 1974). Despite the
lessons learned by RESCUE archaeologists, and their success in
increasing public awareness and government funding from £150,000
in 1967 to £4.8 million in 1982–1983 (Wainwright 2000: 914, 920), the
issue of archaeological communication in general (that is, not just as
it related to site preservation) and the media's role in it only gathered
momentum slowly. By the end of the 1980s – notwithstanding the
pleas of some (Bray 1981: 221; Fowler 1981: 64; Hodder 1992 [1984]:
128; Prince and Schadla-Hall 1987) who recognised that professional
neglect of one's public was, as one put it, a 'near suicidal stance'
(Stone 1989: 203) – archaeology had reaped the consequences. The
mass media and the public, whose appetites for archaeology had been
whetted in the previous age, were finding their nourishment elsewhere, notably in 'fringe' archaeology and Indiana Jones.
    This phase saw an increase in archaeological publishing (Peters
1981: 198), assisted by the launching of specialist book clubs, but it
also witnessed a downturn in factual media coverage of archaeology

as the press and television accommodated to growth and new competitors. The last major expansion in national dailies came in this period with the arrival of the *Sun* (1969) and the *Independent* (1986). As competition from television and each other grew, all three sectors of the UK daily press (downmarket tabloids, upmarket broadsheets, and mid-market tabloids) increased in size and repositioned themselves in the marketplace. The downmarket tabloids went more downmarket, the broadsheets more upmarket, while the mid-market papers, sharing the same audience with television, suffered the most in readership loss (Tunstall 1996: 10–11, 185). One of the consequences of this was that press coverage and sponsorship of archaeology moved upmarket, becoming the prime domain of the quality newspapers (Stone 1989: 201), the subject providing ideal material for their new magazine supplements.

Similarly, in television, when the BBC expanded to two channels in 1964, it gave its new 'highbrow' channel, BBC2 – rather than the more mainstream BBC1 – responsibility for archaeological programming. On the initiative of David Attenborough and Paul Johnstone (both of whom had worked on *Animal, Vegetable, Mineral?* and the former having become BBC2 controller), BBC2 launched *Chronicle* in the mid-sixties (Daniel 1986: 251, 260–261). For 20 years, this would be the BBC's primary strand for archaeological documentaries with an audience that grew from one million in 1973 to 2.5 million in 1983 (Norman 1983: 27). The BBC's sponsorship and live coverage of Atkinson's excavation of Silbury Hill in 1968, like its coverage of Alcock's work at South Cadbury, however, produced disappointing results and would make the corporation uneasy about such investments for over a decade (Cleere 2000: 90; Pitts 2001: 353; F. Taylor 2001: 475). Having started broadcasting in the mid-1950s, the commercial television network ITV did not transmit archaeological series until the mid-1960s when Anglia Television – one of its regional suppliers – put Glyn Daniel on its board to oversee its production (see F. Taylor 2001: 472–474). Yet network executives had little confidence in these series, for they aired many of them in off-peak hours. In 1981–1982, some confidence returned, both with the start-up of Channel 4, whose brief to be alternative and to source programmes from independent producers promised to make it 'an ideal home for archaeology' (F. Taylor 2001: 477) and with the BBC's hugely successful 16-hour live coverage of the raising of the Tudor warship the *Mary Rose* (Norman 1983: 27). Nevertheless, it was clear that the 'honeymoon period' was over (Stone 1989: 199) and that, in a more competitive climate, archaeology was struggling to find space on the mainstream media.

Yet the public had not abandoned archaeology. People queued for up to eight hours to see the British Museum's *Treasures of Tutankhamun* in 1972; they chose archaeology over economics, making it 'the most popular subject' in 1960s adult education classes (Fowler 2001: 607); and they campaigned alongside actors when the remains of the Rose Theatre were threatened in 1989 (Blatherwick 2001; Wainwright 2000: 924–925). However, when asked to name an author of archaeology books, survey respondents in 1984 (Stone 1989: 200) 'most frequently named' Erich von Däniken, whose best-selling books – for example, *Chariots of the Gods* (1969) – were anathema to most archaeologists. Ignored by much of the archaeological community, estranged from TV archaeology as it moved off or to the margins of the populist channels, and reduced to being consumers of the 'heritage industry' by government (see Champion 1996: 138), the mass public assuaged its archaeological hunger with alternative theorists and silver screen heroes. By the mid-1980s, as Stone (1989: 201) writes, '[O]nly those sections of the population who enjoy academic-type documentaries, listen to Radio 4, or who read the heavier academic books or quality press are exposed, on a regular basis, to high quality… archaeological information.' Archaeologists and media professionals were thus together responsible in these years for not feeding the wider public's appetite for archaeology.

The Age of Global Communication: 1990 to the Present

Today, we are in the fifth phase of archaeological communication, which began in 1990 with the government-led commercialisation of the archaeological and media professions. In archaeology, the profession was to become 'client-driven and employer-dominated' (Ascherson 2002: 129) with the coming of PPG16, the government guideline that forces commercial developers to take account of and pay for the archaeological impact of their work. This shifting of the burden of funding from government to the private sector has caused 'a fundamental re-shaping of the structure of the profession' with the appearance of contract archaeology and competitive tendering (Wainwright 2000: 929). PPG16 would lead to an almost threefold increase in archaeological fieldwork and assessments between 1990 and 1996 (Darvill and Hunt 1999: 14), with excavations in one county, West Sussex, jumping from one in 1990 to 114 in 1998 (M. Taylor 2001).

Archaeological funding from developers has been estimated as amounting to £30-68 million a year (Lambrick 2002; Wainwright 2000: 929). Yet PPG16's success, as Baker (2002: 26) points out, 'has been compromised by poor coordination with research and communication,' its results 'not feeding back into the wider academic and popular consciousness.' As he adds, this is not PPG16's fault, for its brief was limited to land management. The profession's failure to make adequate provisions for the public dispersal of PPG16 results (beyond being recorded in Historic Environment Records, which are accessible but largely unknown to the public) has increasingly left archaeological communication in the hands of the developer-employers, to be decided according to their publicity needs and capabilities. These changes have unsettled the profession, forcing archaeologists to ask fundamental questions about their place in and value to society. For example, the Institute of Field Archaeologists' annual conference in 2001 was largely focused on how best to live with the developer-led system and the need to reposition archaeologists in society (IFA 2001). This has led to an increased valorisation of archaeological communication and archaeologists' rediscovery of the importance of public outreach (McAdam 1999: 50; Stone 1997: 23).

In the media, the deregulation of broadcasting and the expansion of outlets and markets has resulted in an even more competitive landscape and fragmented audience. Fewer Britons now read a daily newspaper (Tunstall 1996: 215), a trend accelerated by the accessibility of round-the-clock news coverage on TV and the Internet. Although the Internet has revolutionised communication and information sourcing, with archaeological websites providing sophisticated ways of engaging with the public, it has not yet overtaken the press and television as the public's primary news sources (Walker 2000). Since the mid-1990s, the press and television have embraced archaeological news and information. From my research, for instance, the *Daily Telegraph* increased its coverage of archaeological subjects by 600 per cent in the three years between October 1994 and September 1997 and archaeological documentaries on Britain's terrestrial channels increased by 367 per cent between 1998 and 2002. BBC2 and Channel 4, in particular, have used archaeological programming to hold onto audiences in the face of competition from niche broadcasters like Discovery, National Geographic, and the History Channel. The success of this programming has led to archaeology's return to or arrival on mainstream channels like BBC1, ITV, and Five. Book publishing has been reinvigorated by best-selling TV tie-ins and new popular archaeological series, and video games, films, and the Internet have been responsible for firing the archaeological imagination of a new generation.

Archaeologists and the media have together created an age in which archaeological communication would flourish, and the public has welcomed this. Increasing numbers have been cited at sites and museums – the Museum of London, for instance, clocking a 60 per cent rise in visitors between 1997 and 2001 and attributing this to its *Londinium* exhibition on Roman London (Swain 2001). At least until the mid-1990s, student applications for university archaeology courses had 'steadily increased', almost doubling between 1986 and 1995 (Andrews 1999: 92) – a phenomenon often connected to the 'Indiana Jones effect' and latterly to TV's popular *Time Team* series (Hatley 1997: 14). The public became directly involved in several high-profile rescue campaigns, such as Seahenge in 1999 and the Newport ship in 2002, and showed its passive engagement by watching archaeological documentaries on television in ever greater numbers. A new milestone was reached in 2003 when BBC1's drama documentary 'Pompeii: The Last Day' attracted over 10 million viewers (source: BARB, 2003) – that is, 40 per cent of the TV audience and one-sixth of the total UK population.

The Future

Whether this fifth age of archaeological communication has run its course or has many more years to go is, as yet, unclear. There are, I would suggest, some warning signs that this phase may be coming to a close. One is the gradual disappearance of broadsheet newspapers, with the *Guardian* having followed the *Independent* and the *Times* in changing from a broadsheet to tabloid format. This bodes ill for archaeological coverage, for with less text to devote to their stories, tabloids are more circumscribed in their selection and telegraphic in their reporting of news. How complex scientific stories, and especially ones not easily illustrated, will fare is under question.

In 2004, there was also the first decrease for almost a decade in archaeological programmes broadcast on terrestrial channels. The success of dramatic reconstructions, like the above-mentioned 'Pompeii' and Channel 4's 'Ancient Egyptians' (2003), may encourage broadcasters to privilege this format of presenting archaeology on TV over others that deal more directly with archaeological practice and information and offer archaeologists a presence and a voice on our screens. The increasing penetration of satellite and digital television in British homes has, since 2003, finally begun to erode the audience share of BBC2 and Channel 4, both of which had so far escaped the declines seen in ITV and BBC1. The triumph of narrowcasting over broadcasting may push all of TV archaeology onto niche channels, like BBC4, and perhaps this will encourage more innovative and challenging programme making. Yet, it could be argued, mixed-diet, public service broadcasting that seeks out and engages the widest possible audience is healthier for public discourse.

Even if these forecasts were to become reality, the strength of the bonds among archaeologists, the media, and the public that was developed in recent years may give us some hope for the future. One would hope that the public would not overnight lose its appetite for archaeology. As the public's choices in media consumption further expand, so will its responsibility for seeking out, selecting, and evaluating archaeological information. Having established such a large public constituency for archaeology in advance of this further democratisation of archaeological communication may prove to have been essential for archaeology's future. Equally, one would hope that archaeologists have learned enough during the last decade about the public and its interest in and value to archaeology (and about the media and how they operate) that they will build on this knowledge and keep public communication flowing. Archaeologists are keenly aware that the stakes are high, that if they abandon the public and the media as they did 40 years ago, they are undermining their own future. But it has happened before, and although the world within and outside the archaeological profession has changed immeasurably since then, we can neither be too arrogant nor too complacent to assume it could never happen again.

Conclusion

Recounting the history of archaeological communication even in this brief form has hopefully dispelled any notions that the relationship among archaeologists, the public, and the media evolved in a linear path, that communicating with one's public is a 'new' role for archaeologists, or that the present age of high synergy is unique. It has also underlined the dynamism and complexities of the relationship, a necessary antidote to accounts that judge the present in isolation or that privilege the perspective of one partner in the relationship over the others. Having insights about the history that consciously or unconsciously colours each partner's attitudes towards archaeological communication makes it easier to understand the contemporary relationship and may help to prepare us better for the future.

5

IN THE CAMERA'S LENS

An Interview with Brian Fagan and Francis Pryor

Interviewed by Marcus Brittain and Timothy Clack

Each with over thirty years experience with the media, Brian Fagan and Francis Pryor have broadcast their message of archaeology through many different media and in their own individual ways to audiences around the world. Having written extensively on many archaeological themes for academic and public audiences, public archaeology in the United States and the UK has grown and matured through their combined experience and would be much the poorer today if not for their continued passion and energy. When placed together in the following interview (carried out via email correspondence in the summer and early winter 2005), their views regarding current themes from 'archaeology and the media' offer insightful glimpses into the connections and distinctions between British and American perspectives.

Could you briefly outline your experience in communicating archaeology via television and radio broadcasting?
Pryor: In the days before 'client confidentiality' became such a big issue (i.e., after PPG16 in 1989), people who sponsored archaeology were always keen to get good publicity. So I started

phoning press and broadcast journalists as soon as I began directing my own digs in 1971. I've no idea how many news stories I have dreamed up, but it must be hundreds – ranging from Radio Cambridgeshire to Radio 4's *Today* programme ('Bronze Age Cowboys of the Fens'). I'm the proud possessor of two Blue Peter badges. My first big opportunity was in 1988 when I presented my first documentary, a half-hour programme for BBC2, directed by David Mitchell. Then, in 1989 and 1990 (I think!), I presented two series for Anglia TV, one on the Bronze Age and one on connections between England and Holland; both were directed by Paul Jordan. In 1990. I presented *Now Then*, a series of six 25-minute programmes for BBC1 Children's Television. Then things went quiet as I withdrew to spend five years writing up my two major digs at Etton and Flag Fen in north Cambridgeshire.

I came out of self-imposed purdah in 1996 (I think!) when Mick Aston and Tim Taylor asked me to do my first *Time Team*, which I loved. I've done two or three Time Teams each year ever since, including the first special (they are now referred to as TT Documentaries) on Seahenge (1999) – an idea that Tim Taylor and I hatched up together. In 2002 and 2004 I presented two series for Channel 4 based around my books *Britain BC* and *Britain AD*; both were directed by Tim Copestake for Diverse Productions. This year, I took part in the Big Roman Dig for a week and another 'live' two-day show on 'Foamhenge' [a full-scale polystyrene reconstruction of Stonehenge] for Channel 5. I also do the occasional short film for BBC South's contributions to the regional show *Inside Out*. I'm currently in the final throes of a three-part series – *The Real Dad's Army* – for Diverse and Channel 4 based around the CBA's [Council for British Archaeology] award-winning Defence of Britain Project. After that, Heaven knows what, but something will turn up: Roy Ackerman, who is in charge of programme development at Diverse, still seems to think I'm okay. So my fingers remain optimistically crossed. With luck, I'll still be doing the occasional Time Team. I honestly don't know – which is all part of being freelance.

Meanwhile, I'm writing a big book for Penguin, which won't appear for three years and may well have some sort of TV spin-off. If pressed, I think (in fact I know) that I'd rather write books than make films – the reason being that one can establish a more intimate and altogether closer relationship with a reader than with a viewer. This becomes very apparent when one talks to readers, as opposed to viewers: the readers seem to know one as a friend or family member, whereas viewers only see what the programme makers want them to see – which is often something approaching a caricature of reality. At least, I hope it is. If not, I shall shortly be seeking a high cliff above a rocky foreshore.

Fagan: Unlike Francis, I have never hosted a television series or even a programme. But I have been interviewed for numerous programmes on PBS [Public Broadcasting Service] and the Discovery Channel. TV channels over here insist on celebrity hosts, which is the way they want it. My main role over the years has been as an advisor behind the scenes. I was senior adviser on the Time/Life *Lost Civilizations* series some years ago, a very successful project, and have been involved with other series on early humans. I spend a great deal of time fielding questions about potential TV programmes and series – which is time consuming – and almost invariably hear nothing more. I wish TV researchers (and the BBC are naughty about this) would realise just how much time this takes when one is busy and fighting deadlines oneself. But it's important to provide accurate information and insights, of course, which is why we all do it – but sometimes one feels somewhat exploited, as if one is a convenient resource rather than a human being.

I have been interviewed on radio many, many times, and, in many respects prefer it to TV as it's more spontaneous. Back in the 1980s, I wrote a three-year radio series called *Patterns of the Past*, supported for National Public Radio [NPR] by the National Endowment for the Humanities [NEH]. It consisted of one five-minute and one two-minute spot a week, aired on the NPR satellite. It was apparently very well received and is certainly something worth pursuing as a format in the future. We failed to get long-term sponsorship, unfortunately, and the idea died.

What makes a good archaeological television programme?

Pryor: That's easy. Both good books and good radio/television programmes must tell a good story. A bright idea is not the same as a good story. Nor is a big discovery. Stories, like good solos in jazz, must have a beginning, a middle, and an end. They must be disciplined and not self-indulgent. They can have a twist at the end, but not predictably like a Somerset Maugham short story. They can also wander from the point to increase the tension. But everything that happens must ultimately advance the story. David Collison, one of the best directors with whom I ever had the pleasure to work, would always ask, 'Does that advance the story?' If it failed that simple test, it was out – even if the delivery was brilliant and the photography superb. It had to be relevant. Julian Richards's *Meet the Ancestors* had a format, but it didn't dominate the show and Julian was able to do what he does naturally and with such warmth, which is to tell a good story. *Time Team* also works well because the format, which is vastly more elaborate and perhaps slightly better thought out, does not dictate the content. Each programme must tell a story, which is why *Time Team* can be good and not so good. Even the poorer ones are vastly superior to some of the lamentable clones that have been produced with TV license payers' money; the clones failed because they allowed (or worse, were encouraged to allow) style to dominate content and narrative. As a result, they patronised the viewer. Archaeological programmes must rise above considerations of mere format. We owe that to our great subject – and to our viewers who are growing increasingly discerning.

Fagan: An ideal TV programme is one that takes the viewer along with a scientist as he or she makes discoveries, and above all shows how scientists reach the conclusions they do. I've found that people are far more interested in archaeological detective work than they are in travelogues or sensationalism. American TV tends to be more superficial and sensation loving, which is why there are so many programmes on Egypt and mummies and such things as mysteries of the pyramids.

Is American TV missing out, then, on a format that could result with potentially higher viewing figures and a much more lucrative market – one that is also presumably more attuned to the process of archaeological interpretation?

Fagan: American TV is a highly fractured marketplace, with so many cable channels. Many people seem to think that it's only PBS and the Discovery Channel, but there's much more – even the Archaeology Channel, which broadcasts nothing else. No one here does what the BBC or Channel 4 does, there being an emphasis on celebrities, sensational discoveries, and docudramas. We are long overdue for a first-rate series on archaeology that reaches the standards set by the BBC and Channel 4. Raising the money will, however, be very difficult.

Remember that archaeology is not a very popular TV subject here compared with Europe, partly because much of it is concerned with native Americans, who are not considered by many people to be 'our' history.

More recently, Brian, you have suggested that radio is an untapped forum for archaeological communication. Could you explain further how and why you foresee radio as a useful communication device for archaeology?

Fagan: I think radio is an untapped resource for archaeology in the United States, especially through satellite radio and other outlets that have not yet been harnessed for such programming. Radio has the advantage of being cheap to produce, easy to disseminate, and very immediate. It is far more cost-effective than television or film. Short radio spots can be produced quickly, reflect very recent discoveries indeed, and are easily copied and used in the classroom. I regard them as an ideal, and little used, way of reaching a very broad audience with up-to-date archaeology. Radio does not have the prestige or cachet of TV, but how else can you get a discovery literally from the ground out to a broad audience within hours? (I have done it.)

Radio is a wonderful way of getting short snippets about archaeology out to very broad audiences. This works very well with audiences that listen to the radio in their cars. The approach has been used successfully with astronomy by the University of Texas for years. In *Patterns of the Past,* the NEH-sponsored series I was involved in during the 1980s, we did two- and five-minute spots that were heard by millions of people. With careful writing, you can produce vivid images in the listener's mind without using pictures. We focused on ideas, discoveries, methods.

Pryor: I think Brian's right and largely because – to use an old cliche – the pictures are better. Julian Richards has done some splendid stuff for Radio 4. I tend to work with programmes, such as Radio 4's *Open Country*, which are not specifically geared towards archaeology but integrate it with other aspects of rural Britain. Incidentally, Maisie [Taylor] and I are recording something tomorrow for them to do with the history and exploitation of oak trees. I think that's what I like about archaeology on radio – somehow the medium is less inclined to force our subject into a narrowly defined pigeonhole. Archaeology is, after all, about the totality of the past. It's more than a speciality interest – or should be.

Do you think it is becoming more acceptable, specifically in academic circles, to write general – yet serious – archaeological works that explore and communicate a wider picture to a 'discerning' public?

Pryor: I wish it was; instead, I think that the Research Assessment Exercise [RAE] is having precisely the opposite effect. None of the last six books I've written (two for Tempus and four for HarperCollins) would have counted towards the RAE. Now, I gather that journals are to be graded so that some are better than others. This would mean that the best and most original piece of scholarly/academic work I ever wrote – the *Fengate Third Report* [Northamptonshire Archaeology Monograph 1/Royal Ontario Museum Monograph 6, 1980] – would have scored lower than, say, a short note in *Antiquity*. This is the sort of thing that happens when cretins – themselves incapable of original research (because otherwise they'd be doing it) – take charge of 'standards' in higher education. Incidentally, I don't see why, as your question implies, one should necessarily write for a 'discerning public'. Surely, it's just as valid – maybe more so – to write for an undiscerning public; these, after all, are the people we need to win round to our cause.

Fagan: In a world over here in the United States where the publish-or-perish system is intensifying in the face of increasing competition for fewer academic jobs, I would say that writing any general book for the public or a broader audience is unlikely to do you much good in the research university environment. Conventional wisdom argues that it's better to do it once you have achieved tenure. The language of publish or perish culture is 'peer reviewed articles in established journals' and peer-reviewed books published by university presses. The fact that most general books get far more scrutiny than peer-reviewed publications seems to have escaped notice. Another factor that comes into play is the increasing specialisation within archaeology, which makes it harder for people to contemplate writing a book, say, on the archaeology of Alberta or New Jersey. The near frenetic insistence on publication credit is one reason for the proliferation of specialised edited volumes, which to my mind are one of the curses of modern-day academia.

Although many archaeologists recognise the importance of communicating with the wider audience, it is often still considered (for all the denials) to be 'lightweight' and marginal – which is, of course, arrogant nonsense. Writing for general audiences, including textbooks, is the hardest thing I've ever done archaeologically.

How well equipped are archaeologists for dealing with the media in its varying formats?

Pryor: By and large, archaeologists in the UK get precious little training for dealing with the media. In fact, I think it's getting worse. Certainly, I find interviewees are becoming less and less willing to speak succinctly, which is the entire secret of good broadcasting. The less you say, the more will be transmitted. Having said that, I now do lectures for Mike Parker Pearson at Sheffield University and these seem to go down quite well with the students. But then you can't pack a lifetime's experience into an hour a year.

Fagan: American archaeologists are generally poorly equipped to write for general audiences and for dealing with the media. Generally (and this is of course a gross generalisation), they receive specialised graduate training that exposes them to the formulae for writing academic papers and reports. Add to this the generally appalling standard of writing in high schools and at the undergraduate level, and you have a lot of impenetrable writing about the past. I have on occasion been asked to rewrite a technical report *for archaeologists!*

Although this is changing very slightly, American graduate students receive absolutely no training in dealing with the wider audience or the media. They learn this as they go along on their own. The great explosion of cultural resource management [CRM] is changing this somewhat, but major graduate research programmes are not changing with the times. Remember that the PhD is a specialised research degree, not a degree in how to live in the real archaeological world.

I have no idea how this compares with Britain, although archaeology enjoys a much higher public consciousness in the UK thanks to TV and radio, also the press. We have the added complication over here that a great deal of archaeology is the anthropology and history of native Americans, the history of 'them' rather than 'us', although this issue has received little attention. For all the common methods and theoretical approaches between North America and Europe, they are two very different archaeological worlds – and I'm not talking about the archaeological record here.

In Australia, 'indigenous media' is one of the fastest-growing sectors, having arisen from a growing discontent with mainstream media misrepresentation of indigenous affairs. How extensive is indigenous media in the United States and is it something that archaeologists should take note of, or indeed work with?

Fagan: Archaeologists here generally take no notice of indigenous media. There is a great deal of interaction with Native Americans going on at the moment. Indeed, there are Native American archaeology units, like the one run by the Zuni nation, which are very successful. The overlay of private sector CRM – which takes up a great deal of energy, time, money, and attention – diverts a lot of archaeological attention as well. I wouldn't say that indigenous concerns are all that high on the archaeological agenda here. But there is certainly concern about communicating with Native Americans. What I was talking about was the public perception of American history, which very much begins with Columbus.

Do archaeologists fear the images created of them in the media?
Fagan: No, they do not. And there is no reason to fear them, as the popular stereotype of the archaeologist as a treasure hunter is dead as the dodo over here. Most media here seem to do their best to communicate accurately, and if there is a problem, it's usually a chasm of misunderstanding during an interview. I have found most journalists over here to be even handed, interested in doing a good job, and concerned to be accurate. But we do not have the tabloid interest you do in the UK (they are absurd here). And remember that archaeology is generally not an important story in the United States. We are very low on the totem pole.

Pryor: For the UK? It's hard to say. And besides, I'm not sure that the media does 'create' an image. Phil Harding [of *Time Team*], for example, is like that in the flesh. He is a larger-than-life character, which is one of the reasons he comes across so well on the screen. But he also has very firm views on what does and does not constitute good archaeological practice and woe betide anyone, media or non-media, who tries to make him do anything he isn't happy about doing. My advice to anyone who seems a bit hesitant or fearful is to act yourself. Don't pose because that always appears what it is – phoney.

How challenging has it been to become literate in the language of the media? Is the media now becoming literate in the language of archaeology?
Francis: As I've always been interested in photography and filming, I haven't found it at all challenging, but then I'm not sure to what extent I have 'mastered' mediaspeak. Certainly, when we're doing a 'live' broadcast, the stuff coming into my ear from the mixing truck is incomprehensible – involving strange things like 'Astons'. Being interested in process – all process, be it archaeological or broadcasting – I'll ask what these terms mean, not just because I'm curious but because it's a good way of finding out about other people's careers and lives. 'Astons' incidentally are those strap lines that appear on screen when one starts speaking: 'Dr. Francis Pryor, Bronze Age expert', or whatever.

Fagan: There are two magical words when dealing with the media, or the public as a whole: *common sense*. I have found that if you are open, cooperative, and answer questions clearly, you will have no problems – but I am not dealing with English tabloids. I would not describe myself literate in the language of the media, although I work with them a lot. I don't know what that means! I work with them, they have deadlines, it seems to work out fine. I have never had a problem. The media over here are no more literate in archaeology than they are in physics, global warming, or rugby football. It's whatever crosses their desks, unless of course you are dealing with science journalists at publications like the *New York Times* or *Time magazine*, who often know more than you do.

Have you ever felt that you have compromised your intellectual credibility in a dispute with a producer, and could you explain the best practice for negotiating conflicting ideas with media producers?
Pryor: If in doubt, say no. A year or two ago, I was approached by a broadcaster as a possible presenter on a series. After several phone calls, it became clear to me that the series would approach the subject from – how can I put this without betraying the series that was eventually made – a (*very*) non-archaeological perspective. But I needed the work. So I was determined to have a nose-to-nose with the producer if I got the job, and if he or she didn't satisfy my concerns, then I'd decline the offer. I don't see what else I could have done. In the event, thank Heavens, they found someone very much more decorative than me. No, in my experience most producers are reasonable people and very rarely want to make their contributors feel uncomfortable – because it'll show in the finished product.

Fagan: My experience with TV has been very eclectic. I have generally had few problems with producers, indeed have had some excellent experiences. The best ones have a strong visual sense, are not interested in egos and tantrums, and are utterly professional. I live only two hours from Hollywood and know enough people that I can get a quiet lowdown on most individuals who approach me, which saves trouble. But most people I have dealt with have been cooperative and professional.

How do you feel about the programmes with which you have been involved becoming material culture that will be interpreted by media archaeologists in the future?
Pryor: Any work you do – be it written, radio, or television – becomes grist for the historian's mill. If that worries you, then you shouldn't publish in any form. I've always tried to speak the truth and sometimes, being human, I get things wrong. Even so, it doesn't worry me too much because any historian worthy of the name will assess past work in the contexts of its time. I can't say I share politicians' obsession with their 'legacy' – something which seems to be bothering our respective leaders at present.

Fagan: I think that 'media archaeology' is a completely frivolous idea and certainly not a worthy academic pursuit. There are far more important things to study. I doubt if any programme with which I have been involved with over the past 40 years will ever yield any revealing information on 'historically situated social patterns', whatever they are. Most producers I have encountered are well aware of trends and past programmes. The less archaeology has to do with 'media studies,' the better in my view. In my experience, the best archaeology programmes and series are those made with passion by people who *believe* in what they are doing and care out it. Francis is a stellar example, so is Mick Aston [of *Time Team*]. You don't need media archaeology to tell you that.

To paraphrase the words of Noel Annan to Glyn Daniel in 1955, will archaeology survive the meretricious image of being a television star?

Pryor: I remember that – it was unusually pompous for Noel Annan, who was actually a nice person. I also recall Cyril Fletcher's better use of the word at a Pantomime in the Arts Theatre, Cambridge, in the 1960s: 'Meretricious and a Happy New Year to you all!' Where was I? Ah yes, improving relations with the media: personally I don't think we should give it a moment's thought. As soon as we start to think about and then manage our relations with the media, we'll all relapse into PR babble and produce the sort of safe and dreary corporate 'ideas' that might please certain middle-of-the-road programme makers. Programmes assembled by committees (and I have taken part in one or two) are a yawn to make and even worse to watch. It seems to me that archaeology's greatest strength lies in the individuals who practice it. We should cherish them and their individuality, and if this produces good programme ideas, then well and good. If it doesn't, then too bad. The world won't end if archaeology is off the television for a few years.

Fagan: I suggest that archaeology continue doing what it is doing: use common sense when talking and dealing with the media. There will always be a few archaeologists who will become TV personalities, and they will deserve it. I find most media people are very professional and expect the people they deal with, whether archaeologists or frog experts, to be the same. But I think it's important that we realise that the old stereotype of someone who deals with the public, writes popular works, or – horror of horrors – appears on TV is not a sound archaeologist is now dead as the proverbial dodo, and was never anything but arrogant nonsense anyhow.

6

DARKNESS DISSEMINATED

Lennart Larsen's Images as Photojournalism, Pop Archaeology, and Works of Art

Christine Finn

I first saw his twisted face in a photograph
(Seamus Heaney, 'The Grauballe Man').

The key line in this poem, as it relates to this chapter, is 'in a photograph'. For all that has been written about the influence of *The Bog People*, P.V. Glob's classic work about the northern European Iron Age on the work of the Nobel Prize winning poet, Seamus Heaney, one personality rests in the shadows outside of his own country: Lennart Larsen. Larsen, who took the Grauballe Man photograph and many others that continue to narrate Glob's excavations, is archaeology's lesser-sung hero. And yet his photographs allow a continuous and – significantly - universal reading of the extraordinary phenomenon of the bogland, 'the strange powers' that Glob captures so vividly in his text. This chapter brings together various components: brief biographies of Larsen and Glob, Heaney's response to *The Bog People*, the context of the book's publication, and the dissemination of Larsen's images over the past 40 years (e.g., Figs. 6.1–6.2). It includes my responses to both the original photographs and those produced by a photographer, scientist, and artist, the

Figure 6.1   The Grauballe Man emerging from bogland (Lennart Larsen).

resulting exhibitions and multimedia presentations, and lesser academic findings from the World Wide Web – where one site describes
the Tollund Man with much enthusiasm, as 'a veritable poster boy for
ritual sacrifice'[1].

Peter Glob, who died in 1985 at the age of 74, joined the National
Museum of Denmark in 1934. From 1949 until 1960, he was professor
of northern archaeology and European prehistory at Aarhus Museum
in Jutland; during this time, he was called to Tollund bog one May day

Figure 6.2   Head of Tollund Man (Lennart Larsen).

to examine a peat cutter's curious find. He then became state antiquary of Denmark and director of the National Museum, during
which time he wrote *The Bog People*, first published in Danish in 1965
as *Mosefolket: Jernalderens Mennesker bevaret i 2000 Ar* (Copenhagen,
Gylendal). Reviewing its 1974 sequel *The Mound People*, about Bronze
Age Denmark, Seamus Heaney wrote in his poem 'The Grauballe
Man' that Glob's 'piety towards objects, as well as his archaeological
passion that distinguishes his writing, and no doubt accounts for its
popularity' (Heaney 1974).

Popularisation and Response

Glob's articles in the popular press about the discovery of the Jutland
bog bodies led to extraordinary interest from all over the world. In the
foreword to the book Glob, recalls that excitement: 'Scholars asked for
details. Children write thanking me for a thrilling story and saying
that they included me in their prayers at night'. One of those letters
came from a group of English schoolgirls at the Convent of the

Assumption in Bury St. Edmunds, Suffolk, a landscape resonant with a bogland of its own. The girls asked where they could find the Tollund Man 'because we want to visit him when we are older'. Glob sent them more information and the enthusiastic letters received from the schoolgirls in response set Glob a task to write 'the "long letter" in the following pages for you, for my daughter Elisabet, who is your age, and for all who, like you, wish to know more about antiquity'. The 'long letter' was the hugely popular account *The Bog People*. Glob's book mediated between the pragmatism of scientific analysis and the wonder of discovery, and through it Heaney felt able to respond to feelings of his own that were outside the traditional dialogue of archaeological science. Opening up the metaphorical ground, Heaney is both participant and observer of the events laid bare in Glob's book. Heaney once said of archaeology, 'I know that no one works in this field without feeling something of what I felt. Reverence, after all, expresses itself every bit as convincingly in tender and devoted scientific action as it does in the reverence of the poet' (n.d.).

Seamus Heaney was born into a world in which archaeology was a defined discipline that was fast capturing the public imagination, being communicated through visual media as well as text. As shown above, he was sensitive to archaeology and certainly aware of its practice, not least through his friendship with Tom Delaney at Queen's University, Belfast. Delaney, an archaeologist who died young, is remembered by Heaney in the poem 'Glanmore Sonnets', published in the 1991 volume *Seeing Things*. Heaney's dig into the metaphor of the bog body was a revelation; it enabled him as a writer, presenting him with the facility to link the bog bodies – which had been analysed in their archaeological context and featured in the press as sensational discoveries – with the victims of Sectarian killings during the Irish troubles, whose stories also appeared in newspapers and other media during the 1960s and 1970s.

Critical consideration of Seamus Heaney's 'bog poems', which reinforced his status as a major poet during the 1970s, considers the direct archaeological association of his poetry with archaeology, and the archaeology with his poetry (Finn 1999a, 1999b, 2003, 2004a, 2006; Stallworthy 1982). This conjunction is illuminated, not least, by the explanatory words of the poet himself (Heaney 1991, 1999). Even if Heaney later expressed a wariness of continuing the dialogue of 'S.Heaney = Bog Poems' (Heaney 1998: personal communication), others have taken up the mantle of this connection, thereby creating a narrative that links (at one end) the turf cutter who first exposed the Tollund Man during an everyday domestic practice and (at the other) the artists who have transformed the archaeological data into art. This all by way of Glob, Larsen, Heaney, and a series of overlooked figures: the journalists who reported on the discovery on a global scale; the editors who used Larsen's photographs to illustrate the story; the classroom of English schoolgirls who inspired him to write *The Bog People*; the English translator, Rupert Bruce-Mitford; and the audiences for the artists, writers, and educators, who are continuing to disseminate Glob's work – and thereby Larsen's work – even further.

The discoveries at Tollund in May 1950, at Grauballe in 1952, and several subsequent finds in the boglands of northern Europe were initially disseminated through the press. It was as a direct result of that publicity that the book was written. Glob dedicates the work to the group of schoolgirls from Bury St. Edmunds who had seen the account of the finds and who, Glob noted, inspired him to write a popular book – for them and his daughter Elisabet, who was of similar age. Glob's book became a classic from its publication in Denmark in 1965 and at once began to inspire a generation of archaeologists. Used in schools and read by laypeople, it was also read by academics. Central to its success was the fact that Glob, an eminent archaeologist, was also a consummate storyteller who captured his readers' imagination from the opening lines.

> Evening was gathering over Tollund Fen in Bjaeldskov Dal. Momentarily, the sun burst in, bright and yet subdued, through a gate in blue thunder-clouds in the west, bringing everything mysteriously to life. The evening stillness was only broken, now and again, by the grating love-call of the snipe. The dead man, too, deep down in the umber-brown peat, seemed to have come alive. He lay on his damp bed as though asleep, resting on his side, the head inclined a little forward, arms and legs bent. His face wore a gentle expression - eyes lightly closed, the lips softly pursed, as if in silent prayer. It was as though the dead man's soul had for a moment returned from another world, through the gate in the Western sky. (Glob 1965: 1)

The Enduring Image

While the words are evocative, the nub of this chapter is the central role played by the images, and particularly photographer Lennart Larsen. The man who enabled Heaney to write in all truthfulness (in 'The Grauballe Man') 'I first saw his twisted face/in a photograph', had a sympathetic eye; the images he produced are both examples of photojournalism and works of art that, 50 years later, are the subject of aesthetic veneration, as discussed elsewhere (Finn 2000b, 2004b, 2006).

Lennart Larsen was a photographer for the National Museum of Denmark and a colleague of P.V. Glob. His published work ranged from ceramics to textiles, but it is the photographs from the extraordinary series of bog finds in Jutland that captured the imagination of the Danish public and appeared, in various formats, all over the world. Larsen's best-known portrait shows the Tollund Man lying, as if asleep, on his mound of peat. It offers an easily accessible, and generally acceptable, face of ancient death. Compare this, for example, with the somewhat contorted stare of the Tyrolean Ice Man, now in Bolzano, Italy, who adorns not only book covers but is positioned on postcards as a tourist image beside mountain scenes and Alpine herds.

While the Grauballe Man's face is distorted by the weight of bog above him, the Tollund Man's head is preserved with a certain dignity that is intensified by Larsen's choice of perspective. During excavation, the head was first brought back to Copenhagen; Kit Weiss, Larsen's assistant at the time, once explained to me that she had to produce the head from a bucket of water at the required time – such was concern for its conservation. The resulting image taken by Larsen has more the quality of a bronze portrait head than the better-known image of the lying head with its body in situ. Today, Larsen's name is little known outside Denmark. However, Heaney relied on Larsen's gaze for his best-known 'bog body' poem 'The Tollund Man', from *Wintering Out* (Heaney1972), written before the poet had made his first visit to the actual body in Denmark. Such was the impact of seeing Larsen's black-and-white images in Glob's book that Heaney continued to draw on them for his next volume, *North* (Heaney 1975), in which he continued to reconcile the ancient and contemporary in his poetry. As he wrote in the essay 'Feeling into Words', 'The unforgettable photographs of these victims blended in my mind with photographs of atrocities, past and present, in the long rites of Irish political and religious struggles' (Heaney 1980: 57–58). Further, responding to the archaeologist's idea that such sacrifices were a response to crises such as famines or attacks, he continues, 'This too corresponds with what was happening in my own case, since the poems I wrote after reading Glob's book were in fact exactly that: responses to a crisis inside myself prompted by events outside'.

Heaney made his first visit to Aarhus in October 1973, keeping a promise in the first line of 'The Tollund Man' that he would go to 'see his peat brown head'. He has described this visit as a form of pilgrimage (Heaney 1998: personal communication) and the impact of seeing Larsen's image fleshed out was considerable. When Heaney first cast his eyes on the Tollund Man in the Museum at Silkeborg, he acknowledged a reverence more intimate than a simple cultural familiarity. 'It was the kind of face I had known as a child, the slightly moustached face of an old countryman such as much Great-Uncle Hughie, a man whom I first saw standing tall in a turf-cart, as lean-featured in life as he would be when he lay in his coffin in death – exactly as if he were the Tollund man lying in peace and profile on the turf of the Jutland bog' (Heaney 1999). Years later, opening an exhibition that brought Denmark's bog bodies together for the first time, Heaney made his apology to the people of Aarhus, explaining that the word 'Silkeborg' would not have scanned (Heaney 1999). This poetic licence was a subtle distinction, as it is another bog body, the Grauballe Man, that lies at Aarhus.

Around the time Heaney was working with Larsen's images, his bog poetry was being published, and the public was reading *The Bog People*, John Berger's influential series *Ways of Seeing* was broadcast on BBC Television. The accompanying book of the same name (Berger 1972) was a work of collaboration, of which the central thesis – 'The way we see things is affected by what we know or what we believe' – was itself influenced by Walter Benjamin's essay 'The Work of Art in the Age of Mechanical Reproduction' (Benjamin 1992 [1936]), which is duly credited in the text. A few lines by Berger remind us of the role played by photographers, among them Larsen: 'Every image embodies a way of seeing. Even a photograph. For photographs are not, as if often assumed, a mechanical record. Every time we look at a photograph, we are aware, however slightly, of the photographer selecting that sight from an infinity of other possible sights' (Berger 1972: 10; see also Shanks 1997: 73–107).

The image described so vividly in Seamus Heaney's poem 'The Grauballe Man' can be read as an act; it is an arresting example of liminality as a part of the excavation process. In the full-page photograph that appears in Glob's book, we see the head and shoulders of the Iron Age man apparently suspended between the prehistoric world, in which he lay undisturbed for some two thousand years, and the contemporary world of 1950s Jutland. Upright in the landscape, his body is held fast by the bog, his grave and protector, and held also as a moment in time and archaeological discovery (and a memory) by Lennart Larsen. Other Larsen photographs showed the first instance of discovery – a slice of tanned leg glimpsed by a turf cutter gathering fuel, a partly excavated and less well-preserved body of a woman – but it is this image that arrests for its direct analogy with a portrait taken as a part of an archaeological news story, destined as much for the popular reader as the academic.

The progress of the images taken by Lennart Larsen also charts, in their way, the development of archaeology as a popular subject. Unlike the stark photographs of the Windeby Girl that Glob uses in

The Bog People and which also inspired Heaney in 'Punishment' and *North*, Larsen's compositions are artistic constructs. Although he was taking the photographs as archaeological records, being part of his work for the National Museum in Denmark, the works draw viewers in rather than turning them away. The extraordinary beauty of the Tollund Man's foot is so detailed that we might imagine him walking the Danish boglands; a close-up of the Grauballe Man's hand reveals trimmed nails; the line of his body, out of the bogland and laid in the museum, is – as Heaney describes – 'the black river of himself'.

The photographs of the Tollund Man and the Grauballe Man are at the same time forensic and aesthetic. When we gaze at the Tollund Man's face in close-up, we are distracted from the noose around his neck, which conceals beneath it a cut throat. Larsen's tender focus captures the 'dead or asleep?' paradox of the bristled chin as the man lies in foetal repose. Other images are arresting for their ability to shock; the sodden peat bearing down for 20 centuries has distorted the face of the Grauballe Man into a grimace, as earlier we see him 'born' out of the bog. The contrast is made with bog body images taken by other photographers, among them the more stark portrait of the Windeby Girl, the subject of Heaney's 'Punishment'; she is pitifully vulnerable in Glob's book, with her blindfold, her shaven head, and the accompanying image of the pale coral form that is her exposed brain.

As well as Glob's book, Larsen's images of bog people illustrated Palle Lauring's award-winning literary account *The Land of the Tollund Man: The Prehistory and Archaeology of Denmark* (Lauring 1957) and were commended by the eminent archaeologist Glyn Daniel as 'some of the finest archaeological photography that has ever appeared in a book'[2]. They also appeared in Geoffrey Bibby's evocative account of archaeological practices, *The Testimony of the Spade* (Bibby 1956). So significant are Larsen's images to Danish visual heritage that *Faces from the Past*, a volume of Larsen's images of prehistory, commemorated the fiftieth birthday of Queen Margaretha of Denmark in 1990 and was accompanied by an exhibition of his work.

Contemporising Larsen's Bog Bodies

On a personal note, which does have a bearing on my own perspective of Larsen's work, I came to *The Bog People* in 1992 as a mature undergraduate archaeologist at Oxford, exploring the reading list for Iron Age archaeology. I was captivated by Glob's text and, in particular, its accompanying images. As a former journalist, I recall being surprised to be coming to *The Bog People* for the first time, but soon established that by the 1990s the book was out of popular cultural currency. It was often to be found in second-hand shops but it was no longer part of common parlance. By coincidence, Heaney was then professor of poetry at University and I quickly felt this dialogue of archaeology and poetry deserved further exploration. This became the subject of my doctoral thesis (Finn 1999a). I first presented a paper on this association at the conference convened for the Silkeborg exhibition in 1996[3]. In 2003, I received an email from Stephen Vaughan, a professional photographer who had viewed this site, asking if I might write an essay to accompany his work – a long-term project of photographing bog people and bog landscapes in Denmark and the UK – in which I could explain his own captivation for its myth and archaeology. Vaughan, who was directly inspired by Larsen and Heaney, had grown up in Cheshire near the find site of the best-known UK bog body, the Lindow Man. This, and the fact that his father was a gardener who worked with bog, had shaped his sensitivity for the landscape and its finds. In particular, Vaughan was concerned about its conservation at a time when the Lindow Moss bogland was under threat of development for housing, an issue that is unresolved today.

Vaughan sent me a set of his photographs and encouraged me to critique them – a request that provided him with his first contextual analysis and me with a new challenge to articulate the continuing resonance of Larsen's work, using the language of contemporary art rather than academia. Below is the resulting essay, which accompanied Vaughan's prints to the Fotofest event in America.

OPENED LANDSCAPE   A response to Stephen Vaughan's photographs by Christine Finn

'The wet land. Bogland. Where a body lies dead still in almost-water, an inner narrative hidden in its chemistry: layers of bone, flesh, skin. Colour merging into damp, hues deepening in cool water.

Stephen Vaughan's photographs evoke a landscape of duality. A place where wet meets dry in an empasse of the known and the unknown, where men, digging down through centuries of peat, exposed a catacomb of lost souls from 2000 years ago. In an act of transformation, they lifted them from the earth into the air. Digging deeper still, they found a battleground of prehistoric wood-limbs which lived long before the pace of men.

People were buried here. Sacrificed to the earth in celtic ritual - an appeasement, or a punishment, the origins obscure. Tollund, Lindow, Grauballe, Borre Fen, Windeby - the placenames naming men and women. Their immortality claimed by archaeologists' tools, and the still of display. More dubious are deaths of others who may have buried their own selves, stepping out onto the bogland without thought of the hungry land sucking them in.

The bodies hung in peat, suspended between the ancient world and the now, until peat-cutters, searching fuel, reached their layer. And horrified, fell back as half-men, half-landscape, emerged. They had cut into a liminal world, where known and unknown blurred as bog. Their metal tools were wands; conduits to the ancient land which magicked earth from flesh and bone; being, remaining, stains beyond imagining.

On a crisp day in Denmark 50 years ago, a photographer, Lennart Larsen, went to work, and transformed his museum science into art. A poet, Seamus Heaney, rescued the bog bodies with honed words spanning millennia. With a nod to both, Vaughan celebrates his home land, revisiting and reworking the land's look, celebrating the interregnum, and the pulse over time. He is witness to a series of temporalities.

A tree-sentinel marks the spot, a spot, of something undefined. A leaden bog swallows sky to take a plate of silver in its maw. Impendingness lurks behind a corner of fern. Wavelets of pale grass frame a dark, black pool. A benign treescape is restless with a path cut through, to where? For whom? A tramped field is scarred with signs of recent removal. Snow and ice glaciate the bog, sealing some thing in.

The prints are colour, and yet most seem to have been bled dry of it, as much as the bog bodies who leached their life into the earth. When shades appear, they are ghostly apparitions. A blur of pale blue. A shimmer of sunlight.

Sometimes, though, colour appears to shock. Mercurial pools emerge. Bubbles of fluorescence evidence life surfacing. Moss appears as churned green sheets on a grassy bed. The trail of golden coins scattered as leaves on another path. The same path which heaves up to split the land into two events. The untramelled, soft, bog with its crown of tangled wood; and the scraped land of fresh-removed history.

In one image, both sides of the landscape are shaved bare, with bog hair left like the stubble on the Tollund man's face, and bog-water rippling through as blood dripping from a nick.

A trackway, slightly kinked, is defined by the Lindow light, and journeys on. It is perilously weighty on the already weighty peat. How has it stayed upright, when men and women can sink and disappear for millennia? What is the secret of its bogland embrace?

Vaughan's photographs encourage us to look beyond and beneath. The archaeologist, and the poet, are seers. They, too, probe and work away at layers, respecting each as a testament. Transformation takes place in the dark. Brain works away from the light to hone and chip at words; the body coagulates in the privacy of the soil; beneath the camera's dark cloth, and in the dark room, the photographer maintains an evasive dialogue with the light.

The iris opens and closes. The sound of a shutter in the pale twilight is a slow sigh. Otherwise stillness, only the sound of water and air across the surface of the bog, and the slow movement of the body in the earth as it contorts under the weight of its creeping, leaden, shell. The final weight of the bog on softened skull, and a sigh longer still.

The image is etched onto the ground-glass, read upside down, refined and distilled to expose, just so. A stillness in the dark. The poet stops short of shaving his words to bare point. The archaeologist resists another layer. The bogland holds back complete dissolution of the body, and holds it. Just so.

These images are incidents of memory. The fall of the sun. Shadows. The photographer embossed into the landscape by the light-play. Elongated stumps spear the earth and the sky, as sticks held down the women whose crimes wrought their punishment in the bog. Bedded forever with the land. In the land. Becoming the land.

As if in pliant observation, trees cower on the far horizon. Their limbs shake. Perhaps, you next. Sharp grass erodes to softness. But it is a trick of the light. The downy profile is a ruse. Stay back. The bogland will take you. The camera shifts, as if to look away means rescue. But the simplicity of a cut vein of bog reveals a seepage. It disquiets.

Stephen Vaughan could have charmed us with the landscape of his childhood. Instead he takes us to look at the detail, to see beneath the surface and grasp the unnaturalness of this natural scene. The track is not salvation, he says. It takes you in deeper. The sunrise is a blaze just here, but look how quickly the bogland gulps its raw colour.

Don't be deceived by this land. It is water by another name. Bog land. Wet land. It has witnessed history. Come in closer. Closer still, and it will speak to you. Confide. Take you in.'

Past and Present Image of Bog Land and Bog Body: An Exhibition

In 2004, I invited Stephen Vaughan to present his first solo show in an exhibition I was curating at the University of Bradford's Gallery II. *Strange Powers: Bog Bodies and Bog Lands* had two aims: to bring together Heaney's words and Larsen's images together for a new audience, and to celebrate Larsen's contribution to the bog people narrative by conjoining his work with Vaughan's made 50 years later, but using the same photographic process.

The exhibition ran for one month, between February and March 2004, and attracted nearly one thousand people in. The audience was mainly Bradford University undergraduates and staff, with some visitors from the surrounding areas, either regular visitors to Gallery II shows or drawn in by the publicity the exhibition generated. The audience was generally not conversant with bogland archaeology, Heaney, or Larsen. I wrote a series of panels to accompany the images and Heaney's poetry; ran workshops; hosted talks by Vaughan and Andrew Wilson and Tim Taylor, two of my colleagues from the Department of Archaeological Sciences at Bradford; and also directed a theatre piece, *Shikha*, which was devised by two Bangladeshi actors which reflected the cultural make-up of Bradford's student population. Also included were two film showings: a preview edit from *The Cutting*, an independent film made by Brian Catling, head of sculpture at the Ruskin College of Fine Art and Drawing, Oxford, and Tony Grisoni, a Hollywood scriptwriter, and again inspired by Glob and Larsen; and *I Went Down*, a popular Irish road movie made in 1997 and set in the central Irish boglands. Its director Paddy Breathnach, a former documentary filmmaker in Ireland, had earlier told me about a particular sensitivity towards the bog's aesthetic possibilities; the film was scripted by Conor McPherson, whose award-winning theatre work regularly draws on the myths that emanate from that same intensely potent landscape.

Gallery II is an exhibition space next to a cafe and a busy student thoroughfare. Visitors were guided into the exhibition by a panel containing this quotation from an old Danish almanac, which appears in the preface to *The Bog People*.

> There is a strange power in bog water which prevents decay. Bodies have been found which must have lain in bogs for more than a thousand years, but which, although admittedly somewhat shrunken and brown, are in other respects unchanged.

Inside, Vaughan's prints presented a striking visual effect, positioned on white walls in semi-darkness and spotlit; the accompanying descriptive panels about Glob, Larsen, Heaney, and archaeological science (on the nature of the bog and its preservative qualities) were positioned together with examples of Heaney's bog poems: 'Bogland', The Tollund Man', Grauballe Man', and 'Punishment'. At one end of the gallery was a DVD projection of *Strange Powers*, a series of photographic images with music and a voiceover of Seamus Heaney's commentary and poetry, taken from his spoken word cassette *Stepping Stones*. The images included the first known photograph of a bog body, included in Glob's book; several Larsen images intercut with Vaughan's landscapes; and close-ups of his father's head and hands, the latter meeting my special request to allow me to juxtapose Larsen's 1950s image of the Grauballe Man's peat-tanned hand with that of Vaughan's gardener father. The sequence ended with photographs by Andrew Wilson, who works on bog bodies in the Department of Archaeological Sciences at Bradford; they are scientific images of actual specimens from the Jutland bodies.

As I wrote in the catalogue, 'This installation and exhibition brings together the worlds of science and the arts to explore a curious phenomenon: bog bodies and bog lands. Its inter-disciplinary approach explores the way in which the strange power of bog water, with its potential to preserve, has captured the imagination of archaeologists, artists, filmmakers, photographers, and poets' (Vaughan 2004). The exhibition was reported in the regional press, local radio, on arts and Irish cultural websites, and in the university's in-house publication. I also persuaded the university to open the venue at the weekends, which enabled me to talk with visitors about their response to the work. A visitors' book encouraged responses that brought an interesting range of views from 'disturbing' and 'scary' to 'fascinating' and 'thought provoking'.

Conclusion

The digital film of *Strange Powers* is continuing to reach new audiences: since March 2004, I have shown it as a DVD at a Computer and Archaeology Workshop in Austria, at the European Association of Archaeologists conference in France, in Italy, and at the Theoretical Archaeology Group meeting in Scotland. In March 2005, a version formed part of a collaborative art exhibition, Memoire Collective, in the crypt of St. Pancras Church in London (see Finn 2006) and it was later screened at an archaeology film festival in Rovereto, Italy. Stephen Vaughan has continued to work with Larsen's photographs and showed his *Opened Landscape* prints alongside Larsen's at the Photofusion Gallery in London in 2004. The gallery's website included this text accompanying the show: 'Stephen Vaughan's project is primarily concerned with the layering of time within the landscape. With qualities of stillness, silence and clarity, his photographs resonate with connections to archaeology, history, memory and myth'.[4] *Opened Landscape: Lindow, Tollund, Grauballe* is a series of large-format colour photographs of three sites: Lindow Moss in Cheshire, with accompanying sequences made at Bjældskovdal (Tollund) and Nebelgard Fen (Grauballe) in Jutland, Denmark.

These sites are linked by the three most significant discoveries of preserved, Iron Age, sacrificial bog burials and have been the undisturbed resting places of preserved human bodies for two thousand years. The bodies have been almost perfectly preserved by the unique qualities of the acid bog water. As sites of ritual and sacrifice, these 'opened landscapes' occupy a place between the known and the unknown, between being and remaining, where the preserved surfaces of accumulated centuries rest in a state of liminality, awaiting the peat cutter's spade and the scrutiny of archaeologist, poet, or picture maker. Vaughan's photographs show a vivid representation of the bogland view taken with a large 8 x 10 inch format camera, while also emphasising the landscapes' surface in minute detail. Scrutiny – like that of the archaeologist – creates the potential for discovery and gives

Figure 6.3   Invitation from *Strange Powers* exhibition (Matthew Lupton).

Figure 6.4 Photograph of bogland (Stephen Vaughan).

heightened significance to each fragment of the landscape surface. For the photographer and viewer, the act of looking is transformed into an act of investigation – a search for evidence and meaning (Opened Landscape' exhibition, Photofusion Gallery, London, 19 November 2004 – 16 January 2005 [see Figs. 6.3–6.4]).

Other creative projects inspired by the bog bodies, and Larsen's images in particular, include a series of paintings by Kathleen Vaughan, a Canadian artist whose work accompanied a tour; she describes her epiphany on her website[5] (for further discussion of this, see Finn 2006). In February 2005, another touring show, *The Bog People*, opened at the Museum of Science and Industry in Manchester, a location appropriate for the Lindow Man site in Wilmslow. Stephen Vaughan showed his photographs and I spoke about Heaney, showed *Strange Powers*, and – in the exhibition space – gave writing workshops to adults and children. These mysterious bog people are finding a new generation to enthrall. A Google search on the subject throws up many sites, including, not least William Clark's sideways reverence: the Tollund Man as a 'virtual poster-boy for human sacrifice'[6].

Notes

1. http://www.mesh5.com/tension/febmarch/bog.htm (accessed 15 November 2005).

2. http://www.mesh5.com/tension/febmarch/bog.htm (accessed 15 November 2005).

3. The conference report was posted on the web at http://www.ucl.ac.uk/prehistoric/past/past25.html#Bog (accessed 15 November 2005).

4. http://www.mesh5.com/tension/febmarch/bog.htm (accessed 15 November 2005).

5. http://www.akaredhanded.com (accessed 15 November 2005).

6. http://www.mesh5.com/tension/febmarch/bog.htm (accessed 15 November 2005).

PART III

HAS THE MEDIA CHANGED ARCHAEOLOGY?

7

ARCHAEOLOGY AND
THE GERMAN PRESS

Marion Benz and Anna Katrien Liedmeier

Introduction

For more than ten years, German archaeologists have focused
on the relationship between archaeology and popular culture.
In most cases, their studies have concentrated on museums,
films, and TV documentaries (Denzer 2004; Felder et al. 2003;
Stern 1994; Schmidt 2000). In the print media, the focus has been
on headlines and pictures. Whereas there have been some valuable studies in Scandinavia, Great Britain, and the United States
a similar analysis of the German press is only in its infancy. One
example is Cornelius Holtorf's study of the Anglo-Saxon print
media (Holtorf 2005c); and another is a seminar series at the
Department of Near Eastern Archaeology at the University of
Freiburg, where some aspects of the German print media were
analysed for an overview. These analyses are based on the perspective of the archaeologists, looking at how their profession
and most importantly they themselves are presented to the public. Needless to say, the results are rarely to their satisfaction.

The aim of this study is different. We tried to find out how
journalists create an interesting story using archaeological information and which factors guide them in their choice of subject,
matter, and style. It is only when we understand these factors and
the point of view of the journalists that it might be possible to

further improve the communication that is – at least in Germany – still often dissatisfactory. If the cooperation between media and archaeological science was better, it would be a win-win situation. Readers could profit from informative and entertaining articles about archaeology; journalists would get first-hand information more easily; and archaeological research would be better promoted in popular culture.

Method and Questions

During research on scientific journalism at the Department of Near Eastern Archaeology at the University Freiburg, Germany, led by one of the authors (M.B.), numerous students (see database and acknowledgements) compared the archaeological content of German and Swiss newspapers and magazines. Several questions were posed.

- What significance does archaeology have in popular journals?
- What editorial choices were made regarding archaeological topics, the associations evoked, and the style of the texts? Moreover, do they mirror the profiles of the magazines and newspapers or represent the archaeological research?
- Are archaeological articles used to project our own values and wishes onto the past?
- What picture of archaeology, archaeologists, and our ancestors is presented?

Database

The selected newspapers and magazines comprised a variety of styles. A conscious decision was made to only include popular journals to which mainly journalists rather than archaeologists contribute. Magazines like *Abenteuer Archäologie* or *Archäologie in Deutschland* were therefore excluded. The database included runs of monthly and weekly magazines and weekly and daily newspapers (see Table 7.1).

The Significance of Archaeology in the Print Media

Archaeology has garnered a great deal of interest during the last few years. High-profile events such as the *Tutankhamun* (2004) and *Troy* exhibitions (2001–2002) attracted millions of people and were big media spectacles. Yet it is questionable whether the significance of archaeology in the press is as important as these mega-events imply.

Table 7.1   The study database including runs of monthly and weekly magazines and weekly and daily newspapers

Publication	Title	Analysed period
Magazines (weekly/monthly)	Bild der Wissenschaft (BdW)	2000–2004
	GEO	1984–2004
	National Geographic Germany (NG)	1999–2004
	Der Spiegel	2002–2004
Newspapers (weekly)	Die Zeit	2004
Newspapers (daily)	BILD	2004–2005
	Frankfurter Allgemeine Zeitung (FAZ)	1993–2004
	Neue Züricher Zeitung (NZZ)	2002–2004
	Süddeutsche Zeitung (SZ)	2003–2005
	Südwestpresse (SWP)	2003–2004

A preliminary assessment of the glossy magazines suggests an increasing interest in archaeology. A number of new magazines, such as *Abenteuer Archäologie* (founded in 2004), have recently appeared on the German market. Eight of the 12 front pages in the German edition of *National Geographic (NG)* issues published in 2003 showed pictures of archaeological topics. Since June 2004, at least one archaeological article has appeared in nearly every second number of *Die Zeit*. The question is whether this is only a short-lived trend fuelled by important recent events such as the Olympic Games and the appearance of the two Hollywood blockbusters *Troy* and *Alexander the Great*. But even in *GEO*, the number of longer articles has risen in the last 15 years. Between 1985 and 1988, not a single real archaeological article appeared, while seven were published between 1990 and 1994. Between 1995 and 1999, the number rose again to 13, and the figure has remained relatively constant since then (2000–2004: 12). In *Bild der Wissenschaft (BdW)*, a magazine of popular science, the number of articles published since 2000 has also remained fairly constant. Whereas in 2000 and 2002, archaeological articles were featured in nearly every issue, in 2001 and 2003 the number was marginally less: nine and 10, respectively (Fig. 7.1). Most of the articles were written by the editor, Michael Zick. In 2001, when he wrote only two articles, the total number of archaeological articles also decreased – as compared to 2002, when he wrote eight articles. The number of articles written by other authors also increased in those 'bad' years but never reached the number under Zick. This suggests that the content depends to a large degree on the activity levels of the editor.

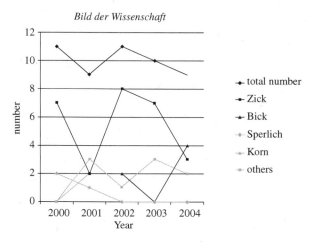

Figure 7.1 **Number of archaeological articles in *Bild der Wissenschaft*.**

The journals and newspapers described so far attract a highly educated readership. The picture changes, however, for the more popular journals (Fig. 7.2). In *Der Spiegel*, a politically oriented weekly magazine (circulation one million), long archaeological features are quite rare. Between 2002 and 2004, only 32 longer articles on archaeology were published. In 2002 and 2004, the number was 14 and 15 respectively, but in 2003 this figure fell to three. The number of articles in *Der Spiegel* depends primarily on the productiveness of Matthias Schulz. He, like Michael Zick, is part of the editorial team and nearly half of the articles (44 per cent) are written by him. In regional newspapers, archaeology is virtually always limited to local archaeological themes and the significance shrinks considerably. Nevertheless, between 2003 and 2004 in the *Südwestpresse (SWP)*, we could observe a general increase in nearly all archaeological topics. Prehistoric archaeology and provincial Roman archaeology in particular were increasingly featured. In the *Süddeutsche Zeitung (SZ)*, which has a relatively young, educated readership, only 31 longer articles on archaeology were published between April 2003 and February 2005 (Fig. 7.3). Seventy per cent of these articles featured local sites, but only one appeared in the section covering 'Wissen'. As this is quite typical for daily newspapers, we will take a closer look at this division. Archaeology obviously has yet to reach the 'standard' of the hard sciences. The newly created science magazines of the *SZ* and *Die Zeit* underline this fact well. Not one article on archaeology was

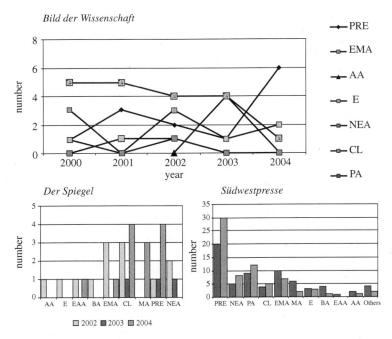

Figure 7.2   **Significance of topics in** *Bild der Wissenscahft, Der Spiegel,* and *Sudwestpresse.*

published in the two *SZ* magazines until April 2005. The *Zeit Science Magazine* did at least feature one, in the second edition of 2005.

This aspect of 'intellectual standard' deserves a digression. On the one hand, archaeology garners interest – among other reasons – because it appears to be understood very easily compared to mathematical equations or chemical formulas. 'Nice finds' and the 'adventure of discovering a treasure' do not seem to deserve a scientific education. But this attraction masks a big problem for archaeological reports. Few local editorial teams can afford to have archaeologists writing for them. An exception is the *Neue Züricher Zeitung (NZZ),* which has at least six archaeologically educated authors contributing regularly. But as we shall see later, the *NZZ* also differs in other respects from the other newspapers. On the other hand, local journalists often feel unable to cope with all the archaeological dates and facts (Kapff 2004: 127). They are interested in the subject matter but lack the necessary background knowledge to present the results in a wider context. This suggests that scientists presuppose too much basic knowledge and do not present their facts at an understandable

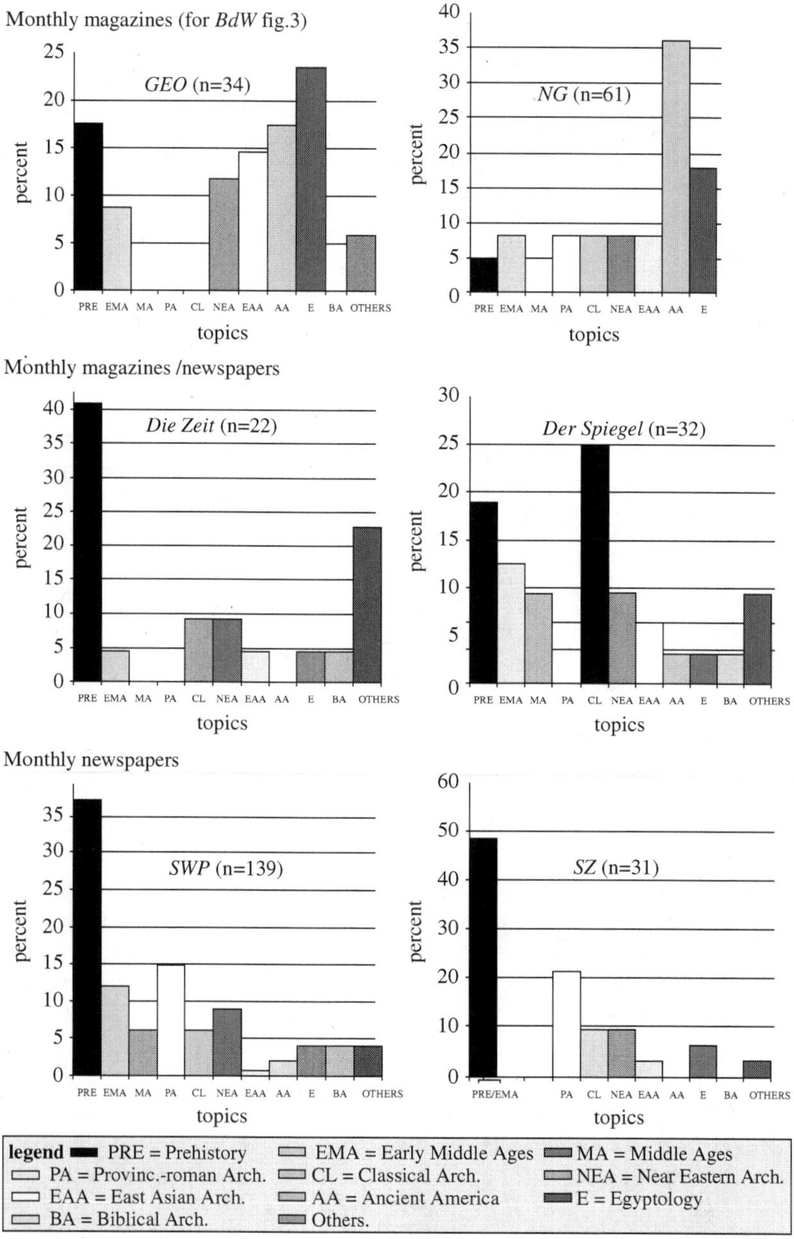
Monthly magazines (for *BdW* fig.3)
GEO (n=34)
NG (n=61)
percent
topics
PRE EMA MA PA CL NEA EAA AA E BA OTHERS
Monthly magazines /newspapers
Die Zeit (n=22)
Der Spiegel (n=32)
Monthly newspapers
SWP (n=139)
SZ (n=31)
PRE/EMA PA CL NEA EAA AA E BA OTHERS
legend PRE = Prehistory
EMA = Early Middle Ages
MA = Middle Ages
PA = Provinc.-roman Arch.
CL = Classical Arch.
NEA = Near Eastern Arch.
EAA = East Asian Arch.
AA = Ancient America
E = Egyptology
BA = Biblical Arch.
Others.

Figure 7.3a Relative frequency of topics in monthly, weekly and daily German newspapers and magazines.

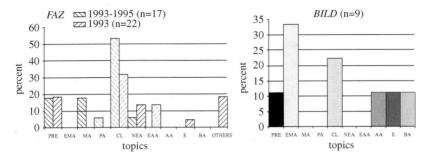

Figure 7.3b   Relative frequency of topics in daily newspapers.

level. The results are often disappointing. Just one of many examples is 'Gegen Ende der Jungsteinzeit vor etwa 15 000 v. Chr. tauchen keramische Funde auf' ('Ceramic finds appear at the end of the Neolithic period approximately 15,000 years ago')[1]. Neither the date nor the fact that 'ceramic finds appear at the end of the Neolithic' are correct, but especially in local newspapers – where no specialists are at hand – wrong dates and the wrong denomination of cultures and phases occur on a regular basis. So the easy comprehension that appeared to be an advantage becomes on closer inspection a problem for the communication between science and the press.

The high number of articles on prehistory in *Die Zeit* points to an even more fundamental aspect of this problem. Once a journalist has established good contacts with an archaeological team, he or she automatically becomes an 'expert' on this topic. In consequence, as an 'expert' his or her interest in the topic increases and he or she – consciously or not – publishes more articles on this topic. So the well-written press releases of the Department of Early Prehistory and Quaternary Ecology Research in Tübingen on Palaeolithic art in the Swabian Mountains led to a couple of articles on prehistory in *Die Zeit*. Urs Willman, editor of the science section of *Die Zeit*, reflects, 'I am glad that the archaeologists of Tübingen provide us regularly with a lot of information' (2006: personal communication). This means that it is not scientific results but the regularity and quality of press releases that is decisive in gaining wider publicity. Furthermore, good public relations not only improve the publicity of one particular project, but also of the topic in general.

To return to our analyses: whereas in the local newspapers there are few archaeological articles, they are at least informative. In the *BILD*, the significance is very different. This newspaper, founded in 1952 imitating the *Daily Mirror*, now – unfortunately – has the highest circulation. Nearly four million copies are sold daily. The newspaper claims to have a readership of over 12 million Germans. Archaeological themes are surprisingly frequent. Between 1 November 2004 and 9 January 2005 (70 days), nine relevant articles were published, which translates into approximately one article per week. At least there seems to be good potential, which could be improved in quality if the information flow from the scientific section to this newspaper were better.

In sum, we have seen that there is a relatively high interest in archaeology. But the more popular the print media, the more the archaeological results are used rather to entertain than to inform – two aspects that do not exclude each other at all. In good popular science articles, both aspects are combined. Yet knowing the different styles and aims of the different newspapers, we are sure that scientists – or the responsible press offices – could increase the number of articles and their quality. Instead of overloading the journalists with spectacular finds or results, one should also furnish them with understandable background information. Another aspect that also reveals itself obvious is the power of individual members of the editorial team.

Coverage of Archaeological Reports

One trend apparent in the German press data is that the choice of topics reported does not primarily reflect new research results. Results (remarkable or otherwise) are often quite old when they are published in the public media. Only scientific scandals are jumped on at once, like the incredibly infantile 'new battle of Troy', where scientific differences in interpretation resulted in mud-slinging in the media. The conservative *FAZ*, the liberal *Der Spiegel*, and nearly all the local newspapers reported on this debate. Beside this voyeuristic aspect, the factors that have the greatest influence on the choice of topics are:

- Relevance ('News you can use').
- Proximity.
- Currency (especially for weekly magazines and daily newspapers).
- Sensation.
- Competition.

Relevance

What do the archaeological results mean to the reader? A survey of 100 people conducted by the University of Freiburg showed, for instance, that people are most interested in learning from the ancient Egyptians when it comes to the present and the future (Efthymiadis and Heinz 2003). The diagram of division of themes in *BdW* shows some very interesting trends, which also appear in other magazines and newspapers as well. We note a steep increase in prehistoric themes in 2004, whereas classical archaeology is almost non-existent. The same trend can be observed in *NG*, *Der Spiegel*, and the *SWP* (Figs. 7.2, 7.4). The increase in features on classical archaeology in these two newspapers is most probably due to the Olympic Games and the film *Troy*, which provided all magazines and newspapers with an occasion to report on antiquity. The increase in articles on prehistory is also seen in *Die Zeit* (9 of 22), the *SWP* (prehistoric archaeology rose from 29 per cent in 2003 to 42 per cent in 2004), and the *SZ* (prehistoric archaeology: 48.5 per cent; provincial Roman archaeology: 21.2 per cent [Fig. 7.3a]). Even in *GEO* – which, in contrast to other journals, reports regularly on archaeology worldwide – both archaeological articles published in 2004 were on prehistory.

How do we interpret this trend? Does it reflect a search for an identity in the past? If so, it is not surprising that 'in the Rhineland and the south, the Romans form part of regional cultural identities, while in the north of Germany, megaliths give access to the past' (Schmidt 2000: 245). The less interested a newspaper's readership is in science, the more the spectacular finds are predominant. As one student put it, 'Readers of the *BILD* don't want boring scientists, but spectacular finds' (Oliver Scheek 2006: personal communication). But even in the

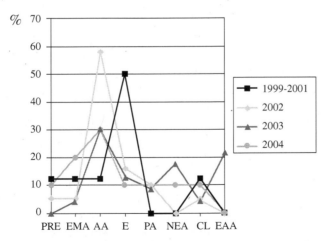

Figure 7.4 Topics per year in *National Geographic*.

FAZ in 2004, most of the archaeological articles dealt with new finds. Although this conservative nationwide newspaper has an educated readership, it is apparently still addicted to the nineteenth century classical *Bildungsbürgertum* (the educated middle classes) ideal of collecting beautiful antiquities (cf. Gero and Root 1994).

Proximity

Since the crisis in the print media of 2001, many newspapers have changed their strategies, trying to provide more reader-oriented 'infotainment'. The increasing interest in local archaeology mirrors this desire to produce spatio-temporal, affective, and social proximity to the reader (Lüger and Schäfer 2004: 51). Whereas temporal and affective proximity is mostly reached through style, the choice of topics shows the concern for spatial and social proximity. Local newspapers can achieve this quite easily since they concentrate on local finds. Seventy per cent of the articles in the *SZ* were reports on local archaeology. Such patriotic attitude can be taken so far that even the Bavarian custom of the 'maypole' (a decorated post erected on May 1st of each year) is placed in the same line of tradition as an ancient rite from the Near East. Even when the theme was archaeology in foreign countries, the tribute to local patriotism can be seen in the titles: 'The Man of Munich' for excavations in Egypt[2] or 'Munich Archaeologists… in the Euphrates Valley'[3]. In the *SWP*, too, articles of local interest dominate. The desire to serve the readers' interest is also shown by the important role classical antiquity plays in the *FAZ* – owing to its conservative readership (Fig. 7.3b).

The dictum of proximity is also relevant for nationwide magazines. The steady increase of portraits on the front page of *GEO* illustrates the tendency to produce social or affective proximity quite well. In 1999, eight out of 12 titles were illustrated with people; in 2000 and 2001, the number rose to nine, in 2002 and 2003 to 10. In 2004, it reached a peak at 11 out of 12. The strong personification of scientific research in *GEO* is also well illustrated by the seven archaeological stories that figured on the front pages between 1999 and 2004: 'Der geheimnisvolle Pharao' and 'Wer war Jesus' (2004); 'Hatschepsut' and 'Tschingiskan' (2002); 'Neandertaler' (2001); 'Tutanchamun' (2000); and 'Ramses' (1999). Archaeology is thus reported from the perspective of charismatic individuals. Furthermore, the high percentage of articles on Mesoamerican archaeology (36 per cent) in *NG* can also be explained in light of the desire to produce proximity, as *NG* is originally an American magazine. It is therefore not surprising that in

2002, just after the sad events of 11 September 2001, there was an increase in the number of articles on this topic, from 12 per cent to nearly 60 per cent (Fig. 7.4). Aside from an emphasis on American issues, the interest in German topics is not negligible either. Asked to publish an article on excavations in Tunisia, the typical German editor's first question is whether there were German archaeologists involved in the digging! A full comparison of topics shows that there are some regions of the world that are seldom or never represented in German print media (except in *GEO*): these are Africa (with the exception of Egypt), Southeast Asia, East Asia, and Australia. Obviously, in these cases the proximity is not there, either culturally or spatially.

Currency

This does not refer so much to the currency of the find, but rather to the currency of other public events connected with the topic – be it the sad events of the Iraq War, the Olympic Games, important exhibitions, newly released motion pictures, or publications. All are welcome opportunities to publish archaeological articles, but are not necessarily correlated with currency of scientific results.

Sensation

Needless to say, the words 'sensation', 'sensational', or 'spectacular' appear in nearly every article, either to disguise the fact that the results are rather boring, or to mask the inability of the author to evaluate the meaning of the find. In fact, really spectacular finds are quite rare from the point of view of scientific research. But if a find were really spectacular, it would be one of the most important conditions for a subject to be chosen.

Competition

Competition is an internal factor in the media that is often neglected (Kapff 2004: 129). When one important newspaper reports on an archaeological theme, the regional newspapers are practically forced to write about it as well. This means that once you have convinced influential editors to write about your excavation, you have achieved an important step towards more publicity. This effect is shown in recurring themes, such as the 'Frozen Fritz' of the 1990s or the 'Himmelsscheibe' of Nebra of 2003–2004. However, it must be stressed that there are some subjects that are practically excluded from publication – e.g., archaeological theory and methodology. Occasionally, there are reports on new scientific methods (such as x-ray[4], anthropological, or archaeobiological analyses[5]), but as we have seen before, the *NZZ* is exceptional in so far as it has archaeologically educated authors. In this case, Geneviève Lüscher wrote both articles. Cultural-theoretical methods in archaeology are consequently neglected by the press. We can only think of one example of such a background article, on the importance of context in archaeology[6]. The choice of this topic was entirely due to a former editor and would be unthinkable today.

Before concluding this section, we want to discuss another factor that influences the choice of a topic: the power of editorial decision making (Fig. 7.5). We can only show this effect in two magazines, *Der Spiegel* and *BdW*; the data of the other newspapers are either not detailed enough, or there are so many different authors that no single author holds the power of decision. In *Der Spiegel* and *BdW*, Matthias Schulz and Michael Zick write most of the archaeological articles. As the figures show, both hold a lot of the decision-making power. It is obvious that the topics they prefer are also those that appear most often in the paper. For Schulz, this is prehistory, as well as classical antiquity and the early Middle Ages. Zick's preference is for Near Eastern archaeology. What is striking is their method for keeping the power in their hands. In *Der Spiegel*, every freelancer – with one exception – wrote only one article. Freelancers mostly wrote on those topics that are not among Schulz's favourites. Thus, Schulz maintains his power by diffusion. The freelancers are given freedom when it comes to style, and their styles differ from the provocative style of Schulz.

Zick uses a different method. He has some authors at his disposal who write for him on a regular basis. The one who is most established is Almut Bick. She writes on prehistoric archaeology, a topic Zick has not reported on in the last five years. Although Zick chooses articles on Near Eastern archaeology from other authors, it is interesting to note that not one freelancer has written more than a single article on Near Eastern archaeology. The difference between these two editors becomes even more obvious when comparing their styles.

Textual Analysis

Associations

The media are fond of language that convey emotions and provides the reader associative space. We therefore analysed which associations

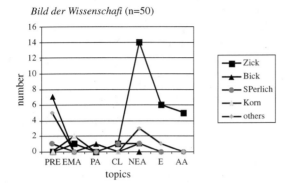

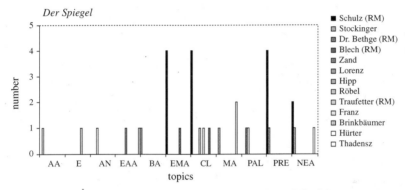

a) number of archaeological topics per author (for abbreviations cf. fig. 3a)

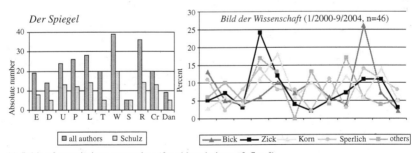

b) fields of associations per author (for abbreviations cf. fig. 6)

Figure 7.5 The influence of the editors in the choice of topics and style in *Der Spiegel* and *Bild der Wissenschaft*.

the authors use to attract the reader's attention (Fig. 7.6). For example, a 'grain chamber' becomes a 'treasury' because 'treasury' catches the eye and interest of the reader. Associations of riches and power are evoked. Phrases like 'No gold, no temple were found, but...' are used to disguise the fact that there is no spectacular discovery. Such phrases or terms can be divided into certain 'fields of associations'. In articles on archaeology, the association of 'religion/cult/myths' is of great importance. In all the media analysed, this field was commonly used: in the *NZZ*, *FAZ*, *NG*, and *BILD*, it ranked first; in *Der Spiegel*, it came second; and in the *SWP*, it ranked third just behind 'riches'. Aside from the opportunity to connect with the reader's feelings and fantasies, it is also an association that is commonly viewed as a typical aspect of ancient societies. The frequent use of these associations shows that answers to religious questions are sought in the past. In all the newspapers and magazines, the associations 'power/riches', 'luxury/gold', and 'war/catastrophe', were commonly used. These associations give the impression of touching world history and offer an opportunity to link our modern world with ancient prosperous empires. It seems illuminating to us that in *BdW*, a popular science magazine for the upper-class educated reader, 'power' is the association employed most frequently, whereas in the *BILD*, 'power' ranks at the bottom of the list.

In the diagrams of associations by author (*BdW* and *Der Spiegel*), we see the two different ways in which the editors influence the style of the archaeological articles in their journals. Schulz does this by writing many more articles than his freelancers. The curve of associations in all articles closely parallels his curve. Zick also chooses those freelancers who most often use similar associations to his own: 'power/riches' and 'luxury', as well as 'downfall'. It is also striking that women use different associations than men. Women emphasise 'cult/religion' and the 'oldest/unique', whereas male authors prefer 'power/riches', 'luxury', and (to a lesser extent) 'downfall/destruction' and 'war/catastrophe'. Associations that generally play a minor role are 'exotic', 'sex/love', 'unknown', and 'medicine'. The 'unknown' and the 'exotic', which appear to have been a point of attraction in former times, have been replaced by proximal concerns. In the *SZ* and *Die Zeit*, both of which claim to have an educated readership, 'civilization' ranks highest. 'Crime', 'adventure', and 'danger' are mainly used in magazines with picture reports. For *GEO*, the danger for the archaeologists is of great importance. '*Raubgräber*' (tomb robbers) lurk everywhere and the archaeologist has to work with a high personal commitment in order to escape the danger (cf. Gero

Monthly magazines

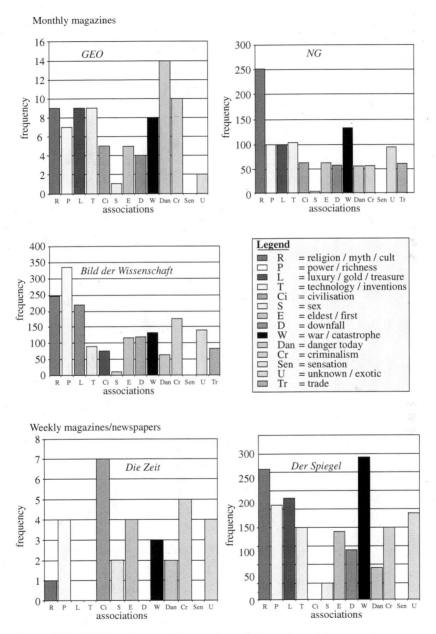

Figure 7.6a   Fields of associations of monthly and weekly magazines.

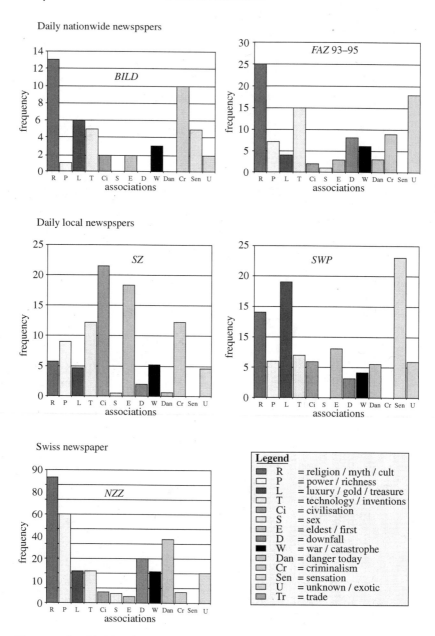

Figure 7.6b **Fields of associations of daily nationwide and local newspapers.**

and Root 1994). But the incidence of such words is not as frequent as one would suppose. The proximity to the reader has become more important than transporting him or her into another world. Finally, the words 'first/oldest' are employed to show the sensational element of the 'discoveries'. The *NZZ* and *FAZ* use far fewer of these terms and try to appear matter of fact and serious. The local journalists in the *SZ* and the *SWP* primarily use words that are linked to 'first/oldest' and 'sensation', even more so than the *BILD*, although generally this is the province of the tabloid press.

Style and Construction

The media personalisation of archaeology is on the increase. There are many interviews and portraits of archaeologists and the narratives are often told through personal experiences or from a point of view. Moreover, another means of creating a sense of proximity is to use the historical present. Apart from these trends, of course, the various media have their own house style. The *BILD* reports are short and sensational. The texts are often very cleverly constructed so that news of mediocre potential becomes unique. The facts are presented in such a way that the interpretations given are not correct, but not completely wrong either. The *FAZ, NZZ, SZ*, and *SWP* endeavour to write correctly and seriously. Stylistic devices such as pictures and metaphors are seldom used. First and foremost, their texts provide facts. Nevertheless, they try to avoid technical terminology, and if it is used, it is explained. An exception is the *NZZ*, whose readers should preferably have had a classical education, incorporating ancient philology and biblical studies. But even here, scientific circumstances and complex themes are often reduced by presenting only one view, because both time for research and space in the newspaper are limited.

In contrast, the magazines use a wider range of stylistic methods. Their first aim is to entertain by telling an exciting story. *Der Spiegel* belongs to this group, as does *Die Zeit* to an extent. Their formulations are vivid and pictorial. In both the titles and texts, they frequently use neologisms and anachronisms to create a sense of proximity to the reader and make the text more colourful. The articles are often so easy and thrilling to read that one would suppose that archaeology is viewed not as a science, but a sport. These authors like to show the different interpretations of researchers. But seemingly this is not out of respect for the complexity of the science, but rather only another stylistic device to make the text vivid.

The Picture of Archaeology and Archaeologists

The resulting media portraits of archaeologists are diverse. Within the same medium, we can find the 'worldwide famous [archaeologist]' alongside dismissive descriptions (*Der Spiegel, NZZ*). In *NG*, archaeologists are tough, active guys searching for ancient bygone cultures in exotic landscapes (Gero and Root 1994). In local newspapers, they are often portrayed as experts. They work meticulously and accurately, scraping every piece of evidence like good detectives (*SWP, SZ*). But all too often, they are uncertain: 'We know virtually nothing', is one of the many sentences quoted (cf. *BdW*)[7]. Archaeologists can also be saviours of our civilization (*BdW*) or at least revive the past like magicians. It is interesting to note that in those magazines that support their own archaeological research, the description is quite positive (*NG* and, in one case, *Der Spiegel*). At the other end of the spectrum lies the picture of the chronically under-financed, shrewish freak, fighting with bureaucracy (*BdW, SWP, Der Spiegel*).

As far as archaeology as science is concerned, the picture is reduced to excavations and high-tech work in laboratories or the field. Sometimes we also find the complex puzzle of putting material sherds together. However, theoretical aspects and the time-intensive work of textual studies are not mentioned at all. In the journalists' view, it is most often chance rather than well-guided research that leads archaeologists to find something spectacular. In the *BILD*, archaeologists are rarely mentioned. Obviously, authors of the *BILD* suppose their readers to be interested only in the 'treasures' archaeologists discover rather than in science. Although the standard cliches of archaeology are reported again and again, it should be stressed that in some journals, the aim of the archaeologists to reconstruct a holistic picture of ancient cultures, and the importance of the context of archaeological finds, are also mentioned (*SWP, FAZ*).

Thus the picture of archaeology and archaeologists strongly depends on the tenor of the article. If one wants to underline the importance of the article, the archaeologist is described as an expert. But if one is reporting on a debate in archaeology, the picture might change to the other end of the spectrum, depending on the position of the journalist. When an excavation has been sponsored by the press, you can be sure of a positive report.

Images of the Ancestors

The images of our ancestors can be divided into two kinds. The first is that 'our ancestors' were simply perfect. They were everything the reader wants to be. They were mighty rulers with huge empires and possessors of gold and luxury. Their civilisations were prosperous and their trade relations were far reaching. Since they developed culture and important technologies, we are strongly influenced by them. Yet there is a difference in how this perfect image is dealt with.

While *BdW* suggests a closeness between the people today and our ancestors (the Neolithic farm house is seen, for example, as 'the archetype of the huge farms in Germany' *BdW* 2/2004), *NG* always maintains a distance from the deceased. While *BdW* sees the ancestors in a rather positive way, *NG* also considers the negative view. The negative side includes the idea that life in former times was influenced by cults and religion. The myths are interesting but strange and the rites were often barbaric. *Der Spiegel* uses mostly degrading stereotyped images such as 'Rambo', 'rude fellow' (*Grobian*), or 'corrupter of the Olympic ideals'. Moreover, in the daily newspapers except the *BILD*, you can find all these aspects in reduced form. In the *SZ* and the *SWP*, the image of the ancestors is nearly always positive. They both stress that our ancestors were gregarious. In the *SWP*, we can find plundering Teutons, cheerful musicians, and Neanderthals pottering about. Articles on scandals or brutal rituals are exceptional. In this case, the ancestors are used as a negative mirror of our own advanced society (*Der Spiegel*, *BILD*). In all the print media analysed, archaeology is partly used for the search for identity, but for the local newspapers, this is obviously the crux of the matter.

Conclusion

We conclude that print media interest in archaeology is high. Nonetheless, readers are thought to be interested not so much in the hard facts of archaeological science as in sensational discoveries – the glitter, glamour, and power of ancient civilisations. Creating a feeling of proximity to the reader and an appeal to the reader's emotions seem to be the main aims of the journalists. This influences their selection of topics and style. We could show that the various media differ in their choice of themes. Local newspapers are particularly interested in reporting on local excavations. The tendency in nationwide journals with national prehistory coming increasingly to the fore can be interpreted in the same way. It is thus not very surprising that non-European archaeology – with the exception of Egypt and ancient Mesoamerica – is seldom featured. Archaeology gains its attraction from the 'fun-action-factor' or the fascination for the exotic and unknown alone, as is still the case in *NG* (Gero and Root 1994). To a great extent, archaeology is attractive because it produces a proximity to the ancestors and therefore provides orientation from the past for the present. As a consequence, the archaeologist often appears as a mediator between past and present.

Detailed analysis of the texts has shown that by using neologisms and anachronisms, by the 'wrong use' of the present time for prehistoric settings, and by citations, proximity is produced. In magazines in particular, the archaeological findings and results are often disguised by a story to entertain. As the analyses of the associations made clear, themes like cult, religion, power, and riches are often highlighted. Also, by the choice of words and adjectives, an atmosphere of glamour or of mystical tenure is produced. This mirrors more the dreams and wishes of the authors – and those supposed to attract the reader – than the archaeological results. Often the choice of topics, the images of the past, and the style of the articles are determined by the preferences of the editor. In this sense, reporting on archaeology is still a male domain. Associations used by women and men in *BdW* differ in some ways. So we argue that if more women were to report on archaeology, we might get a different picture of the past. There is no real perception of the scientific work archaeologists do.

The picture of the archaeologist – in most cases male– is ambivalent. If the author wants to stress the correctness and importance of his or her article, the archaeologist is an expert. In other respects, archaeologists are notoriously under-financed, opportunistic, sceptical, and often uncertain. Readers should then witness the moment of discovery. Thus, not only spatio-temporal proximity but also social and emotional proximity is produced. Our ancestors are more and more portrayed as the bringers of civilisation or as mighty sovereigns, with whom readers like to identify in one long line of tradition. Articles on archaeology thus betray more about our own desires than about archaeology. In this context, it might be interesting to remember what Jan Assmann (2002: 297) wrote some years ago: 'Erinnert wird Vergangenheit nur in dem Maße, wie sie gebraucht wird und wie sie mit Sinn und Bedeutung erfüllt ist' ('The remembered past is only meaningful and coherent when being used').

Acknowledgements

We owe our thanks to the following students for their excellent work, and are grateful to them for putting their results at our disposal: Ulrike Bößmann, Christopher Burtzlaff, Isabella Denk, Jana Dümmler, Sebastian Finger, Anne-Sophie Heinz, Esther John, Marco Kircher, Petra Kohler, Sarah Lange, Julia Linke, Jens Reinecke,

Catherine di Ronco, Katrin Rackel, Oliver Scheek, Nicolas Tomo, Sebastian Wall, and Alexandra Walther.

Notes

1. *Süddeutsche Zeitung*, 22 November 2004.

2. *Süddeutsche Zeitung*, 23 June 2004.

3. *Süddeutsche Zeitung*, 20 August 2004.

4. *Süddeutsche Zeitung*, 30 October 2003.

5. *Neue Züricher Zeitung*, 12 May 2004, 23 June 2004.

6. *Basler Zeitung*, 12 February 2003.

7. *Süddeutsche Zeitung*, 22 October 2003.

8

GREAT WAR, GREAT STORY

A Personal View of Media and Great War Archaeology

Jon Price

The archaeology of the Great War is a comparatively recent field of study (see Desfossés and Jacques 2000; Price 2004; Saunders 2002; Schnapp 1999). The archaeologists involved are a small group who work together closely. The short time for which they have been working means that in reality there has been little discussion of their activities in archaeological publications. This paper is written as an informational document. It is not intended to reiterate widely known historical information and is based on observations in the field. As a consequence, there will be little in the way of bibliographic justification of data or theories. Neither does it set out to be a comprehensive listing of all media productions touching on archaeology and the Great War, but merely a contribution to the studies that others might carry out.

The Media and the Great War

The Great War is greatly misunderstood. This misunderstanding starts with the question of when it happened. Most people would say that it ran from 1914 to 1918, yet many war memorials in Britain are dated 1914–1919 and the Commonwealth War Graves

Commission records casualties overseas in this conflict through the early 1920s. British troops conscripted for the duration of a war against Germany were expected to carry on fighting in a new war against the revolutionary armies in Russia. Chinese labour battalions sent by Allied warlords to the Western Front remained on the battlefields for several years after the Armistice, carrying out clearance of unexploded ordnance.

Despite this vagueness about dates, the Great War was the first war in which modern mass media played a part. Still photography of wars first made an impact in 1854 with images of the battlefields and soldiers of the Crimean War. The telegraph, and Mr. Reuters's reports, made an impact soon after; Friedrich Engels, for instance, relayed the daily movement of troops in the war of 1866 from Germany to the *Manchester Guardian*. The Great War, however, saw the first large-scale introduction of moving pictures. The British army employed cameramen to record significant battles, and copies of the films produced were rapidly copied and distributed to cinemas throughout Britain.

The filming took place within a well-defined media context. British cinemagoers of the time were used to going to the cinema to see themselves. The majority of early film production in Britain was made up of films of ordinary people going about their ordinary lives. Film crews visited towns to film people leaving factories. Film of events was largely made up of slow panning shots of audiences or static cameras filming moving processions or parades. These films, which preceded the feature films in a cinema programme, were designed to attract viewers who hoped they might see themselves or their friends, relatives, or neighbours on the screen. The films from the battlefields were largely made up of similar shots. A large part of the film *The Battle of the Somme* consists of soldiers moving past the static camera in columns. To a modern audience, these war films are strangely unexciting. The contemporary audiences that saw them watched in the expectation of seeing people whom they knew. The interaction between observer and observed took place within a clearly understood framework. The result of this media exposure was a much closer identification with the war on the part of the population at large. After the war, it did not take long for filmmakers to realise the potential of the subject, and in 1925 King Vidor made the dramatic depiction of the lives of ordinary soldiers in *The Big Parade*. The population of Britain experienced the war through the filter of the latest mass media, both during the war through documentary and after the war through drama. This was the first time such mediation had happened.

The Media and Archaeology

Egotists and self-publicists have always been engaged in archaeology and have attempted to use whatever media was at their disposal. Schliemann's photograph (taken in the 1880s) of his wife as Helen of Troy is an early example. It is also the case that more powerful agents have controlled the media representation of archaeology for their own purposes. Film of archaeological activity, whether documentary (such as the Ford Motor Company filming the exhumation of Native American burials [1937] or the Nazi films of excavations of early German settlements [1930s]) or dramatic (such as *Raiders of the Lost Ark* [1981]), has always been driven by factors other than the archaeological intent.

The arrival of television appears to have changed this. Mortimer Wheeler's appearances on the BBC TV quiz show *Animal, Vegetable, Mineral?* (1952–1960) marked the beginning of a very different relationship between the media and archaeology. While admittedly not being completely in control of the mediation process (although Glyn Daniel was a director of Anglia TV), the archaeologist's concerns, expertise, and knowledge appeared to become more central to the production process. The use of the *Chronicle* documentary brand in the BBC's sponsorship of the British Archaeological Awards, from 1976 to 1984, made this relationship clearer. In 1991, the *Time Signs* series was broadcast, presented by archaeologist Mick Aston, who with Tony Robinson produced a pilot in 1992 for a new series: *Time Team*. The pilot programme, which was never screened, was used to persuade Channel 4 to commission the first series of *Time Team*, filmed in 1993 and released in 1994. Once it became clear that archaeology could be used to make good television, production companies began to explore the possibilities of archaeology-based TV and the archaeology series became commonplace. At this point, however, most TV archaeology dealt with existing projects.

In 2005, the Newcastle University Archaeology Department website cited being 'interested in archaeology documentaries on TV' at the top of a list of ways to tell whether an archaeology degree 'could be the course for you'.[1] The symbiotic relationship between archaeology and TV is thus complete. In most cases, this symbiosis involves TV watching archaeology. Archaeology is still most likely to be funded through statutory bodies such as English Heritage in Britain and DRAC in France, or through research grants or by developers. In 2002, Tony Pollard fronted a TV series that took things further. The *Two Men in a Trench* series used media money to fund a series of excavations of battlefield sites in Britain.

Archaeology and the Great War

Is the Great War a suitable area for archaeological activity? The events of the war were, until recently, still in living memory. In addition to the usual panoply of historical sources, there existed a vast amount of film media. Of course, archaeology is by no means simply an alternative to be used when no historical sources are available. In one sense, this question was resolved in 1984 when the media-sponsored British Archaeological Award was given – in its last year as the Chronicle Award – to Henry Wills for his study of pillboxes from 1940. An ostensibly well-documented modern conflict was accepted as a valid field for archaeological investigation. It was made clear that archaeology is defined by methodology, and thus the use of methodology validates archaeological activity. If archaeology can show relationships or activities in a new light, it is valid – no matter how recent, or in principle well documented, the subject is.

Until recently, the archaeology of the Great War was accidental, with French archaeologists finding Great War material while looking for earlier evidence. Some of these archaeologists (such as Alain Jaques) began to take the Great War material seriously, rather than seeing it as an unfortunate intrusion into more important remains. As interest grew, the tension between amateur and professional about who should do the archaeology of the Great War was stimulated by the media.

The Media, Archaeology, and the Great War

In 2000, London Weekend Television (LWT) made a documentary that featured a Belgian amateur archaeological group called the Diggers,[2] who were digging on Great War sites around Ieper/Ypres with the permission of Belgian authorities. An indication of the relationship between the media team and the Diggers can be gained from the title of the documentary, which was aired as 'Battlefield Scavengers' (2000). As a result, there was a great deal of negative press coverage in Britain[3], with much debate on British discussion websites that focused on the Great War. It is clear from reading what was posted on these sites that the participants in the discussions, none of whom were directly involved in the war, were absolutely convinced of their own connection with the war and their ownership of the cultural resources, even though those cultural resources lay in French and Belgian territory and were thus covered by French and Belgian antiquities law. In part, it seems likely that the impact of the original media coverage of the events of the Great War has contributed to this sense of ownership.

Nevertheless, the pressure brought to bear – and transmitted at parliamentary level – led to an eventual agreement by Belgian authorities to professionalise the archaeology of the Great War. Things were, however, not as straightforward as they at first seemed. In July 2001, the Broadcasting Standards Commission upheld a complaint by the Diggers and found that they had been unfairly treated in the LWT film. It is clear that the LWT documentary set out to expose a sensational story and the production used language that was not supported by evidence. The inquiry process itself stimulated further media interest and a rival media team, Maya Vision, produced the documentary 'The Forgotten Battlefields' for the *Meet the Ancestors* series for the BBC, which was aired in March 2002. This was interesting in that it did not make judgements about the Diggers, instead presenting their activities in a relatively neutral way. From an archaeological viewpoint, it was possible to view the activities represented with a critical eye, but this was not an inevitable response and most viewers would have simply seen an archaeological excavation in progress (Fig. 8.1).

It is clear that the media had discovered the potential for using Great War archaeology. In 2003, Maya Vision made contact with our group, which is now No Man's Land. Rather than filming the archaeological process, and then making a story out of it, the Maya Vision people had a new proposition. They wanted to make a *Meet the Ancestors* programme dealing with Wilfred Owen, the Great War poet, and they wanted an archaeological excavation of the location where he first experienced combat and that was the stimulus for many of his later poems (Fig. 8.2). At that time, No Man's Land was a self-funded team, carrying out limited excavations in the rear battlefield area at Auchonvillers on the Somme. Over several years, we had developed methodology – and understanding – that enabled us to achieve professional results on Great War sites. We had made contact with the new official archaeological team working on the Great War in Belgium, and it had visited our site to compare methodology. Cooperation with Maya Vision was seen within our team as a way of broadening our activities (as the excavation would be funded by Maya Vision) and gaining profile and we hoped, credibility. It is important to realise that although Maya Vision was impressed by No Man's Land's methodology and professional approach, it was because No Man's Land is fronted by Andrew Robertshaw – a senior manager at the National Army Museum, London – that Maya Vision was prepared to go ahead with the project.

As we had expected, given its track record, Maya Vision produced a very creditable documentary that did not traduce the archaeology;

Figure 8.1   Single hand excavated at Auchy-Les-Mines by No Man's Land (Jon Price).

however, the process of collaboration generated some interesting problems. It was clear from the start that the creation of a story on film and the methodical excavation of a site do not necessarily go together. Participation in the necessary fictions of story making would certainly increase our profile, but there were concerns within the team that choices made by the media team during and after the excavation would severely damage our credibility by misrepresenting chains of command, chronological sequences, and methodological choices. Despite these concerns, it was clear that the relationship between our archaeology and the media was likely to continue.

The chief problem with filming archaeology is that you do not always find what you are looking for. This was the first archaeological excavation of the front line on the Somme to be carried out by a professionally competent team. We had clear ideas of the probable

Figure 8.2 Maya Films with Peter Owen, descendent of Wilfred Owen, filming for *Ancestors: Journey to Hell* at Serre, on the Somme (Jon Price).

geology, stratigraphy, and finds. In all these areas, we had some surprises, though from the media point of view, it made more sense to show us finding what we thought we would. The single biggest problem for the media was that we kept finding bodies. We knew this would happen, and we were prepared for the eventuality, but it interfered with the story the media wanted. The result was that we generated our own story, which we took elsewhere. In the end, we fully identified two German soldiers and an individual British casualty by regiment only. None of this information was used in the documentary. As an interaction, the whole project was very successful. Maya Vision got the footage it needed to produce a good documentary. No Man's Land got valuable experience, we expanded our team to involve a colleague from Belgium, we began to address the complex issue of Great War casualties, and we improved our media profile. Beyond this, we were able to provide closure to an extended family in Germany – whose father/grandfather/great grandfather was finally buried – and we stimulated interest in two villages in the fate of their missing soldiers.

As a result of the Maya Vision production, we became involved in a much bigger media project: *Finding the Fallen* (Fig. 8.3). This project was a five-episode production by YAP Films, from Canada, filmed in early 2005 and aired in November that year. YAP was particularly interested in our success at recovering and identifying Great War casualties and proposed to fund a series of excavations covering each of the five years of the war. Each programme would create a story based

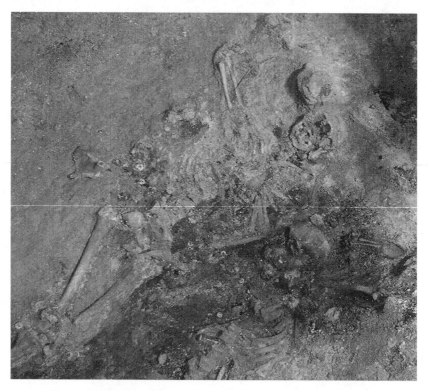

Figure 8.3   The first of six bodies of German soldiers uncovered at Auchy-Les-Mines during the filming of YAP Films' *Finding the Fallen* (Jon Price).

entirely on the excavated evidence. YAP hoped that each excavation would produce a number of bodies whom we would identify. This was not an unreasonable proposition. Over 400,000 British soldiers from the war have no known grave; the numbers for the French and Germans is considerably greater. Our own experience – and that of the Belgian excavators – combined with known casualty figures and lists of missing soldiers, led us to believe that there would be a likely frequency of one missing soldier for every ten metres of front line we excavated. This proved to be the case.

In addition, the money from the production company was not simply funding No Man's Land. The Belgian group set up under the auspices of the West Flanders Archaeological Institute to carry out work in advance of the A19 near Ieper/Ypres had run out of money, and in order to continue the work, two of the programmes planned for the series were scheduled to take place on sites of interest to the Belgian institute. The forensic identification of human remains was a central and essential element of the excavations funded by YAP. Unlike the Commonwealth War Graves Commission, which is funded by the member governments, the German war graves organisation (the Volksbund Deutsche Kriegsgräberfürsorge) is an NGO and has insufficient resources to deal with the large numbers of German war dead that continue to be found in Western Europe, North Africa, the former Warsaw Pact countries, and the former Soviet Union. The media funding permitted forensic identifications to be made, soldiers to be buried, and families to gain closure.

The Conclusion of a Beginning

The media's relationship with the Great War originated on the battlefields while the battles actually took place, and now the media exploits the resource of its own archive, as well as interacting with the archaeological creation of new texts. The media's relationship with archaeology, and more recently with Great War archaeology, began with the media observing the practice of archaeology and the activity of archaeologists. It now is engaged as a full partner with the conduct of archaeology and the creation of archaeological texts. The media, however, is always likely to be a fickle partner.

There are now several projects under way in which media companies are working with Great War archaeology. It is clear that the media has been involved in stimulating, and then funding, Great War archaeology. It is also clear that this is creating new ethical problems for the archaeologists involved. It is clearly risky to have to rely on media funding, yet the field is too new to have yet developed viable research-funding agendas. If the field is to develop, the participants must work through the existing agencies to develop research and funding strategies.

The problem of the recovery of unidentified soldiers will continue to be significant, with or without the availability of media funding for forensic work. Before the arrival of good archaeological technique, the identification frequency for recovered Great War human remains was pitifully low. The availability of media funding has enabled a much higher rate of successful identification. The continuation of this process is a moral and ethical imperative. At some point in the future, the media will lose interest and move on to new areas of popular significance. If Great War archaeology has not developed and matured sufficiently to mainstream its funding requirements, then it will subside and disappear like the traces of the Great War battlefields themselves.

Notes

1. University of Newcastle http://www.ncl.ac.uk/undergraduate/course/V400/profile/Do-you-enjoy-watching-archaeological-documentaries-on-TV (accessed November 2005).
2. The Diggers http://www.diggers.be (accessed November 2005).
3. 'Ghouls Dig Up the Bodies of Our Hero Tommies: Trading on the Sick Black Market', *Sun*, 11 November 2000, pp. 6–7.

PART IV

VISUAL ARCHAEOLOGY

9

SCREENING BIASES

Archaeology, Television, and the Banal

Timothy Taylor

> Television… [has] succeeded in lifting the manufacture of banality
> out of the sphere of handicraft and placed it in that of a major
> industry.
>
> *(Sarraute 1960: 371)*

Introduction

The provocative words of French novelist Natalie Sarraute now
seem prophetic. It was still only an assertion in 1960 that television
was a major industry, and to characterise it as the major industry
of the banal seemed rhetorical or cynical or exaggerated (or some
combination). In 2005, after nearly a half-century of subsequent
broadcasting expansion, it is hard to argue that Sarraute was not
essentially correct. Yet there is a hidden implication in her judgement that depends on the value that banality is accorded. I want
to subvert what I take to be Sarraute's negative implication by
suggesting that banality is television's main strength, and I want
to argue that it is this aspect that makes it compatible with – and
important for – archaeology and archaeologists.

   In this paper, I draw on experiences and observations from over
a decade of involvement in radio and television programmes (as a
researcher, interviewee, and consultant) to argue not only that

media work is an important form of public mission – part of the social justification of a discipline that does little (directly) to save lives or put food on the table – but more contentiously that television can change the background expectations of what human subjects are. I argue that television has the power to reveal and reflect prejudices concerning plausible patterns of human behaviour and that it has the potential, through its ability to draw comparisons and contrasts widely in space and time, to challenge such prejudices to the point of allowing new sorts of professional inference to be made within the discipline, or old and discarded inferences to be revived. I will try to make this case in relation to a theme with which I have been most recently involved in television: the presentation of controversial data and arguments for the so-called 'extreme' human behaviour of cannibalism.

The Banal and the Sensational

The word 'banal' originates in a feudal concept connected to compulsory service. Its modern sense is derived from its meaning of something (the squire's corn mill, for example) that is available to an entire community, and which that community is obliged to use. With certain caveats, this is what television is. The public service remit of the British Broadcasting Corporation and the blanket collection of a licence fee, irrespective of actual viewing habits, make this explicit.

Soap operas are the epitome of banal in its received sense. Take the listings magazine *Radio Times*, when its front cover claims an 'exclusive': 'Who's the greatest soap star of all time? – Find out in RT's State of British Soaps survey' (17–23 July 2004). This 'all time' seems at first sight desperately parochial: understood in an archaeological time frame, it hints that Hilda Ogden of *Coronation Street* has out-competed everyone in a history of performing arts stretching back at least as far as the Middle Upper Palaeolithic. But 'all time' is not meant to be understood archaeologically, geologically, cosmologically, or in terms of theoretical physics; it spans the 44 years from AD 1960 to AD 2004 and circumscribes a minor social cosmos, the limits of a known contemporary world in a particular country. The banality of this kind of television is that it epitomises (or anatomises in a manner that is frequently only lightly editorial) central aspects of current social life: 66 per cent of the *Radio Times* survey correspondents agreed with the statement 'Soaps can give useful insights into everyday problems'.

Such shows aim to show us as we are – rather than as we would like to be – and help form parts of our communal character and identity. They contain much potent (although usually tacit) information about a society's contemporary view of itself and how it understands its own, usually fairly proximal, historical origins. These types of collective representations (to borrow Durkheim's term) have much in common with the reconstruction of archaeological contexts by skilled prehistorians. These typically seek to deconstruct origin myths and reveal something of day-to-day realities in particular times and places in the forgotten past. Many of the social worlds that archaeologists study are likely to have had a cosmic horizon (in terms of detailed practical knowledge of real people and events) that extended back over something of the order of the 44 years of the soap stars' 'all time'. In short, the potential recovery of what was commonplace, common, trite, trivial, and petty (*Oxford English Dictionary* definitions of the banal) for a particular prehistoric culture is one of our discipline's principal aspirations.

From documentaries to soap operas and reality shows, television can both reveal and undermine particular sources of bias in archaeological inference. Because watching television – by contrast to reading a novel or absorbing a work of sociological analysis – is essentially passive, it is a very immediate way to reflect on our own lives. Television provides not a replacement for but an everyday alternative to the depth psychologies of novels; archaeology provides a counterpoint to the thick and nuanced accounts of individual intentionality that historians specialise in producing. Television archaeology is a means of presenting the everyday lives of people in the past, employing the same format used to present ourselves to ourselves in the present day.

As a university-based archaeologist, I am not unusual in having developed several different levels of research commitment and using different voices according to the needs and knowledge level of a particular audience. It will be useful to briefly outline the sorts of archaeology that I do and the sort of media interest and involvement this has led to. My areas of expertise are the later prehistory of Eurasia, with a particular focus on precious metalwork and iconography. Concomitantly, I have an interest in particular areas of theory, such as semiotics, ethnicity, gender, death-related behaviours, slavery, and materiality. Building on these interests, I have written two books in the popular science genre, on sex and death respectively: *The Prehistory of Sex* (Taylor 1996) and *The Buried Soul* (Taylor 2002), both with UK and U.S. paperback editions and translated into several languages.

These books are not conventional in their form of argument and have provoked a wide range of responses both academically and generally. They deal with subjects like childbirth, forced weaning, eroticism, transvestism, rape, ritual killing, child sacrifice, torture, and cannibalism. These are obviously 'media-friendly' themes, in that they involve material that is thought of as 'sensational' and can be treated in a sensationalised manner. It is worth distinguishing between the *sensational*, which arouses in us an unmediated, viscerally engaged response and thereby commands our attention whether we like it or not, and the *sensationalised*, which is spuriously coloured with the sensational, typically to make a serious but possibly boring subject hold our attention by way of an injection of inappropriate and manipulative detail (the latter often characterisable as 'explicit' in some way).

This distinction is an important one. If, for example, we professionally avoid dealing with the contents of the classic collocation 'sex and violence' because we look down on it as potentially sensationalising (which it is), we are in danger of removing sex and violence from prehistory, a period during which – in the absence of television and improving literature – there may have been few other pursuits. It is extraordinary that some of the most fascinating aspects of prehistory, from Bronze Age rock engravings of human-donkey sex and the graphic iconographies of Roman brothel tokens through the realities of Inca child sacrifice and the viciously dispatched bog bodies of Atlantic Europe, have been pushed to the disciplinary edges. They surface in footnotes and volumes for the precisely engaged specialist, although there is as much evidence from which to make inferences and interpretations in relation to these themes as there is for prehistoric subsistence activities or transport technologies.

Working in Television

Before the publication of these books, I had had some association with television and had learned about some of the pitfalls and frustrations. Following my first degree, I was employed briefly as a researcher on an archaeology series, but this did not lead further (see Hills 1983). I did not consider television as relevant to what I wanted to do until 1992 when, following publication of some of my research on the Gundestrup cauldron in *Scientific American* (Taylor 1992a, 1992b), I was contacted by *Down to Earth*, the Channel 4 archaeology magazine programme produced by David Wilson. *Down to Earth* was supported by educational publication aimed at a general audience (Taylor 1992c), which helped me feel comfortable that there was something to leaven the unavoidable sound bite style. I enjoyed working with Wilson, and as I had by then commenced research on what was to become *The Prehistory of Sex*, he and I sought a television link-up for the forthcoming book. We tried hard for several years, and failed. Although Granada Television optioned the book after its publication in 1996, all that happened was that its content was embargoed for other media uses for a year.

This was a frustrating period. I learned that academic agendas could be very different than the ideas of commissioning editors, and it became obvious that the way I wrote and would always want to write – even when presented within the genre of 'popular science' – would not produce material conducive to easy television transfer. Nevertheless, after *The Prehistory of Sex* appeared, producers started to contact me and I agreed to appear on Channel 5's *Good Sex Guide Late*. On the couch opposite presenter Toyah Wilcox and Susie Hyman of *Forum* magazine, brandishing replicas of what may be Ice Age dildoes, I said what I wanted to say on the basis that a television audience, like a student audience, would take what it wanted and understand what it was prepared to grasp. Contributions to several other programmes followed, including 'A History of Sexuality' (MPH Productions, 1997); 'Stonehenge: The Secret of the Stones' (Yorkshire Television for ITV, 1998); 'Pornography: The Secret History of Civilization' (World of Wonder for Channel 4, 1999); 'Sins of the Flesh: a History of Sex and Religion' (BBC 2, 2000); and 'Sex BC Programme 1' (Optomen/Channel 4, 2001).

Television programmes with which I have since been involved include those for BBC Timewatch, ITV1, and Channel 4 (UK terrestrial broadcasting and international syndication), National Geographic, HBO, and the History Channel (USA and syndicated), as well as for independent companies with documentary specialisms. The latter include Café Productions, founded by anthropological filmmaker André Singer, and 3BMTV, Emmy award winning producers of factual documentaries specialising in history, science, arts, and current affairs. In addition, I have been interviewed for state networks in Ireland, Germany, and Spain. Radio work has included the real pleasure of Laurie Taylor on BBC Radio 4's *Thinking Allowed* (2002) and strangely enough – following the publication of *The Buried Soul* in 2002 – contributions to a BBC Radio 2 programme on Kurt Cobain in which I was able to discuss artistic immortality, hero myths, and the public ownership of death, linking prehistory with contemporary culture (*Lamacq Live*, 2004).

One major theme of *The Buried Soul* was cannibalism, and while I was writing the book, I became a consultant for the 3BM/Channel 4 (later HBO) three-part documentary series *Cannibal* (2001; Korn et al. 2001). Since its publication, I have done more on cannibalism, including interviews for Michael Hoff Productions/National Geographic

Channel's 'Are We Cannibals?' (2004) and consulting for Engel Brothers Media's documentary 'Cannibals' for the History Channel (2005). The latter received both critical acclaim and ratings of two million viewers for the first showing and the History Channel commissioned two further documentaries. The result was that what has now become Engel Entertainment funded radiocarbon dates for important archival material in connection with a programme of English Heritage-supported threat-led fieldwork on a putative prehistoric cannibal site in the Yorkshire Dales National Park in summer 2005 (the new programme was screened in March 2006).

Because archaeology is widely popular, and British and American television has a global reach, it is hard to know where material to which I have contributed has been or is being broadcast. One unforeseen and (broadly) welcome aspect of appearing in this medium is that many old friends and colleagues from other countries send cheery emails about what one has said in a way that almost never happens with contributions to international journals (this has some interesting, perhaps even serious, implications that I will return to below). Another benefit is in attracting overseas PhD students: the quality and content of English-language documentaries is such that they can provide an attractive shop window for scholarly activity.

Formats and Genres

In a way, it was television that attracted me into archaeology too. Born in the same year in which Sarraute passed her judgment on banality, as a child I was profoundly affected by watching the BBC series *The World About Us*, a social anthropology and nature magazine programme that introduced me to my planet and my human compatriots in a way that until that point had been quite impossible. There is nothing less parochial than showing the mundane of a different culture. The double meaning of my title 'screening biases' is meant: television, although certainly reflecting our own prejudices, can also help us to screen them out by presenting a broader view of what it is to be human.

It is unfortunate that there currently seems to be much less will to make social anthropological programmes than there once was, and in some ways archaeology has taken over the mantle. The reasons for this can only be speculated upon, but may include the costs and liability issues involved in filming among remote peoples when compared to the relatively static nature of archaeology. It is also a sad fact that the number of distinctively indigenous peoples is shrinking. There is little romance in the images of shanty towns, sneakers, and

Coke cans that press forward as picturesque nakedness fades. Archaeology is thus perhaps perceived as providing a purer access to another world. But it may also be that archaeology seems to promise producers greater editorial freedom for 'making it up' and thus controlling and formatting content. Perhaps cued in by the iconic image of Raquel Welch in *One Million Years BC*, prehistory documentaries allow the re-emergence of the savage, in the form of the semi-clad reconstructors' risque but safely constructed alienness (see Fig. 10.4; also Stern in this volume).

It would be unfortunate if television archaeology were no more than a pretext for camping it up. There is no general template for how televisual archaeology content is initially defined, included, excluded, censored, or transformed through a series of academic, editorial, commercial, and sociopolitical decisions involving chains and networks of financial decision makers, programme makers, technicians, journalists, professional researchers. and subject specialists. There are format programmes like *Meet the Ancestors* and *Time Team*, which are almost archaeological soap operas. Fairly much the same thing happens in each episode, the presenters get muddy and argue, and there is no particular challenge to our idea of what it is to be human. Then there are the prestige documentary series that are sold to the public as being about archaeology but tend towards the fanciful.

These have recently included Richard Rudgley's *Secrets of the Stone Age* (in book form as *Lost Civilizations of the Stone Age* [Rudgley 1998]) and Graham Hancock's *Quest for the Lost Civilization* (in book form as *Heaven's Mirror: Quest for the Lost Civilization* [Hancock and Faiia 1998]). Aside from a civilisation being lost in each case, there is a similarity in terms of overstated claims and overly reduced causal mechanisms that one suspects only non-archaeologists could convincingly present. Aside from a civilisation being lost in each case, there is a similarity in terms of overstated claims and overly reduced causal mechanisms that one suspects only non-archaeologists could convincingly present. In both cases, the key ideas are simple to grasp: Rudgley claims we have been very sophisticated for longer than we think (based on observations concerning 'Palaeoscience' and Neolithic writing) and Hancock's theory proposes pyramids as a worldwide phenomenon and the fingerprint of a lost master civilisation.

The positive reviews from journalists and non-archaeologists of Graham Hancock's exhumation of hyper-diffusionism made depressing reading. Under the guise of uncovering mysteries, data were shoehorned into a version of an old 'master race' theory. Archaeologists tend to think that large architectural structures in different parts of the world were built with wide bases and narrow tops more due to the ubiquity of gravity than any global diaspora of astronomer-priests from a super-sophisticated ancient Antarctican civilisation destroyed by tectonic upheaval. The real (messy and convoluted) story of the demonstrably historically independent rise of astronomy, writing, and numeracy worldwide, and the developing need for public monuments, was turned down in favour of a quick fix. Television would not – except as a spoof – show an astronomy series in which celestial objects were claimed to be made of cheese, so why allow Hancock to present natural rock formations off the coast of Yonaguni (east of Taiwan) as the putative ruins of an astronomical observatory? Perhaps the reason was that Hancock had been smart enough to link archaeological data to a form of argument that the public increasingly accepted as 'scientific' – that explanations should be reductive and the truth 'simple and sayable' (Taylor 2001a).

Add glamour to simplicity and you have a winning combination. Television companies throw massive budgets at this kind of thing because they sell something acceptably exotic, the Fantasy Island to *Time Team*'s Brookside. But between these types of programme, which may have benefits in bringing people to archaeology through attraction to the camaraderie (*Time Team*) or the sites themselves (the 'lost civilisation' genre), there is much that can be truly challenging.

The Sociological Paradigm

The acceptance and analysis of a broader view of life has been formative in the development of archaeology and remains of central importance. The ethnographic observation of people using stone tools as a primary technology informed the birth of analogical thinking in the seventeenth century, with the Tradescants' distinction between 'Naturalls' and 'Artificialls', or what we now call natural history specimens and artefacts. Acheulian handaxes, previously commonly placed alongside fossil sea urchins as curiosities of nonhuman origin, were now recognised as the products of prehistoric culture. In the nineteenth century, John Lubbock justified his methods in his works *Pre-historic Times* and the *Origin of Civilization*, saying that the study of the customs and practices of modern 'savages' allowed a better conceptualisation of the ways of life of our remote ancestors, the newly conceptualised 'Palaeolithic' people of Europe.

The multi-stranded way in which antiquarianism developed into archaeology is well documented (Trigger 1989). The history of scholarship is perhaps best understood as characterised by a staggered form of paradigmatic development, rather than the neat shifts with which Thomas Kuhn understood changes in the experimento-predictive or natural sciences (Kuhn 1962). However, although Trigger notes Masterman's distinction among 'metaphysical', 'construct', and 'sociological' paradigms in the social sciences (Masterman 1970), he builds on the idea little further than to say that her analysis provides a way of understanding the existence of a shifting pattern of partly overlapping and sometimes synchronic and rival schools of thought (which he terms 'movements').

The clearest example of the independence of these paradigms is the observation that when, from the 1830s onward, C.J. Thomsen and Jens Worsaae crystallised the ideas of the closed find and stratigraphic succession to establish the Three Age system as the sequential technological paradigm for European prehistory, their data sat comfortably within the short biblical-literalist chronology in which the world was considered to be a mere six thousand years old. In Masterman's terminology, this was a shift in 'construct' paradigm, a purely epistemological development relating to the methods and procedures by which knowledge was obtained within an unchallenged metaphysic of a God-created earth. The paradigm shift at the metaphysical level came only with the application of similar stratigraphic methods to geological and archaeological contexts (where the results were clearly antagonistic to a literal reading of Old Testament ancestral genealogies) and was not really formally complete until the publication of Darwin's two main works – *Origin of Species* and *Descent of Man* in 1859 and 1871, respectively.

It is Masterman's third paradigm, the sociological, that has received least attention and is, for present purposes at least, the most interesting. Her thesis is that what is accepted as knowledge is not merely affected by the methods that produce knowledge (the construct realm) nor the fundamental *concepta* of metaphysics – the often implicit understandings of the nature of time (linear or cyclical) and cause (human agency or divine will), or essentially materialist or idealist outlooks in particular branches of scholarship. Knowledge is also affected by what we find plausible, and this is particularly true in the social sciences. The sociological paradigm labels the realm of prior beliefs conditioned by the currently familiar social world. Because it is little analysed, it is potentially the most biasing in its operation on what kinds of interpretations are accepted. In short, the suggestion is that only behaviourally 'comfortable' inferences are accepted.

Cannibal Controversies

Within archaeology, there has been only a small amount of significant discussion of the issue of how inferences are made acceptable, notably the paper by Tim Murray and Michael Walker on meaningfulness and plausibility (Murray and Walker 1988). I have been well aware that in writing about viscerally engaged subjects such as cannibalism, I run up against the sociological paradigm. However, the way that I have framed my interpretations – within a book-length treatment that develops a continuous argument that is not easily (or perhaps plausibly) abstractable – means that I have not been able to effectively signal the paradigmatic issues.

The form of some academic response to my interpretation of cut-marked human bones from a communal grave in Iron Age Siberia was telling. The bone data had been published in *Antiquity* by Murphy and Mallory (2000), in a paper concluding that the evidence was consistent with ritual funerary defleshing rather than the funerary endo-cannibalism described for this region and time frame by the classical author Herodotus. The details of my dissent from this interpretation are given elsewhere (Taylor 2002: 82) but centre on the observation that the cut-mark pattern is wholly consistent with the classical account (Murphy and Mallory had pointed out the significant difference between what they saw and the trait list for aggressive exo-cannibalism drawn up by Christy Turner for the American Southwest [see Turner and Turner 1999]). The ensuing debate, started in the pages of *British Archaeology* (Taylor 2001b), was picked up in the editorial of *Antiquity* (Stoddart and Mallone 2001), where my position was portrayed as overheated and the original interpretation as sensibly cautious.

What is of interest here is that my interpretation was (and is) demonstrably *parsimonious*, while that of Murphy and Mallory requires additional mechanisms. That is, next to Herodotus' description of forms of funerary (and also aggressive) cannibalism among three tribal formations of the Scythian period on the Black Sea steppe, they had to add a behaviour not attested by any ancient author. The reasons for ritual funerary defleshing without ingestion of the defleshed portion were given in terms of a solution to problems with grave digging in frozen winter ground and a need to arrest decay. In reality, we know from the frozen tombs of Pazyryk that the Scythian cultures were adept at embalming and organic preservation, and their methods for doing this are described in considerable detail by Herodotus – whose description, in that case at least, is thus fully vindicated by archaeology (Taylor 1994, 2002). Why then, in diligently applying Occam's razor and refusing to needlessly multiply entities in my explanation, was I seen as fanciful and less scholarly? The answer to this, I believe, is that my reassessment of the data was not *sociologically* parsimonious.

Of course, parsimony in explanation – especially of human phenomena – itself requires justification and, fetishised, can lead to reductivism. The essential point is that my reasoning, which involved a higher level of consilience to available data sets and was therefore epistemologically conservative, was perceived as baroque. The sociological paradigm in this case involves the comfortable modern assumption that because we are not presently cannibals, it is not in our nature to be.

That customary cannibalism is an empty myth is the line taken in two influential academic works (Arens 1979; Peter-Röcher 1998). These contain many arresting examples of illogic and stem, as I have argued elsewhere from (on the one hand) misguided political correctness and (on the other hand) a habit of mind characteristic of post-industrial consumer societies that I have termed 'viscerally insulated' (Taylor 2002: 56ff., 273ff.). The attempt at political correctness is very clear in Arens's *Man Eating Myth*, where the author casts doubt on Hans Staden's sixteenth century account of witnessing aggressive warfare-driven cannibalism among the Tupi (or Tupinamba) of coastal Brazil, principally because the protagonists are described as women (Staden 1929 [1557]). Arens concludes that 'prejudices depicting the unsavory nature of a minority have little if any bearing on empirical reality' (Arens 1979: 26). Why Arens thinks Tupi women were a minority is puzzling (as men seem more likely to have died in the conflicts that produced the material required for the cannibalising of vanquished enemies, it is likely they were a majority) but it is clear that he finds it 'unsavory'. He recoils at the fact that the woodcuts that accompanied Staden's publication are 'most graphic', implying that this also must cast doubt on veracity. His recoil is characteristic of 'visceral insulation' and his scepticism is actually a form of inverted imperialism. What he says, in effect, is that cannibalism is nasty because we do not do it, ergo people described as cannibals are being slandered. Like the cheesiest of archaeological reconstruction tableaux, this is the sort of anthropology that can only cope with a mild exoticism – Western mores in tribal garb.

I have little doubt that if the technology had allowed it, Staden would have brought in a film crew. Film crews did accompany later anthropologists, such as Shirley Lindenbaum, who studied the Fore of highland New Guinea during the period of their *kuru* outbreak.

Kuru was a disease later identified as a prion-protein pathogen similar to mad cow disease, and it mostly infected Fore women because they were the principal cannibals (although, unlike the Tupi, within the reverential setting of funerary endo-cannibalism). Footage of the affected population was used in several of the documentaries for which I have consulted, but none of it definitively shows human meat going from 'body to mouth'. Although Arens and others use this as ammunition for their assertion that all claims of customary cannibalism are misinformed or deliberately slanderous, the testimony of the people themselves and Lindenbaum's recounting of her experiences can leave doubt only in the minds of those who have a prior and external emotional attachment to disbelief. Lindenbaum says the women told her that they ate their dead because the dead were 'delicious' (Lindenbaum 1979).

As archaeologists, we can never see activities directly, and the closest the cannibal camp (in which I include myself) has come to absolute proof of ingestion is the famous Cowboy Wash coprolite, shown to contain the distinctive human myoglobin protein (Marler et al. 2000; Taylor 2005). But there is really no epistemological problem unless we construct one. In short, applying in the first instance a principle of parsimony, if we have a cut-marked deer bone, we say that people were eating venison; if we have a similarly cut-marked human bone, we should say that people were eating each other. More often, however, we say that in the latter case people were doing something funny that we would not do ourselves – but if it involved cutting meat off, then something other than ingestion awaited it. Precisely what might be done with human flesh removed like this is never specified. Rather, we are supposed to nod in sage agreement at this point, relieved that the author has not required us to make an uncomfortable leap in our conventional and homely understanding of ourselves as human.

Conclusion

The cannibal documentaries in which I have been involved have tangibly changed the climate of public and thus, to a degree, scholarly opinion. Of course, I cannot quantify this, but I now teach a cohort of students for whom there is no systematic barrier at the level of the sociological paradigm to inferring cannibalism if the evidence is potentially congruent with it. The episodic, case-based nature of the documentaries referred to here, coupled with the sheer number and variety of cases, and – perhaps most importantly of all – the ability to see experts in diverse fields talk about their data and observations, erodes the comfortable position of so-called scepticism. We see the evidence of starvation cannibalism in the Old West, Soviet Russia, and China and on voyages of discovery that went wrong. We follow the gruesome tales of psychopathic cannibalism in the most celebrated criminal cases worldwide, and compare their patterns and warped justifications with the embedded and often highly logical reasons presented by indigenous peoples (and by the anthropologists who have studied them) for reverential funerary cannibalism and aggressive warfare-driven cannibalism.

The success of such filmmaking is in its conversion of the sensational into the banal. The viewer's journey starts with horrid fascination and reaches a measured understanding of another place and time where other circumstances, customs, and imperatives governed the everyday. These documentaries present social anthropology, archaeology, modern psychology, and psychiatric analysis as facets of a complex intersect of behaviours, norms, contentions, and beliefs. Even if the way in which content has to be presented means that arguments are streamlined and subtleties sometimes lost, the critical business of challenging preconceptions concerning the nature of the human subject succeeds. Because it acts directly at the level of the sociological paradigm, it does what a dozen specialist papers and a heap of academic books can never achieve: it changes the geometry of the plausible. All archaeology (and anthropology) works with a model (or models) of what the human subject is and what behaviours are plausible as explanations for cultural phenomena. These require continuous reevaluation if we are to convincingly recover dimensions of the past that are genuinely unlike the present. If academics are brave enough, not only is the interest there among programme makers and the viewing audience for critically engaged archaeology, but there is an opportunity to attract a new generation into the discipline with minds already broadened.

Television presentation is not a substitute for data presented in scholarly written format, and it cannot always reflect the full spectrum of debate. For example, although some cannibal 'sceptics' like Andrew Darling (see Darling 1999) have agreed to put their cases on screen, William Arens has pretty much left his book to do the talking. This is unfortunate, as television can provide important supplementary evidence – not just in terms of what is said, but how it is said. Through television, we have an opportunity to 'visit' sites and laboratories in the company of enthusiasts and expert advocates. We can see Christy Turner's face and eye movement as he handles cut-marked and exfoliated Anasazi culture bones - an experience that can be linked to reading his and his late wife's works (e.g., Turner and Turner 1999). When set in context with the testimony of other scholars expressing a variety of opinions, such footage facilitates the formation of more mature judgment of the status of Turner's methods and theories and cannot fail to deepen our understanding of the terms of the debate. The power of documentaries is not in telling people what to think (which is rarely successful), but in providing material for our critical faculties and thereby stimulating new ways of thinking.

I began this paper by saying that banality was perhaps the most interesting point of similarity between archaeology and television. Strip the banal of its pejorative connotations and it becomes what a society normally expects – its commonplaces. The commonplaces of ancient societies were not ours, I think, unless prehistory is more like geology that I can be persuaded to believe. Human subjects and societies are volatile and vastly various in terms of their customs, beliefs, social structures, and motivations. There are of course universals (or near universals) in what is true of people, but what is most interesting about archaeology – both for us as practitioners and for the general public – is the patent, undeniable *difference* it continuously reveals.

Acknowledgements

I am grateful to many people for the opportunity to work in television, but I would like to single out David Wilson and Dan Korn at Discovery; Simon Andreae at Fox; Marion Milne at 3BMTV; Jess Beck, Mo Smith, and Meredith Fisher at Engel Entertainment; John Hays-Fisher at the BBC; and Peter Bate, Jimmy Duggan, and Guillermo Santamaria for particular thanks.

10

'WORLDWONDERS' AND 'WONDERWORLDS'

A Festival of Archaeological Film

Tom Stern

[*Translated by* Georg Hartung and Timothy Clack]

Archaeology, re-creating never seen and experienced matters, requires pictures and feelings. Film, always a phantasm and dream, depends on truth and visions.

Early Film

Archaeology and film began their relationship in 1897 when three 'passion films' emerged roughly simultaneously in France, Great Britain, and the United States (Bamberger 1968: 8). In the American silent film tradition, the productions of the 1920s dealt with biblical themes, depicted the ancient civilisations of Egypt and Rome, or concerned Palaeolithic humanity in the 'slapstick-love story' style[1] (Stern 1994: 9–13; see Figs. 10.1–10.2). Similarly, the first German archaeological films, mainly from Ufa-Produktionen[2], fit into this scheme (Bock and Töteberg 1992: 32). This paper will necessarily concentrate on the German film traditions as the author has most familiarity with these, but where appropriate other media is considered.

German archaeology of the early twentieth century was characterised by a zealous interest in national ancestry advanced

Figure 10.1   On-screen titillation *Natur und Liebe* [Germany 1927] (Ruhrlandmuseum).

Figure 10.2   The girls of *The Three Ages* [USA 1923] (Ruhrlandmuseum).

through the culture-historical approach (see Kossinna 1936) and used innovative methodologies, techniques, and technologies (Stern 1992: 49). Some early films reflect and document this sense of experimental and nationalistic delight. The original film documentaries[3] and reconstructions[4], which covered excavations and other archaeological matters, were implemented and filmed by scientists and/or archaeologists. In the Ufa documentary films[5], archaeological reconstructions are pursued but these films are generally identifiable in their censorship of sex (Kracauer 1979: 161, 398). The silent film *Die Hermannschlacht* (1922–1924), however, is best categorised as a reactionary attempt to establish superiority over the French (Tode and Stern 2003: 168). Also during the 1930s, archaeology attained a presence in newsreel reports; the first educational film was produced (Drößler, 1988); and the first publications on archaeology and film were published in the academic journal *Archäologischen* (Zotz 1933a, 1933b; Pittioni 1936: 217ff.).

The 'instructional scientific film' became, according to the perfidious logic of National Socialism, dominant in archaeological films between 1933 and 1945 (Stern 2001: 145; 2002: 213 [see Fig. 10.3]). Even the titles of some of these productions, such as *Flammen der Vorzeit* (Flames of the Future) or *Wir Wandern mit den Ostgermanen* (Following the Teutons), make reference to the underpinning ideology of this archaeology (Zotz 1986)[6]. Conversely, greater reflexivity and scientific refinement characterise the film archaeology of the postwar period. These films can be grouped into excavation documentaries[7] and those

Figure 10.3 Nazi propaganda *Germanen genen Pharaonen* [Germany 1939] (Ruhrlandmuseum).

with creative/fictional outlooks[8]. Both the pre- and postwar instructional scientific films offered a means, using the instruments of treasure, exotica, and time travel, to acknowledge the oblivion of history – an understandable characteristic given the temporal-political context, but nonetheless problematic for the precipitation of a collective historical awareness. Similarly, these films served as devices of optimism allowing for and anticipating better times both in the past and in the future. The historic retrospection of films catalyses the creation of new futures – and this is as true for the films of the Third Reich as it is with all others.

In the 1950s, distant archaeological topics (Egypt, Italy, Japan, Yemen, etc.) tended to dominate the newsreel. Indeed, only one lone film contribution (in 1956) dealt with indigenous Germanic archaeology[9]. The following year, with the foundation of the Institut für den Wissenschaftlichen Film (IWF) in Göttingen (which included a 'history' section), new standards were established for the filming of archaeological themes[10]. Furthermore, the newly developed 'Pantoffelkino' communicated the first new archaeological-historical reports[11]. Moreover, towards the end of the 1950s, the competition of television became such that motion pictures (in particular Hollywood and Cinecitta productions) reacted by increasing the levels of elaboration and costume (Smith 1990).

In the 1960s, growing audiences witnessed a modification in the style of German reportage. These cohorts of spectators watched variations of the cultural journey[12], in which the histories of foreign groups and individuals were played out on screen. Moreover, the primordial German was seen to be one who would travel into the unknown/alien. In this sense, 'worldwonders' and 'wonderworlds' vitalise the humanity and character of the domestic condition[13]. Both adults (Fig. 10.4) and children are the intended recipients of these messages, but importantly for the younger generations, history is no longer encountered out there but rather takes place in the cinema[14].

The archaeological films of the 1970s focused on the Stone Age, but more than that they were characterised by the mystification of archaeological content and interpretation. The educational film of the time – with postwar productions on the state of Palaeolithic and Neolithic research[15] – concentrated on the early human being and debates involving whether our ancestors were hunters, handcrafters, or farmers. The place of the early human within the wider conceptualisations of social structure and society membership was theorised.[16] In comparison, funded by public money, dreams, secrets, treasures, gods, and immortality were covered by domestic television output[17].

Figure 10.4 **The playmate look** *One Million Years BC* **[UK 1966]**
(Ruhrlandmuseum).

Thus, in the 1970s it was the cinematic topics of the 1960s that were, in a different guise, screened in the living room. As part of this trend, for example, the second public channel (ZDF) aired its first evening programme, which involved an archaeologist racing to Hungary to collect some record of the ancient Alderberg culture with – as might be expected – generous helpings of adventure and intrigue supplied[18]. Meanwhile, the cinema began at this time to use the archaeological genre to produce sex films[19]. The processes of archaeological mystification had truly begun.

Trends in the 1980s and 1990s

Beginning in the late 1970s, archaeological-historical topics were broadcast on television during prime time. The series *Länder, Menschen, Abenteuer*[20], and later *Terra X*[21], were regularly broadcast on the main public channels. Stylistically, their mix of exotic, cutting-edge technology and adventure – frequently mixed with dramatic reenactments – caught the public imagination. In regular 45-minute programmes, the engaged spectator interested in culture and adventures was informed about global archaeological topics, and at the same time entertained. With C-14[22], the ZDF successfully produced a new archaeological media vehicle 10 years after the onset of prime-time archaeology. In collaboration with domestic archaeologists, initiator Giesela Graichen deliberately gave primacy to the highlighting of 'national archaeology' (Graichen 1996: 118). The show embodied the form of a telemagazine, with contributions lasting from three to 10 minutes. Excavations and excavators, research themes and research sectors, techniques and sponsors of the old and new federal states, were exhibited. In 1995 and 1996, ZDF broadcast 'Sphinx – Geheimnisse der Geschichte', which also copied this new formatting and appearance (ZDF 1994: 10). In collaboration with the German Archaeological Institute, the research of several German archaeologists of international status was explored.

The three segments of Schliemanns Erben (Schliemann's Heirs) – a punchy/effective if ultimately insensible title as far as the public was concerned – reached over 16 million viewers (Graichen 1996: 118) during their peak. In each segment, diverse archaeological projects were combined with investigations into familiar core themes: 'Auf der Spur versunkener Königreiche, Legenden auf der Spur, Auf der Spur großer Kriegszüge' ('the search for forgotten kingdoms, ancient legends, and large-scale historical wars'). Besides searching for controversy and the sensational, the archaeology on television at this time broached issues of national as well as international importance. Although lurid titles often played with standard sensitivities of daily life[23], a technical interest also became apparent[24]. Indeed, another trend in the 1980s and 1990s was a special consideration of archaeological methods and an emphasis on the analytical/interpretive techniques. This is very obvious in the educational films[25]. It would seem that in a technologically competent society, the comprehension of archaeology can be optimally communicated by means of technological analogies. A further tendency of this form of archaeological film contribution, perhaps due to the high mobility of contemporary societies, was a reduction in direct regional reference and the concomitant focus on landscapes and placement[26]. Archaeology in this sense mediates the plane between time and space and hence coordinates individual and group identities. In this context, if one considers the correlative conceptualisation of the future, then the science fiction genre also uses archaeological references and allusions in order to create futuristic-archaic worlds and identities (Kempen 1994)[27]. It is imperative to note these potential forces inherent within the forms of archaeology documentation discussed herein. The depicted past is and can only be an archaeological utopia.

Until the early 1980s, television programmes were publicly regulated and mediated. Moreover, cinematic and educational films dominated other relevant media. Later, a number of commercial television channels were established, the diversity of which were exposed quite rapidly – in the competition for audience rating and promotional revenue – as a monopolistic culture. Yet why should archaeology and history not be commercial? As an example, consider the application of archaeological themes in television and cinema advertising since the early 1990s. Various advertisements clearly apply and promulgate established archaeological stereotypes and cliches. The cosmetic giants Axe and Jade conjure the cloak-and-dagger excavations of the Mayas as an atmospheric backdrop for their aromatic products; the car manufacturer Audi portrays its vehicles in the tradition of a marmoreal sculpture 'Rome, first century after Christ'; the airline Lufthansa refers to the wanderlust of the Vikings; and Punica revitalises ancient Egyptian mummies with its juices. Moreover, one rogue involved in the illicit collection of antiquities is seen to sacrifice his booty for a Magnum ice cream. The thick spread Brunch deliberately associates itself with the opulence of the Roman elite. On the other hand, a car manufacturer, stereo brand, and credit institute like to be thought of as ancient and traditional. The Sparkasse refers to its Palaeolithic payment tradition ('We have always paid this way') and Citroen implies a comforting mode of protection ('Ugga agga!'). The relationship between archaeology and advertising has grown stronger; since the release of the motion picture *Gladiator*[28] (Pausch 2000: 427), the number of archaeologically themed advertisements has boomed.

Should one be concerned with this trend or does this examination merely reflect the author's aversion to specific forms of commercialised broadcasting? The widespread utilisation of archaeological material as well as humour/titillation/shock embodied in specific archaeological metaphors, – e.g., leather and fur dress – to increase profits reflects the centrality of archaeology in the popular consciousness (e.g., the mask in Fig. 10.5). Thereby archaeological material possesses an exchangeability, which allows it to be measured and deployed in the competition for audience rating and market share. After all, everything is in some way answerable to profit margins. The thematic content of advertisements correlate with wider scheduling patterns. A view of the German national 1997 Easter schedule highlights this: from

Figure 10.5 Mask from *The Lost Legions of Varus* [UK 2001] (Tom Stern).

Saturday to Monday, including the advertisement blocks, more than 39 hours of films on archaeology or archaeologically related themes were broadcast (Stern 1997: 1). The highlights of these televisual outpourings were definitely series like *C-14* or *Schliemanns Erben*. However, the combination of professionalism, zeitgeist, and pressure for sustained audience ratings results in all cases in the direct presentation of archaeology to the viewer – allowing no room or occasion for personal understandings or engagement. Without any subjective relation, archaeology and the past remain objects: entertaining, exchangeable, and arbitrary.

Another Way

Is not the defining objective of archaeology to bring into focus an individual moment through the contextualisation of both time and space? And is the individual or spectator not the last and conveying link of his or her own, personal historical lineage?

In the 1980s and 1990s, movies were made that sought to connect – beyond the hype – with the personal conflict of the spectator and facilitate/challenge an individual's learning and understanding. For instance, *Aha!* (1983) showed through the metaphor of a stone axe 'that today is already tomorrow past'. *Capreolus*[29] referred to the tension between the confrontation of text and image: on the one hand, the dissection of deer using silex tools; and on the other hand, lexical texts of archaeological keywords. The historical relevance of Troja and Troas is creatively highlighted by *Laokoons Rückkehr* through an experimental approach to the 'archaeology of the invisible monuments'[30]. Lovingly and ironically, *Unter römischer Herrschaft* (Under Roman Rule)[31] portrayed the life of occupation and power. In a different approach, the documentary movie *Arkona, Rethra, Vineta*[32] casts archaeologists at the centre of the piece, and notes that only through their worlds of feelings and ambitions – and their political-historical context – does the archaeology becomes accessible. Yet other films engage with the younger generation, and in this genre *Sendung mit der Maus* (Transmissions with the Mouse)[33] and *Löwenzahn* (Dandelion)[34] stand out. Another more sculptural example is *Celtic Memory*[35], an installation from Nam June Paik manufactured out of monitors, circuit boards, and video clips, which pushed Stonehenge into the digital and video era.

The filming of archaeology underscores and reinforces temporal and chronocentric interests. Through film ideology and sound bites, histories are made. In these times of neoconservatism and recessive economies, the remote past offers itself up for adoption in the sense of identity creation – apparently unencumbered by the present, which not even as history inspires hope. Moreover, because of academic budget cuts and failing sponsorship, film is gaining primacy as the archaeological medium. The methods of science and the adoption of high technology provide easily mediated images, which deconstruct the associations of stagnant science, burst open the doors of the ivory tower, and create understanding that opens up new research and funding opportunities. Conversely, the repetition of stereotypical imagery, as well as the excessive usage of superlatives and media-friendly sound bites, raises new barriers for archaeology and its communication. These are processes whereby cliches create and simultaneously satisfy expectations. Ultimately, what remains with the viewer is a taste of adventure and the exotic, rather than the comprehension of archaeological routine or exercises in interpretation. The archaeologist, the 'missing link', is actually the binding element between the past and the present. Thus, one must not perform to these mediated expectations, but should hope that through film better archaeological understandings are precipitated. To do this, the archaeologist must radiate some entertainment value and achieve a media presence. However, in this respect his or her screen colleagues have been developing impressive reputations for years and thus have a head start – e.g., Indiana Jones[36], Tom Baxter[37], and even Jean-Luc Picard[38]. Further, other celluloid archaeologists such as Lara Croft[39] or Sydney Fox[40] combine fantasy and archaeology on a sexual as well as fictional level.

Archaeological Film Festivals

Since 1994, the biennial CINARCHEA festival in Kiel has been centrally theorising the archaeological film (broadly defined) on an international stage. It is not the first archaeological film festival; however, it is the only one accompanied by an academic symposium in which filmmakers, media scientists, and archaeologists critically investigate the relation between archaeology and film. Since the mid-1990s, sporadic essays, monographs, and dissertations on archaeological film themes have been published concerning multiple localities (classic archaeology, prehistory, Near Eastern archaeology, Egyptology, etc.).. An overview is provided in the online symposium literature (http://www.cinarchea.com).

The archaeological film festival is not a recent phenomenon and indeed has been relatively commonplace throughout continental Europe for two decades. For example, as part of the North Rhine-Westphalian Exhibition (2005), the archaeological film festival ARCHEO CINEMA was staged; this was principally a retrospective film show without competition. Again, the German Archaeology Institute arranged a film show in October 2005 with '35 mm Persien', in which films from and concerning Iranian archaeology were shown, discussed, and accompanied by talks. In 1980, KINEON in Brussels staged the first archaeological film festival, which focused on archaeology *in* films and awarded high-quality films (after a break of several years, the festival was continued in 1994). Later, in 1986, ICRONOS in Bordeaux examined domestic archaeology films; this was followed in 1990 by a French festival of international flavour, Festival du Film d'Archèologique d'Amiens. In the same year, the annual Rassegna Internaztionale del Cinema Archeologico began in Roverto in Italy.

These were followed by AGON, another film festival focusing on the archaeology of Mediterranean countries. The Musèe de Mariemont in Belgium has arranged regular film screenings since 1998, and since 1999 archaeological films have found a platform in Nyon, Switzerland, with the Festival International du Film d'Archeologique. With the

International Archaeology Film Festival Istanbul (1998) and the regular Archaeology Channel – International Film and Video Festival in Eugene, Oregon, archaeological films have been afforded good levels of publicity and represent an important and (alarmingly) largely unrecognised dimension of archaeology in the media. Detailed insights into the specific festival foci, award-winning films, and contacts are provided by the Europäische Förderation der Film-Festivals über Archäologie und Kulturelles Erbe, FEDARCINE (http://www.fedarcine.com). Prizes awarded are scaled according to various categories – e.g., large festival prize, jury's discretionary prize, spectators' prize. etc. In the past, the French production company Gedeon has won awards at various archaeological film festivals and it would seem prudent to scrutinise its successful strategy.

Good Archaeological Film? Emotional Strategies of Gedeon-Produktion

Have you ever had the chance to watch an archaeologist eat? In asking this question, I am not thinking about an artificially stage-managed final dinner from the German television series *Schliemanns Erben*, in which the cooperation of archaeologists and domestic excavation workers is celebrated superficially, but rather the short scene involving two baguette-eating archaeologists in the film *Au-delà d'Angkor* (1999). In my mind, this is a characteristic element of a good archaeological film: empathic observation. Empathy and observation provide a means of informing views about archaeologists and their work, which can be simultaneously full of humour and melancholy. Most of the following analysis is taken from the contributions of the French production company Gedeon to the series *Uncovering Lost Worlds*. These film contributions have won multiple awards and were very highly thought of by CINEARCHEA jurors. Nevertheless, it would be useful to understand more precisely on what the success of Gedeon-Produktions is founded. The analysis of the material is confined to four aspects: the presentation of archaeological work, narrative structures, application of music, and placement of the past.

The Presentation of Archaeology

At the centre of Gedeon films are the emotions of the archaeologist. The archaeologist constitutes the essence of the film, the key figure who investigates the relics of the past, interprets it, and explains it to the layperson. Essentially, an unobtrusive camera records the archaeologist throughout the excavation process. The extremely long filming time enables the film team to refrain from the common practice of restaging or re-performing discoveries and moments of excitement and to picture the *real* emotions of the protagonist in the context of a *real* finding. The camera records everything. If with desperation, amazement, or luck, something important occurs – e.g., an unexpected discovery of a Roman support arc in a wastewater channel – the spectator becomes an active participant in the events, 'an insider', and undergoes the appropriate subjective experience/response.

The reserved archaeologist becomes human and can be understood as such. Even though the archaeologist is always in the foreground, the processes of working and interpretation are not reduced to his or her individual personhood. On the contrary, a common trait of the Gedeon-Produktion material is the exhibition of teamwork in archaeology. The tension between the forces of the group and the individual allow one to become aware of both. In this way, the specific subject is lost among the interdisciplinary facets of research. Through this contradiction, the cliche of the worldly innocent shows up in association with the loner working or fighting.

For example, in *Sur la trace des Celtes* (In Search of the Celts), the field archaeologist searches for the artefactual relations of the Torques choker. The camera only observes the discussion about the dating but records much more; the archaeologists are talking with each other and not directly into the camera. Examples of teamwork are present elsewhere: through the archaeologists at the card table, those at the evening briefing, or the integration of previous research. The viewer therefore understands archaeology as a process and the interpretation of the excavation as temporary and organic. Many of the scientific methods used throughout the excavation require definition for the layperson. Gedeon's stance is clearly different than more mainstream stylisation that renders and exaggerates the technical and makes the event impressive but incomprehensible. For example, the geomagnetic investigations in *Zeugma und Alexandria* appear to be 'Mickey Mousing' the viewer and the music is mapped to the movement sequences; the technology is communicated at a patronising, popularising distance. The narrator sums up the scientific specialist with a rather belittling comment: 'similar to a fantastical Mars-person with funny equipment'. Gedeon-Produktions distances itself pleasantly from other archaeology films in its visualisation of research results through computer-generated images.

The reconstruction of the lighthouse of Alexandria, only stencilled in for a moment like a vision, enables the viewer to become an imaginative participant in the interpretive exercises of the archaeologist. The integration of soundtrack emphasises the dreaming quality of interpretation and the role of emotion. Moreover, the reconstruction does not appear to be understood as the central technique of conceptualisation, but merely as a means of showing the bias and perspective of the archaeologist. In *Sur la trace des Celtes*, a three-dimensional reconstruction of a Celtic village arising from an excavation plan is provided. Here the images are embellished with bird melodies, cock crows, and dog barks, which contrast abruptly with the sterile computer animations of more common archaeological films. In general, music is limited. This encourages a dialogue of emotional connection to open up between the artefact and the viewer. The viewer is confronted by a past and is forced to actively think and decipher it. The high dosage of synthetic, formulated images is important in achieving connections between common humanity. In *La Mémoire perdue de l' île de Pâques* (Lost Memories of Easter Island), electronic 'morphing' fluently convolutes stone idols into each other. This elegant and simple method is very successful in illustrating for the viewer the stylistic-chronological development of the 'Moai'. Also, the presentation of artefacts in the Gedeon films is significantly different than the conventional methods employed in other screen archaeology. Usually, artefacts will be consistently and deliberately positioned in front of a dark but illuminated background. Gedeon humanises these artefacts by incorporating the archaeologist or restorer within the frame. The artefacts are handled and continually repositioned. This 'presences' the artefacts and makes them meaningful. The viewer engages with the artefact to produce multiple meanings and associations and they are not disengaged but stylistically neutral. All these mechanisms are of course exemplary ways to convey emotions!

Narrative Structures

The narration strategies of Gedeon films are clear especially in regard to their accounting for or representation of the current state of archaeological research. The films themselves have a narrator or commentator posing questions that offer progression, continuity, and linkage. These questions act as reference points or summaries and are subsequently investigated by the archaeologist. Thus, the narrative adopts the archaeological position. In addition, the viewer experiences the processes of archaeology. The Gedeon films allow the viewer to accompany the archaeologist in his or her work by orienting and facilitating empathy. In many productions, this 'connection through accompaniment' is further enabled by artistic direction (see, for example, the work of Thierry Ragobert). In one instance, the camera operator documents two archaeologists' exploration of a sewage system by crawling with them through small channels and wading with them through the dirty water. The viewer becomes there and involved.

The subject and the archaeologist conduct a dialogue with each other even though seldom does either speak to the camera. The traditional interview is virtually absent. Obviously, the accompaniment takes place at the arrangement of the film crew. The archaeology is staged for the camera and editorially reconstructed; however, this is the performance of real archaeological activities. Moreover, even during complex proceedings such as the recording of underwater inscriptions, the viewer remains diligently in attendance and thus observes the realities of work and associated discussions. Time is another important component of the narrative structure. The temporal theme is frequently highlighted and consequently the notion of time pressure remains of constant anxiety. It is emphasised, for example, that the season for diving and underwater activities will soon terminate, that bad weather and natural hazards are impending, or that large-scale construction projects threaten the site. In *Alexandrie la Magnifique*, the excavations are carried out in the normal way, but in the background the landscape is increasingly marked by motorway feeder tracks and numerous other constructions. These subtly remind the viewer of increasing external pressures. The time demands are unsettling and the impending end to the excavations is communicated with an absence of feeling. This numbness is intentionally created by the filmmakers.

Musical Imposition

In contrast to the conventional musical embellishment of the more prevalent archaeology films, which purposefully handle the viewers' emotional arousal through soundtracks, Gedeon films apply carefully chosen orchestral arrangements that seek to construct and develop novel emotional worlds to be experienced by the spectator. The score serves as an empathetic medium that relates the past (as embodied in the archaeology) to the worldly presence of the spectator. This does not necessarily mean that all Gedeon films have contained new compositions, for some have no music at all. The agency of the excavator involved in clearing and brushing away the coverings above hidden mosaic floors, portraying magnificent figures and themes, is emotionally charged. For instance, in the Godard film *Le Mépris* (Contempt), this emotion is expressed through a score composed by Georges

Delerue (1963) that enjoys cult status in France. Furthermore, the film makes reference to Greek mythology – the odyssey is the central theme. The music touches even those viewers who do not know the film allusions of Thierry Ragoberts. The repetition of Delerue's composition, in concert with the gliding tempo, communicates the routine and hardship of archaeological work. The fateful impression of the music, its painful yet sweet melancholic interactions, informs the viewer about the pending ruin of featured places. We are able simultaneously to see the beauty, which was once created here, for a first and last time in context. The site is about to be destroyed but in that moment is captured and experienced. In *Alexandrie – La Septième Merveille du Monde* (Alexandria – The Seventh Wonder of the World), the background orchestral music consists of vibrations, percussions, and oboe tones that place viewers within underwater archaeological worlds and inspires them to use their imagination in the re-creation of the past. The playful, accented tones convey the sense of mystery. Together the picture and the music generate the necessary space for the audience to pursue its own dreamlike reflection in order to conflict the past.

In a similar way, the sad music of the film *Ile de Pâques* (Easter Island) suggests the deep-rooted melancholy embodying a group of island residents mourning the disappearance of their unique culture. In all examples, the music is the carrier of meaning, which enables the empathy of the viewer and brings about an attitude whereby common humanism is recognised. In the same way, the intonation of the commentary conforms to the music and adjusts to be humble, encouraging, or irritating. The voice of the narration itself becomes attuned to the music. The voice is carefully chosen in the same way that a soloist would be selected to accompany an orchestral temper, as can be heard in the version of *La mémoire perdue de l'île de Pâques* and *Sur la trace des Celtes* accompanied by the commentary of Hans Zischler. The accentuation of this timeless and powerful musical composition, which requires little effort to listen to, is basically and refreshingly distinguishable from the awkward tone mapping of other archaeological films, with their typical musical accompaniments that only serve to reinforce the foreignness of the highlighted cultural artefacts.

The Intermediation of the Past

The closing scenes or conclusions of any Gedeon production are highly emotional. The last words of the commentator always attempt to deliver the essence of archaeology, which can be optimally characterised as tragedy. The *Zeugma* film concludes with the accusation that emergency excavations are rarely initiated early enough, bearing in mind the fact that land use schemes are normally proposed a long time before they are enacted. The viewer realises that no apologies can be accepted for destroying any part of the heritage that involves an irreversible loss of a common human past. Therewith in the closing scene in *Zeugma*, melancholic music accompanies an elderly person walking for one last time through the graveyard of his ancestors, at the edge of the oncoming threat. This person raises his hands in front of his face and prays and then looks one final time directly into the front of the camera with a pained expression – a lingering shot, which (as it is shown in the end) results in the abrupt and relentless accusation. This performance subtly questions our (often inattentive) acquaintance to the past, tradition, and homeland. The humanistic attitude, the poetic and fragile melancholy, the empathy with other beings, differentiates the Gedeon productions from more mainstream archaeological films, which make shows of high-tech applications. Thus, Gedeon avoids association with contextless findings and other positivistic-affirmative celebrations. While others get journalistically sucked in to the nowness of the finding, Gedeon films seek to address broader philosophical questions, issues of human identity, and the constitution of humanity.

The feeling of loss and ruin of cultural heritage is permanently stressed in the Gedeon films, where spectators witness the emotions of the archaeologists faced with, for example, the looted temple: discomposure, shaking of the head, grief, and desperation are all mediated. The archaeologist and the audience are almost reduced to tears. Such emotional connection in film is uncommon, which is surprising for archaeology has always been a public enterprise. It is reported in national newspapers and discussed in cafes, and local residents participate in or keenly observe excavations. Thus, for whom should archaeologists conduct their work? The Gedeon films answer that through their humanistic approach, the archaeologist works for all: he or she is a public servant. The narration in the climaxes to these films is emotionally charged. Phrases and terms such as 'integration', 'thirst for knowledge', and 'human heritage' are commonplace. Sometimes one is let go with a positive message – e.g., the foundation of an archaeological protection zone or the return of a piece of cultural heritage, often accompanied with a triumphal parade of citizens viewing particular artefacts for the first time. In these emotionally stimulating final passages (whether melancholy or triumphant), the films create a space for fascination and grace, tenderness and subtlety, but also for selectivity, determination, and protocol. These fragile essential components of the arts combine imagery, metaphor, and philosophy.

Postscript

Quest for the Lost Pharaoh, a Gedeon production from 2003, is in numerous ways markedly different than other archaeological films in the *Uncovering Lost Worlds* series. This film is fundamentally dissimilar, as it does not contain any of the listed qualities and effectively becomes the antithesis of this series: self-congratulatory, unnecessary computer animations, emotional tone-mapping cliches, *Playboy*-style sex appeal, mysterious scenes/discoveries, and the work of the singular archaeologist. Produced for the American Discovery Channel, this film reflects the requirements of the U.S. market; however, it also shows that the archaeological coverage of this production company does not derive necessarily from its beliefs, but rather from market trends and appetites. This insight indicates good news for archaeology, as clearly some European viewers want to or are prepared to empathise with archaeologists and/or their subjects.

Notes

1. *Man's Genesis* (USA 1912), Director: D.W. Griffith; *Brute Force* (USA 1913), Director: D.W. Griffith; *His Prehistoric Past* (USA 1914), Director: Charles Chaplin; *A Prehistoric Love Story* (GB 1915), Director: Leedham Bantock; *R.F.D., 10,000 B.C.* (USA 1917), Director: Willis O'Brien; *The Dinosaur and the Missing Link* (USA 1917); Director: Willis O'Brien; *The Three Ages* (USA 1923), Director: Buster Keaton; *Flying Elefants* (USA 1927), Director: Frank Butler.

2. *Der Sohn des Hannibal* (Germany 1918), Director: Viggo Larsen; *Die Augen der Mumie Ma* (Germany 1918), Director: Ernst Lubitsch; *Die Vase der Semiramis* (Germany 1918), Director: Willy Grunwald; *Veritas Vincit* (Germany 1918/19), Director: Joe May.

3. *Ausgrabungen auf der Wasserburg Buchau* (Germany 1927), Landesmuseum Stuttgart; *Das erwachende Ägypten* (Germany 1928), Bundesarchiv-Filmarchiv Berlin.

4. *Haus im Wilden Ried* (Germany 1921), Landesmuseum Stuttgart; *Pfahlbauten in Unteruhldingen* (Germany 1927/28), Bundesarchiv-Filmarchiv Berlin.

5. *Wege zu Kraft und Schönheit* (Germany 1925), Bundesarchiv-Filmarchiv Berlin; *Natur und Liebe - Vom Urtier zum Menschen* (Germany 1927/28), Bundesarchiv-Filmarchiv Berlin.

6. *Vom Dampfpflug bedroht* (Germany 1934); *Bronzeguß* (Germany 1935); *Zeugen deutscher Vorzeit* (Germany 1935); *Reichsburg Kyffhausen* (Germany 1937); *Germanen gegen Pharaonen* (Germany 1939).

7. *Archäologische Funde - Der Moorboden wird untersucht* (Germany 1947), Welt im Film (WiF) 84/; *Prähistorische Ausgrabungen in Schwaben* (Germany 1948), BiF 29/1948.

8. *Schätze der Pharaonen* (Germany 1949), WiF 208/6; *Wiederaufbau nach 4000 Jahren - Die Tempelruinen von Karnak am Nil* (Germany 1949), WiF 200/5.

9. *Ausgrabungen auf der Hammaburg* (Germany 1956), Staatliche Landesbildstelle Hamburg; *Ausgrabungen aus der Römerzeit unter dem Rathaus in Köln* (Germany 1956), UFA 17/3.

10. *Ein fränkisches Fürstengrab* (Germany 1957), IWF Göttingen.

11. *Das Grabtuch von Turin* (Germany 1958).

12. *Cypern - Insel der Aphrodite* (1968); *Im Lande Kanaan* (1969).

13. *Die sieben Weltwunder* (September-November 1966), Director: Artur Müller, Süddeutscher Rundfunk, 6-teilige Reihe; *Tauchfahrten in die Vergangenheit - Auf den Spuren der Antike* (1967), *Aus der Geschichte der Menschheit* (Germany 1965), 3-teilige Lehrfilmreihe, FWU München.

14. *Asterix der Gallier* (France/Belgium 1967); *Asterix und Cleopatra* (France/Belgium 1968); *The Flintstones* (USA 1960–1966), TV-Zeichentrickserie, 166 Folgen, Pro: Hanna-Barbera Studios.

15. *Die Jungsteinzeit - Der Mensch wird Bauer* (Germany 1970); *Kunst und Magie auf Höhlenwänden* (Germany 1970).

16. *Neandertaler und Höhlenbär - Frühe Gesellschaftsformen der Jägergruppe* (Germany 1972); *Handwerker der Steinzeit - Späte Jungsteinzeit in Mitteleuropa Tl.1 u. 2* (1972); *Mensch und Gesellschaft der Bronzezeit* (Germany 1973).

17. *Träume, die keine blieben - Heinrich Schliemann* (1977); *Geheimnisse des Meeres: Atlantis Tl. 1 u. 2* (1978); *Das Geheimnis der Etrusker* (1979); *Ärger mit der Schatzsuche* (1977); Bayrischer Rundfunk, München; *Länder, Menschen, Abenteuer: Schatzgräber* (1978); *Wege zu den Göttern? Das Geheimnis der Nazca-Linien* (1979); *Das Haus der Unsterblichkeit* (1978).

18. *Semesterferien* (Germany 1972).

19. *One Million AC/DC* (USA 1969); *Creatures the World Forgot* (UK 1970); *Quando le donne avevano la coda* (Italy 1970); *Quando gli uomini armarono la clava* (Italy 1971); *Messalina, Messalina* (Italy 1977); *Caligula* (Italy 1979).

20. *Die Tempel des Schweigens* (1978); *Schatzgräber* (1978); *Eine Brücke ins Morgenland* (1978); *Spuren im Fels* (1981); *Das Rätsel von Lubaantum* (1982); *Neptuns Hexenküche* (1983); *Djebel Chemtou* (1983); *Die Nacht der Grabräuber* (1984); *Expedition Mauretanien* (1984); *Hattussa brennt* (1985); *Das Geheimnis des Ararat* (1985); *Piraten am Meeresgrund* (1985); *Die Ahnen der Inkas* (1988); *Die hängenden Gräber der Huaylas* (1990); *Zeitreise durch Equador* (14 May 1990); *Das Rätsel von Nevali Cori* (1992); *Die letzten Tasmanier* (1993).

21. *Sie brauchen keine weißen Götter* (1982); *Südseeinseln aus Götterhand* (1982); *Die gefiederte Schlange* (1983); *Auf der Fährte des Jaguars* (1984); *Die Spur des Giganten* (1984); *Der Fluch des Pharao* (1986); *Audienz bei der Königin von Saba* (1986); *Mumien im Goldland* (1986); *Im Schatten der Inkasonne* (1986); *Vorstoß nach Eldorado* (1988); *Wo lag Atlantis?* (1988); *Im Kielwasser Sindbads* (1988); *Canyon der heiligen Vulkane* (1988); *Die Inseln des Drachenbaums* (1990); *Die Sternstadt im Chaco Canyon* (1990); *Als die Götter stürzten* (1990); *Kreuzfahrt mit Odysseus* (1990); *Die Reiter der Goldenen Horde* (1991); *Safari in die Steinzeit* (1991); *Vergeßt Kolumbus* (1992); *Das Blut der Azteken* (1992); *Die Geister vom Fluß der Gräber* (1994); *Tod im Schilfmeer* (1994); *Das Schloß der vergessenen Mumien* (1994); *Der Fluch der Pharaonen* (1994); *Karawane nach Petra* (1995); *Die Abenteuernacht* (1997); *Der Fluch von Oak Island* (1997).

22. *Die Reihe besteht aus 2 Staffeln* (C 14 – *Vorstoß in die Vergangenheit*, März/April 1992, C 14 – *Archäologische Entdeckungen in Deutschland*, November/Dezember 1993).

23. *Mord und Gold - Grabgeheimnisse aus Mazedonien* (1981); *Der Fluch des Sonnengottes* (1984); *Engel, Teufel und Dämonen - Die Masken der Sphinx* (1987); *Höhlen - Hexen - Heiligtümer* (1990); *Das Feuer der Menhire* (1995).

24. *Geophysiker auf den Spuren der Wikinger* (Germany 1980); *Sonde 4/82* (1982); *Kupferchlorid-Krebs – eine archäologische Katastrophe?* (1989); *Der hölzerne Kalender - Dendrochronologie in Haithabu* (Germany 1994).

25. *Keramik der Jungsteinzeit* (Germany 1983); *Rekonstruktion römischer Reliefkeramik* (Germany 1984); *Die Römerschiffe von Mainz - Ausgrabung und Bergung* (Germany 1986); *Rekonstruktion eines bronzezeitlichen Langhauses* (Germany 1988); *Geräte aus Stein* (Germany 1990); *Rentierjäger am Petersfels - ein Beitrag zur experimentellen Archäologie des Paläolithikums in Südwestdeutschland* (Germany 1992); *Pretec. Steinbearbeitung* (Germany 1994); *Pretec: Speerschleuder* (Germany 1994); *Pretec: Pfeil und Bogen* (Germany 1994).

26. *Archäologie am Rhein* (1981), WDR; *Landesarchäologie in Bayern* (1983), BR; *Die Römer in Westfalen* (Germany 1989), *Steinzeit in Westfalen* (Germany 1990), Landesbildstelle Rheinland; *Von Rom zum Rhein - Die Römer Tl.1-4* (März 1994), BR.

27. *2001 - A Space Odyssey* (GB 1968), Director: Stanley Kubrick; *Stargate* (USA 1994), *The Matrix* (USA 1999).

28. *Gladiator* (UK/USA 2000).

29. *Capreolus* (BRD 1995).

30. *Laokoons Rückkehr - Die Landschaft Troas als Mahnmal des Krieges* (BRD 1993/94).

31. *Unter römischer Herrschaft* (BRD 1992); Director: Enzio Edschmid, Sabine Wolfram. Großer Preis der internationalen Jury, CINARCHEA 1994 in Kiel.

32. *Arkona, Rethra, Vineta* (DDR/BRD 1990).

33. *Die Geld-Maus* (Germany 1995), *Die Rom-Maus* (Germany 1995), *Die Steinzeithaus-Maus* (Germany 1997), WDR.

34. *Peters Reise in die Steinzeit* (Germany 1993), ZDF.

35. *Celtic Memory* (1992), Folkwang Museum Essen.

36. *Raiders of the Lost Ark* (USA 1980), *Indiana Jones and the Temple of Doom* (USA 1983), *Indiana Jones and the Last Crusade* (USA 1988), Director: Steven Spielberg.

37. *The Purple Rose of Cairo* (USA 1984), Director: Woody Allen.

38. *Star Trek - The Next Generation* (USA 1987–1994); TV-Series.

39. *Lara Croft: Tomb Raider* (UK/D/USA/JAP 2001); *Lara Croft Tomb Raider: The Cradle of Life* (USA/D/JAP/UK/NL 2003).

40. *Relic Hunter* (USA 1999-2003), TV-Series; 66 Episodes.

11

FAKING IT

Why the Truth is so Important for TV Archaeology

Angela Piccini

> Among the various carry-ons under discussion were on-screen
> trenches not meeting health and safety requirements and diggers
> being advised by programme makers to get agents. Apparently
> the team behind one particular series wanted the farmer on
> whose land they were about to dig to greet the arriving archae-
> ologists. The farmer refused, so instead of revising the script a
> camera assistant was dressed up in suitably rustic garb and acted
> out the part of the recalcitrant son of the soil (Neil Mortimer [per-
> sonal communication] on the 2004 meeting of the Institute of
> Field Archaeologists ([IFA]))

Introduction

In 1926, John Grierson[1] wrote in the *New York Sun* that documentary is the creative treatment of actuality. Even so, the cultural significance of the inauthentic and untrue has been at the
centre of anxieties surrounding documentary filmmaking from
'Nanook of the North' (Robert Flaherty 1922) to 'Two Men in a
Trench' (BBC2 2004). Letters to websites and popular magazines
from professional and academic archaeologists and other viewers with a vocal interest in archaeology energetically debate the

accuracy of TV archaeology narratives[2]. This paper stems from my acknowledgement that this anxiety forms the reception context for this programming and my continuing concerns with the tenor of much TV archaeology critique. Why do we fail to consider television production as ritualised industrialisation akin to the magic of the medieval smith? And why do we not take on board the strides made in other subject areas in the arts and humanities to recognise television programmes – not to mention the television set – as material culture (Morley 1995; Silverstone 1994)?

When we watch *Time Team* (Channel 4), we are not simply absorbing a linguistic account, although there is clearly an important aspect of storytelling around the hearth. Beats and rhythms constructed through the montage of editing, drama, and anticipation evoked through sound design, and the inter-relationships among presenter, participant, close-up, and cutaway, are together designed to keep us from changing channels. Short cuts are taken, runners stand in as locals, and elements of the archaeological story are left unvoiced; arguably, that is the condition of industrialised production. That is to say, in a climate of content-focused critique of archaeology documentaries, are we neglecting the opportunity to develop a critical language that speaks about sound *and* vision – cultural performance rather than accuracy alone?

Of course, it will not do to claim that Edward I reigned from 1271 to 1308, or to illustrate the Neolithic with an Iron Age enclosure (*Seven Ages of Britain*, C4, 2003), or to argue that a coherent Celtic civilisation held sway over Europe until those Romans ruined it all. But is this all there is to it? At one time, this was explained as the anxiety of the 'postmodern condition': '[T]here is an escalation of the true, of the lived experience.... And there is a panic-stricken production of the real and the referential' (Baudrillard 1983: 12–13). Yet to focus on that alone is to fail to recognise the dialectical aspect of what it is that we mean by expressing this anxiety (Žižek 1991: 21). In an attempt to map out this crisis of 'truth', I will discuss the institutional and critical frameworks of documentary television production in Britain and then move on to explore issues around spectacle and concepts of authenticity, reality, and truth as they are framed in TV archaeology.

Institutional Discourses

The debates around truth and documentary practice of all kinds gained in frequency and volume through the 1970s and 1980s in the writing generated by the BBC and British Film Institute. Of course, this was the grand age of Marxist thought across the intellectual and creative elites in Britain. Building on Grierson's original commitment to social change through documentary practice and on 1960s direct cinema, cinema verité, and observational cinema, filmmakers and critics promulgated a doctrine of objectivity, quality, and rigour. Whether strictly Marxist in outlook or conservatively paternalistic – '[T]elevision, as the most potent visual form of communication, offers us the best chance we possess to pass on this knowledge to ordinary men and women' (Hearst n.d.: 4) – the bottom line was that the filmmaker had a responsibility to educate the masses.

In *Principles and Practice in Documentary Programmes* (BBC 1972), some of the key aims of the filmmaker are set out.

a) A documentary explores a factual subject in depth. It not only shows, it illuminates. It attempts not merely to inform, but to provoke deeper thought and understanding.
b) A documentary usually presents its subject first hand (e.g., by use of film camera on location) rather than at second hand (e.g., by discussion in a studio).
    ⋮
f) A documentary may confine itself to undisputed facts, or it may be concerned – partly or totally – with opinion. It does not, however, normally make use of fiction.
g) Without departing from his [sic] responsibility to his subject matter, the producer of a documentary sets out to hold the attention of his audience and to entertain them or to move them. He therefore uses the skills of the filmmaker, the journalist, and even the dramatist, in presenting his material.

In another BBC publication, budding filmmakers are advised that although 'television is not a good medium for the dissemination of concentrated factual information', 'the emphasis must be on accuracy and authenticity' (Croton 1989: 14; 17). The Broadcasting Research Unit published *Quality in Television* in 1989; in its section on factual programmes, it stated that the 'standard above all others is that of striving for impartiality. Facts, when facts there are, must be treated with care, accessibly offered, placed in context, obtained with sensitivity and sensibility; and the manner of presentation must be honest, truthful and plain' (1989: 10).

The institutionalised quality narrative was not wholly monolithic, however. In an influential paper, Stuart Hall (1976: 246) problematised the dominant ethos.

Good television captures the on-going form of real life…. Good television… offers a polished professional product, largely in terms of the assembly of material, the smooth management of the transitions. It is 'good television' if there are no breaks or discontinuities…. Television is not a medium for complexly structured or nuanced argument or exposition…. Thus 'good' television must be either plain, simple and straight, *or* it requires the mediation of the explainer/guide/moderator, who 'stands in' for the absent audience and makes the complicated plain, simple and straight.)

Building on this perspective to discuss the role of narrative in 'good television', McArthur argues that while visual records of events are not ideologically neutral, they 'lack total explanatory force and require supplementing by other codes – usually musical or verbal or, most particularly, montage codes – before this explanatory force can *begin* to come into play' (McArthur 1978: 20). He goes on to suggest that 'the central ideological function of the narration is to confer *authority* on, and to elide *contradictions* in, the discourse' (1978: 22). According to McArthur, the ultimate manifestation of this is the placing of the narrator on location, which creates an indexical relationship between the reality of the existing place and the truthfulness of what is being said.

From the publications of this period, it would appear that the mid-1970s marked an intellectual break between those who firmly believed that documentary 'implies a construction of the diegsis as indexally related to the pro-filmic event and this, in turn as "locating" a putative reality beyond it' (Vaughan 1976: 26) – that is to say, those who believed the document gave access to real life and those who argued that this was simply the 'reality effect' (Barthes 1986) of documentary, that there is no 'plain, simple and straight'. Yet, as with the (British) archaeological practices of the period, the apparent conflict between ideological and symbolic perspectives finds a certain resolution in the homology between stripping away 'false consciousness' and stripping back systems of signification. The implication in both is the uncovering of truth. These discussions continue to frame understandings of and writings on the documentary genre. Many documentary practices continue to rely on notions of realism through their use of a 'set of formal markers that confirm to us that what we are watching… is a record of an ongoing, and at least partly media-independent, reality' and of a 'rhetoric of accuracy and truth' (Corner 2001: 127). Although we 'know' that documentary cannot give us access to some pro-film reality, for it to survive on television, it has to assert ideas of truth and authenticity (Ellis 1990: 38).

To set up the transition from this general discussion of British televisual documentary to my specific TV archaeology focus, it is necessary first to outline a key institutional change in broadcast television since the early 1990s (Blumer 1993). Broadcasters view TV archaeology as part of their public service broadcasting (PSB) remit. PSB traditionally assumed that responsibility towards the audience outweighed commercial duty to shareholders. Winston argues that documentary flourished despite (or perhaps because of) this small-audience, duty genre context for documentary (2000: 40). The 1990s pressure on public service broadcasters to operate more like private businesses was coupled with a relaxation and reformulation of PSB. In the context of ratings wars, the presence of documentaries in the schedules became 'a real mark of public service commitment' (Winston 2000: 40). Is it any coincidence that the BBC's Science Department, along with the number of archaeological programmes, trebled in size between 1994 and 1999 (Kulik 2003)? More recently, in 2003 the BBC restructured its factual programming, moving from a split between general factual and specialist factual (including TV archaeology) to six categories: documentaries and contemporary factual; specialist factual; current affairs and investigations; arts and culture; life-skills; and new media (Hill 2005: 43). Within documentaries and contemporary factual is the subgroup leisure, which includes history and many programmes that deal with archaeology. However, archaeology programmes may also be commissioned as specialist factual, along with the sciences. This same inconsistency is found in the BBC's radio output. On BBC Radio 4, archaeology can be found in science (*Unearthing Mysteries* 2004) and history (*Prehistoric Manual* 2004). This perhaps makes manifest at an institutional level the continuing uneasiness about the truth claims of archaeological practice: is it science or storytelling?

The current situation is described via the 2005 Ofcom (the independent regulator and competition authority for the UK communications industries) public service broadcasting guidance consultation exercise. Ofcom defines the four main purposes of PSB.

- [T]o inform, and to increase understanding of the world, through news, information, and analysis of current events and ideas.
- [T]o reflect and strengthen cultural identity, through high-quality UK, national, and regional programming.
- [T]o stimulate interest in, and knowledge of, arts, science, history, and other topics, through content that is accessible, encourages personal development, and promotes participation in society.
- [T]o support a tolerant and inclusive society, through programmes that reflect the lives of different people and communities within the UK, encourage a better understanding of different cultures, and, on occasion bring the nation together for shared experiences.

Both Channel 4 and the BBC have responded to this document with their own publications. Addressing the third PSB purpose, Channel 4 planned to invest £87 million in 2005 with programmes ranging from 'arts, history, science and schools programmes to more informal lifeskills series' (Channel 4 2005: 2). Unlike the BBC, Channel 4 groups all of its history and archaeology programming together, from David Starkey's *Monarchy* series (production Granada Bristol, 2004, 2005) to *Time Team*. While Channel 4 does not recognise the second and fourth PSB purposes as relevant to its history output, the BBC may yet do. The BBC's current Royal Charter and Agreement expire in 2006. Before its renewal, the British Department for Culture, Media, and Sport is undertaking a detailed review. In advance of this, the BBC commissioned a report on the future of PSB. The report foregrounds a concept of 'social captial' as a powerful means by which to justify the continuing provision and expansion of PSB output and appears aimed at a more holistic approach to the Ofcom list (Brooks 2005). Perhaps commissioners will increasingly view history and archaeology positively if programme pitches address more than one of the key purposes.

Inconsistencies in categorisation and the current state of flux with regard to PSB usefully point towards the need to understand institutions (whether BBC, Channel 4, or more broadly mass media itself) as not conceived of 'as an extradiscursive structure which controls the production of films, for example... but as itself composed in part of these texts, as a system of relations discursively ordered' (Copjec 1990: 50). That is to say that institutions are themselves signifying practices and that production, post-production, and viewing of TV archaeologies are themselves part of – rather than dictated by – institutional discourse. Here I find myself sidling up to Lacan. While I neither purport nor wish to engage in a sustained Lacanian analysis of TV archaeologies, there is something to be gained through 'looking awry' at this material (Žižek 1991). Aspects of Lacan's architectonic – the Symbolic Order or 'big Other', the Imaginary and the Real – resonate through televisual archaeologies. While Lacan has informed television and film research (for example, Jagodzinski and Hipfl 2001; Metz 1990; Mulvey 1975), specific televisual documentary has been largely ignored (Steele 2003 is a notable exception). So what role does the industrialised production of archaeological knowledges play in this 'libidinal economy'?

Accuracy, Reality, Truth

She: *'I always speak the truth'— so what do you... say about that?...*
I: *No one ever speaks without at the same time saying, 'I speak the truth'.*

She: *Except for the person who says 'I am lying'…*
I: *And even if I say 'I am lying', I am saying nothing but 'it is true that I am lying' – which is why truth is not the opposite of falsehood.* (Miller 1990: xx)

In her pioneering study of audience reception of reality television[3], Annette Hill cites research carried out in 2002 by the Independent Television Commission and Broadcasting Standards Commission that indicated that 80 per cent of respondents were interested in watching documentaries, with 60 per cent believing they were accurate (Hill 2005: 59). The research also suggested that audiences are more likely to trust dramatised reconstructions than documentaries (2005: 60). This has interesting implications for TV archaeologies. Although television critics overwhelmingly focus their ire on dramatic reconstruction (Caveille et al. 2005: 44–45), viewers repeatedly comment favourably on what they feel they learn about 'life in the past' (Piccini 1999).

Reconstruction may be used to structure an entire programme, although its use from programme to programme is markedly different in appearance and sound. In 'Pompeii: The Last Day' (director Peter Nicholson, BBC1 2003), Tim Piggott-Smith and James Carter perform against a CGI Italy with classic TV drama elocution, while 'The Iceman Murder' (production Dangerous Films, BBC1 2005) used a more 'naturalistic' acting style. More commonly, a reconstruction sequence is embedded within the documentary. From 'Gladiator Girl' (director Jeremy Freeston, Channel 4 2001) to 'Helen of Troy' (executive producer Richard Bradley, Channel 4 2005), stories include reconstruction scenes, very often under-cranked (either in-camera or in post-production) to give the sense of slow-motion action, coupled with grainy visual texture and low lighting and/or sepia tones. Notwithstanding the individual audiovisual treatments, research suggests that viewers place more faith in the accuracy of these overtly dramatic performances than in the academic or expert performances provided by presenters and interviewees.

Viewers believe that they are learning something 'actual', and so at some stage, enter into a contract of faith – or credibility game – with particular aspects of the programme. At stake is the credibility of 'I always speak the truth' (Steele 2003: 330). As Roscoe and Hight suggest, '[E]ven though we may agree that documentary representations are as constructed as fictional ones, the stance that documentary takes toward the social world is one that is grounded on a belief that it can access the real' (2001: 8). Steele argues that truth, fact, and reality are conflated via the truthfulness of the programme's performative communication of the facticity of its content as it relates to a pro-film reality (Steele 2003).

That is to say, our belief in a lived space outside the frame – before and after we press 'record' – is coupled with the fact base of TV archaeology, which then becomes part of the truth of the programme's broadcast. The telescoping of those three elements works powerfully to construct a narrative of 'false completeness' (Steele 2003: 330). In other words, a belief that what we watch is the whole, not the (w)hole, truth (Lacan 1990). And yet how do we account for the fact that viewers believe the drama more than the documentary?

I suggest that a return to Barthes's 'reality effect' (1986) may offer some insight into this process. Barthes asserted that representations look paradoxically more real when they carry a density of details of little, if any, significance. There is ample evidence of such tactics in TV archaeologies. In the long-standing series *Time Team* (series producer Tim Taylor, Channel 4, broadcast since 1993), an array of presenter pieces to camera, cameos, cutaways, mid- and long shots, and both watercolour and CGI reconstructions provide the detail. Series producer Tim Taylor, archaeologist Mick Aston, and directors such as Graham Dixon and Laurence Vulliamy believe very strongly that their attention to detail is a mark of intellectual rigour and faithfulness to the material. No viewer could disagree with the intentions of these programme makers. However, it is useful to consider how the everyday practices of filmmakers, carried out under the extreme pressures of television production, complement the factual content to produce viewers' perceptions of archaeo-historic televisual reality.

Let us take one example. In *Time Team*'s 'D-Day Special', broadcast on 2 June 2004, the director and editors establish the truth value of the programme with an initial sequence in which presenter Tony Robinson speaks with a war veteran on the 'actual' beach at Normandy. From the use of location to establish truth (McArthur 1978: 29), the sense of authentic place is extended with a bird's eye map view of the Normandy coast. Normandy is no longer a single location on the map; it becomes a landscape of conflict. Stewart Ainsworth then discusses an aerial photograph of the area, which is followed by a cutaway to a layer of maps and images, with hands moving over their surface, retracing the boundary and location marks.

In BBC2's *Time Flyers* (series producer Steve Evanson 2002–2003), not only is location filming used to bolster the credibility game, but the presenters themselves fly over the landscapes in the programme's helicopter. All the detail is thus laid out beneath them as utopian surveillance, with nothing to be missed. There really *is* something (under) there. Of course, that focus on the aerial, or bird's eye view, is a key marker of the archaeological 'gaze'. From O.G.S. Crawford's early use of aerial photography during the First World War to the big-budget, thematic TV archaeologies such as 'Seven Ages of Britain' (producer Justin Pollard, Channel 4 2003) or 'Britain AD' (producer Timothy Copestake, Channel 4 2004) and the CGI reconstructions of 'Pompeii: The Last Day' (producer Alisa Orr, BBC1 2003), most of what appears in the frame is extraneous to the archaeological narra-tive – thus heightening the 'reality effect' of this 'complete' gaze that can never be complete.

Returning to earth, in *Time Team*'s 'D-Day Special', Robinson claims that 'we use archaeology to unearth the lost secrets' but then turns to one of the team experts, Francis Pryor, and questions, '[H]ow can you as archaeologists tell this story'? Pryor responds, '[F]irst we have to get rid of all the vegetation' while Phil Harding chimes in, 'I want to get on and do some digging'. There follow cutaway shots of saws, pickaxes, and strimmers. Later, we see Pryor describing how the team will 'put a trench through the trenches', with a jump cut to the JCBs clawing away the layers of topsoil. I suggest that such scenes con-struct a creative, audiovisual account of Lacan's premise 'I love you, but there is in you something more than you, *objet petit a*, which is why I mutilate you' (Žižek 1991: 169). The libidinal activities of these men and their machines, as screen narrative, points towards an archaeological desire commingling with a desire for truth, even as the insistent percussion of the show's music marries the pagan beat of the machine and trowel rhythm with the film beat. That is to say, the cred-ibility of the programme is augmented by the myriad details of tools and what they do, rendered as 'reality effect' by the camera technolo-gies that frame this destruction of the materiality that archaeologist, director, and viewer desire.

In another example, the first programme in the *What the Ancients Did for Us* series, (series producer Ian Potts, Open University and BBC2 2005), 'The Islamic World' combines a wide variety of location shots, cameos, cutaways, reconstructions, and stock footage, creating a rich texture unusual for 'educational' television. Main series presenter Adam Hart-Davis introduces the series by describing how the team will 're-create and test inventions' and 'travel to where it all took place'. The editing rhythm rapidly takes the viewer from Hart-Davis to an establishing desert shot, to co-presenter Amani Zain describing the work of the 'great man, El Sufi, who named all the visible stars', to a mix of tracking and panning shots along the desert landscape, and then into the heart of Mecca to the Al-hajar Al-aswad. The camera moves with Zain and intercuts her pieces to camera with rostrum shots of paintings, manuscripts, and artefacts. Back in Britain, the camera work becomes more static. Hart-Davis and Jamie Darling are filmed with straight-on mid-shots and close-ups from fixed camera positions. There is an interesting structural opposition between the objective, cold light of science to play off Zain's narrative history. There is, too, an issue around gender as both Zain and Hermione Cockburn (who does location presenting for different episodes) are attractive young women and it is perhaps all too tempting for the director not to place them on windswept ridges bathed in golden light.

However, I suggest that of greater interest is how the 'reality effect' of the audiovisual detail – as it animates place and space – also speaks of Lacan's *objet petit a* – 'the object-cause of desire... the nothingness of pure seeming' (Žižek 1991: 94). The images of the 'pure seeming' of Al-hajar Al-aswad suggest this object *a*, the little bit of reality that 'sticks out'. Žižek's reiteration of Miller's 'Montré à Premontré' (1984), in his discussion of Hitchcock's use of the tracking shot, brings *What the Ancients Did for Us* into a frame (Žižek 1991: 93–97). That is to say, Mecca becomes the blot suggested by those seemingly empty tracking shots. There is no revelation to be found at the camera's resting point. Instead, it perhaps illustrates how 'the field of reality rests upon the extraction of the object *a*, which nevertheless frames it' (1991: 94). Mecca is extracted from the shot but nevertheless frames the reality of the desert landscape, and by implication all those unseen objects within it. I would argue that there is something of this in the prevalence of the aerial imagery in TV archaeology discussed above. The archaeology is within the landscape that becomes a field of reality only when the individual feature or set of features is extracted from it. It is the abstraction of the archaeological feature that makes this an *archaeological* landscape.

Catherine Liu argues that television wants to believe that it tells the truth (1991). Despite the IFA scandal cited at the opening of this chapter, most programme makers believe this, too. Yet from Hill's research into audiences, it would appear that viewers have trouble believing, despite the efforts of the documentary industries. To understand this, I wish to return to reconstruction and argue that it is, in fact, within the reconstruction form that we see the fullest expression of Barthesian reality. The visual and sonic richness – the slow-motion film that allows the eye to linger on detailed materiality and the dramatic sound design that allows for more layering and effect than is acceptable in the standard interview – of reconstruction actually provides the evidence for authenticity that the viewer desires. Certainly, viewers do not feel so rewarded with the presenter-led stories. But perhaps the function of those non-dramatic programme elements is in fact to engender viewer *jouissance.* The vigour with which viewers criticise programme makers for 'getting it wrong' would suggest that there is a transgressive pleasure in the active fragmentation of programmes. I will return to the subject of viewer *jouissance* at the end of this chapter, but I wish to turn first to another genre of TV archaeology that trades in authenticity and the discourse of truth: the genre of 'live' archaeology.

Spectacular Liveness

As Jay David Bolter (2005: 9) asserts in the preface to *The Spectacle of the Real*:

> [I]n the current hybrid (analog/digital) media world, the concept of real-time delivery now plays a key role in defining the real or the authentic for our culture. Real-time is televisual 'liveness' as refined by digital processing.

Yet this is only ever near real time, as a gap exists between occurrence and consumption. Those who control the technology can both manufacture and constrain the spectacle within those electronic gaps. On-the-fly continuity editing invisibly transforms real-time TV into spectacular narrative. Those currently writing about the spectacle of 'liveness' acknowledge the key role of Andy Warhol's *Empire* (1964), a six and one-half hour film of the Empire State Building shot from the forty-first floor of the Time-Life Building in New York (Rodney 2005; Steele 2003). Leaving aside the 2001 events at the World Trade Centre, the appeal in *Empire* is the desire for catastrophe: '[I]t is this capacity to capture catastrophe (along with banality) that gives the live cam its currency' (Rodney 2005: 43). We can see this in a range of works, from the first round-the-clock webcammed 'Doll's House' (producer Ian McClelland, Bravo 1998) to the BBC's 'Badger Watch' (Steele 2003: 332). This fascination with the potential for catastrophic occurrence calls up the Freudian 'uncanny' (*unheimlich*), which draws us in not because it is 'something externally alien or unknown but – on the contrary – [because it is] something strangely familiar which defeats our efforts to separate ourselves from it' (Morris 1985). Of course, in the near real time of contemporary television broadcast, the uncanny is massaged. This is not the liveness of performance, where anything really can happen (Phelan 1993); instead, the three-second delay is used to produce the circumstances of the uncanny and heighten its effect.

Archaeology has recently joined the ranks of 'near real-time' broadcasting. *Time Team*'s first live broadcast took place in August 1997, and even at this early date the power of convergent media was recognised – with updates broadcast via the website and a dial-and-listen telephone service. The most recent event was 'The Big Roman Dig' (July 2005), which had full convergence capability with site blogs, webchats, online database, interactive TV content for digital viewers, and online games and virtual tours in addition to its terrestrial television broadcast. This rich content complemented the real-time elements of the television output. 'Big Dig' participants had been wary that events might be 'faked', but Somerset County archaeologist Bob Croft vouched for the 'archaeological integrity of the show' and felt that 'it seems incredibly inclusive… as close as you're going to get [to the real thing]' (Hartle et al. 2005: 57). Those involved in the programme ascribed to its authenticity via the seeming immediacy of the live format, during which the 'unfakeable' uncanny might occur.

Five has recently taken up the challenge of 'live' archaeology with its 'Fighter Plane Dig… Live!' (producer/director James Cutler, 30 May 2003), 'The Golden Mummy Tomb Opening.. Live!' (producer/director Laurence Vulliamy, 12 December 2004), and 'Stonehenge… Live!' (producer/director Rupert Parker, 20 June 2005). These exploit the real-time technologies to provide a richly detailed televisual environment that mixes live, presenter-led commentary with excavation, interviews with experts, and pre-recorded special features or cameos. In this discussion, I focus only on the real-time elements.

The three main 'Golden Mummy' presenters were Guy de la Bédoyère, Kate Sanderson, and Egyptologist Zahi Hawass. De la Bédoyère opens the programme standing in front of a white geodesic dome, bright against the desert night. He tells the audience that 'burial chambers were discovered, just over there' and indicates with his arm an area out of shot and blanketed in darkness. He announces that 'out there is the valley of the golden mummies' and then says 'the digging is ongoing as we speak' although 'it's difficult to see what's happening out here, but believe me, there are tombs everywhere'. This takes the uncanny to its limits as the viewer cannot see the field in which the event is meant to take place.

After an hour of thrilling, real-time excavation, we see the underground stone-built entrance to the tomb. Hardhat-mounted cameras film the frenetic scrabbling while we hear Hawass excitedly calling 'We need to enter! We need to enter!' Behind him, Sanderson gamely asks, 'Can you see, Zahi?' It is her task to encourage the visualisation of the finds as the small camera views become obscured with moisture and sand. Sanderson asks again whether Hawass can see and there follows this exchange.

H: Yes, I can see.
S: What can you see?

Pause.

S: Zahi, what can you see?
H: I can see many rooms and a sarcophagus.
S: C'mon, you gotta tell me what you can see.

After some minutes, Sanderson follows Hawass into the tomb.

H: You know, Kate, you are entering history!

As she enters the tomb, the condensation and sand finally obscure our view completely and Sanderson is forced to leave again in order to present to the camera operators above ground. Just when our patience might be rewarded, the technology of our gaze confounds us. Yet the tantalising glimpse of the tomb nonetheless presents us with evidence for the uncanny, but also points towards a pro-film reality. Just because we are not seeing it does not mean that it is not happening. Yet this 'brush with the Real' perhaps has the unintended consequence of tormenting the viewer with 'both the desire to see everything, to have the world on hand, 'live and raw', and the suspicion, ultimately reassuring, that there really is 'nothing to see' (Lockwood 2005: 77). We return to the fallacy of the whole truth when of course that completeness – like that of 'the entirely false' or 'the solid fact' – is illusion: '[A]lthough saying it all is literally impossible…, it's through this very impossibility that the truth holds onto the real' (Miller 1990: xxiii).

Near real-time programming is thus performative of archaeological truth and particularly the conflation of truth, reality, and authenticity in a number of ways. The indexical relationship of the moving image 'document' to reality links it to the pro-film Real. Place, particularly the powerful wedding of presenter to place, then creates an indexical relationship between the screen work and 'truth'. The myriad visual and sonic details, which are provided by archaeology's attention to the material and fact, combine to enact a Barthesian 'reality effect' that is tied in with discourses of the 'authentic'. In Crandall's terms, '[A]uthenticity arises less from the authenticity of reality *per se* than the authenticity of the means by which reality is portrayed' (Crandall 2003).

Futures

Walter Benjamin's discussion of the 'work of art in the age of mechanical reproduction' still resonates today for TV archaeologies. For

Benjamin, film has 'burst this prison world asunder by the dynamite of a tenth of a second' (Benjamin 1969: 236). Despite the change in technology from frames per second to bite rates, the moving image 'on the one hand, extends our comprehension of the necessities which rule our lives; on the other hand it manages to assure us of an immense and unexpected field of action' (1969: 235). It is therefore useful for me to work towards a resolution of this chapter that considers Benjamin's evocation of the revolutionary aspect of screen practice. From the above discussion, it should be apparent that we will continue to be frustrated by TV archaeology and miss television's generative potential if we reproduce the 'bipolarity of discourses dealing with documentary' – that is to say, if we continue to argue about whether documentary provides access to the phenomenal world or that it is all fakery (Lioult 2005).

With broadcasting commissioners now advising that 'formats should be invisible' (Bailey et al. 2005: 56–57), it may become more of a challenge to pigeonhole programmes and the knowledges that they produce. Yet the need for television to feel that it tells the truth is expressed anew by Roy Ackerman, creative director of Diverse TV ('Britain BC', Channel 4 2003; 'Britain AD', Channel 4 2004), who believes that we should

> find a different way of doing archaeology on television - hands-on but not against the clock... continuing to innovate while involving viewers in the quest for new ways of interpreting the past. Good presenters... new stories... new ways of linking artefacts and sites to storytelling. Less hyperbole, less cheap and cheesy reconstructions. (quoted in Bailey et al. 2005: 56)

It is tempting to consider that the current emergent documentary renaissance indicated by Channel 4's increased documentary investment and the BBC's independent report into the social value of documentary, discussed at the beginning of this chapter – and in other genres typified by the big screen successes of Michael Moore (*Bowling for Columbine*, 2002; *Fahrenheit 9/11*, 2004), *Capturing the Friedmans* (director Andrew Jarecki, 2003), *Supersize Me* (director Morgan Spurlock, 2004), and *Tarnation* (director Jonathan Caouette, 2004) – might be a response to Žižek's assertion that as the perception of 'truth' diminishes, so the desire for it grows (1991: 8). In a Lacanian framework, the crisis of truth in TV archaeology is 'the answer of the real to human praxis' (Žižek 1991: 34).

With that in mind, TV archaeology broadcasters are now in a position to take up the challenge of documentary's recent problematising of notions of the authentic, real, and truthful. Perhaps, as Lockwood argues, when there is no longer an elsewhere, a real, we are driven to the destructive pursuit of authenticity (Lockwood 2005: 74–76). But if television commissioners begin to move away from TV archaeology's use of 'evidence' to plug the gaps in the real towards an acceptance that factual television teaches us how to be do-it-yourself citizens (Hartley 1999), then perhaps we might see archaeo-historic documentary on television that strives to do more than just tell us about the past. As Bruzzi states, all documentary is 'necessarily performative because it is given meaning by the interaction between performance and reality' (Bruzzi 2000: 154). It is certainly the case that producers and production companies make programmes that they believe commissioners believe audiences want. Yet, as discussed, recent commissioning guidelines and broadcasting policy documents appear to point the way towards a more nuanced understanding of increasingly diverse niche markets.

I am not arguing that TV archaeologies abandon well-researched, rich audiovisual detail. Rather, I would suggest that it is what we do with that detail that is at stake. If directors, producers, and editors return to montage as the defining characteristic of moving image practice, then this detail might approach the quality of Benjamin's *Arcades Project* (1999 [1935]), in which there are 'moments when information bristles' (Doane 1990: 228). Rather than these visual and sonic details being used as illustrative, 'authentic' evidence of truth, the juxtaposition of images and sound – when divorced from the idea of linear narrative – might just link us briefly with the Real. While real-time television might provide the thrill of the uncanny, while TV archaeologies might offer its viewers the *jouissance* of transgressing the televised truth via robust fact checking, archaeo-historic television that embraces the strengths of the medium might just take us somewhere different.

Acknowledgements

Since 2001, I have been given the unique opportunity to develop work on mediatised archaeologies through my teaching and curricular involvement in the M.A. in Archaeology for Screen Media, University of Bristol. Successive students and my colleagues John Adams, Jon Dovey, and Dan Hicks have both encouraged and challenged my thinking practices as they sit uncomfortably betwixt archaeology and screen studies. More recently, I have been appointed Research Councils UK Academic Fellow associated with the University of

Bristol Research Theme, performativity | place | space. It is under the auspices of that theme that I present my work here. It should go without saying that any errors or oversights are my sole responsibility.

Notes

1. Following a degree in philosophy (Glasgow University), Grierson became interested in filmmaking during his work in the United States on the influence of mass media on public opinion. His first film, *Drifters*, premiered in 1929. He famously produced *Night Mail* in 1936. Grierson founded the film unit at the Empire Marketing Board and Post Office and, during the Second World War, went on to start the National Film Board of Canada.

2. I variously use the terms 'TV archaeology' (Kulik 2005), 'televisual archaeology', and 'archaeo-historic documentary' in my research to indicate moving image material (primarily for television broadcast) that uses archaeological research practices to structure narrative.

3. This is not the place to embark on a lengthy definition of reality TV. For my purposes, I am content to ascribe to Hill's definition: 'entertainment programmes about real people' (Hill 2005: 50).

12

THE ICONOGRAPHY OF EXHUMATION

Representations of Mass Graves from the Spanish Civil War

Layla Renshaw

Exhuming Iconography

This contribution will focus on the ongoing exhumation of mass graves from the Spanish Civil War. The graves in question contain Republican civilians killed by Nationalist soldiers or militias between 1936 and 1939. The exhumations are part of a broader campaign to acknowledge Republican memory of the civil war and the Left's experience of repression under Franco, still an absolute taboo in many communities in Spain. The exhumation work began in earnest in 2000, 25 years after the death of Franco, and is coordinated by a national network of activists, sympathisers, and relatives of those who suffered in the war or subsequent repression. An oft-cited estimate is of 30,000 civilian victims still remaining in mass graves throughout Spain. Since the Nationalists's victory enabled them to mourn and memorialise their own losses, the vast majority of these graves are Republican, a label encompassing a broad spectrum of left-wing politics.

In order to appreciate the significance of these mass graves, it is important to understand the nature of the violence that produced both them and a level of fear that ensured 65 years of silence on the subject. There is a dominant perception both inside and outside Spain that the civil war was one fought between two armies, however ad hoc and ragged. Yet the civilian graves under discussion here are not the product of this kind of warfare and are numerous in parts of Spain where battle lines were never drawn. For these graves, it is more accurate to use the Nationalists's own terminology of the *limpieza*, or the cleansing of Spanish society. The civil war has rightly been described as fratricidal at times, but it is less often termed 'genocidal' due to the shared ethnicity of victim and perpetrator. In fact, the Nationalists used their biologically determinist, quasi-racial characterisation of both the working-class population, and liberal or leftist ideologies, to justify the mass killings of their own civilians (Preston 2004: 285). This logic and rhetoric makes the violence in Spain more closely comparable with the actions of Europe's other fascist regimes in this period. It is important to acknowledge these points of comparison, so that the contrast in the starkly different trajectories of memory and mourning following the Spanish Civil War and World War II becomes fully apparent.

This quasi-racial logic also helps to explain the repression of surviving relatives 'contaminated' as 'reds' by their relation to the dead. The pervading silence surrounding this violence and the apparent breakdown in the transmission of memory or personal narrative in Spain is easily understood in the light of the repression meted out to bereaved Republican families. In the aftermath of political killings, relatives of the dead suffered incarceration, surveillance, harassment, sexual humiliation, and economic marginalisation to the point of destitution. Children of dead Republicans were often made dependent on Francoist charity, conditional upon religious and political 're-education' (Silva et al. 2004). After Franco's victory, official discourse constantly asserted that the dead had been enemies of the state. To publicly challenge this would have been unthinkable, and silence became a survival strategy. From my own interviews with the surviving children of Republicans, it is clear that for some, this disjunction between public and private memory made remembering the dead unbearably painful and burdensome.

The lapse of 65 years to initiate a popular social movement to redress the breakdown of Republican memory is not a testament to the success of forgetting, but rather a measure of the thorough and absolute nature of Francoist repression (see Fig. 12.1). The dominant group to emerge from this developing social movement is called the Association for the

Figure 12.1   Grave excavated by ARMH that contained 12 residents (thought to include the majority of councillors and the mayor who were loyal to the Republican government) from a small village in the Burgos region of Castille Leon (Layla Renshaw).

Recuperation of Historical Memory (ARMH)[1]. It started as an informal contact and support group, allowing individuals to swap information on the fate of missing relatives, and researching state archives for information on Republican victims. A significant part of its role is the coordination of commemorative acts at cemeteries and clandestine graves to raise awareness of the past through media coverage and give a channel of public expression to the relatives of dead Republicans. The number of exhumations has risen exponentially since 2000, as has the media coverage and public awareness of the movement. It is a grass roots campaign with a predominantly voluntary workforce and to date has received no central government funding. Outside the Basque autonomous region, the majority of these exhumations have no permanent links to any archaeological or forensic institution and have mainly relied on the voluntary participation of archaeologists and other specialists. The physical exhumation of bodies is only a recent part of the broader project of 'recuperating' Republican memory, but since these investigations began, ARMH has gone from being a minority interest group to a loose but influential political entity, instrumental in shaping the national discourse on the recent past. Arguably, this transition has been achieved in large part through the levels of public interest generated by a particular representation of the exhumations by domestic and international news media.

Since 2003, I have visited Spain to work on exhumations and conduct a series of interviews with campaigners, volunteers, archaeologists, and the relatives of those buried in the mass graves. The comments presented here are not the result of systematic media survey but more of participant-observation, watching first hand the interaction among the journalists, photographers, and filmmakers who came to the graves and those responsible for the exhumations (see Fig. 12.2). My examination of the resulting texts and images is from the perspective of an outsider, missing some subtleties that might be apparent to a Spanish viewer. Although my involvement has primarily been in conjunction with ARMH, it is not the only group working in Spain. The re-examination of civil war memory is a regionally and politically diverse movement that I refer to as the Memoria cause, and any generalisations made here entail a degree of simplification. Furthermore, my observations are based on ARMH's first forays into mass media. As the publicity surrounding the exhumations subtly impacts upon popular perception, the campaign's strategy evolves responsively in an ongoing dialogue with public opinion. The constant thread running through this process remains the power of visual representations of the graves to engage the public.

My own interest in forensic archaeology was inspired and shaped by newspaper images of the archaeologists at work on the mass graves of Bosnia in the late 1990s. Involved as an intern in a forensic excavation

Figure 12.2   Documentary film crew interview informants beside a mass grave in Asturias (Layla Renshaw).

in Kosovo, it was possible to see first hand these images being produced and reflect on the symbolic impact of the work and the gap between the meanings encoded in those images and the disturbing reality of a human rights investigation. This is a discipline in which the same scientific practitioners travel from country to country, and the investigative process followed in one country becomes the precedent and paradigm for the next. It is a relatively new subfield, strongly promoting universal protocols and paradigms to gain acknowledgement as a discrete subject. This is very much the case in Spain, where campaigners in favour of exhumation draw on popular knowledge and approval of the truth commissions in Latin America – particularly Argentina – that were extensively covered by the Spanish press.

The Representation of Mass Graves

As the practice of exhumation becomes universalised and gains significance as an act in itself, independent of its political or historical context, it is unsurprising that a prevailing aesthetic emerges in the media coverage of mass graves from around the world. It is an undeniably charged and emotive act, transgressing boundaries between the living and the dead. The symbolic resonance of an exhumation becomes inseparable from its stated aim of investigation or the retrieval of remains. Media coverage in one country builds up a repertoire of images for use in the next. Some examples of newspaper headlines and captions show the common pool of imagery that is drawn upon: from a piece in the *Independent* on Bosnia entitled 'Brave Voice Of The Silent Witness'[2]; from a Spanish student newspaper in 2004, 'Finally The Civil War Victims Will Have a Voice'[3]; or most graphically from the BBC web page on the newly exposed Iraqi graves, 'The archaeologists have to make the corpses tell stories'.[4] The coverage of these three very different countries frames the investigative process in the same way by giving the corpse a form of agency or voice, and portraying the archaeologist as mouthpiece or translator.

It is logical that the prevailing discourse on universal human rights, with its legal paradigm based on the cross-cultural applicability of a judicial or quasi-judicial investigative model serving as precedent between distinct contexts across time and space, will serve to homogenise this process. Comparisons with international precedent weigh heavily on public discourse in Spain, a young democracy still dealing with its post-dictatorship inferiority complex. It is highly significant that the co-founder and president of ARMH is himself a professional journalist, and his founding act was to write an article entitled 'My Grandfather, Too, Was a *Desaparacido*', which made an explicit comparison between Spain's past and the 'dirty wars' of Chile and Argentina (Kolbert 2003: 70). Despite this increasingly homogenised representation of exhumation, it is still possible to detect examples in the current use of imagery in Spain that are particularly relevant to the Spanish political and historical context. By first analysing the common elements in emerging international iconography of exhumation, it should be possible to highlight the specific iconography of Spain's mass graves and the crucial part this plays in the Memoria campaign.

Archaeologists have noted, and to some extent expressed disquiet over, the representation of exhumation in the media. 'Public interest in forensic techniques may be gauged by the prominence of reports in the popular media, especially during the 1990s, concerning the excavation of mass graves. The potential prurience of these reports has perhaps contributed to mainstream archaeology avoiding the topic' (Crossland 2000: 115). This media attention is of course a measure of their belief in a widespread public appetite for coverage of the theme. The multiple strands that fuel this appetite are worth evaluating to help uncover the logic underlying the Memoria campaign's representation of graves.

On occasion during theses exhumations, the potential for representation was placed above the potential for recovery of archaeological evidence. On one site, the process of recording and protecting the small finds – watches, wallets, shoes, and belts – was postponed. A decision was taken to leave personal objects in situ until the visit of a photographer from a national newspaper on the following day. Individuals complete with personal possessions were deemed to have more 'impact'. Aside from an understandable impulse to humanise a group of victims so long dehumanised in official discourse, the precise nature of this impact bears examination. Essentially innocuous objects – the ephemera gathered in a trouser pocket – can, due to their context in a mass grave, turn into matter out of place and capable of immediately encoding the message that something terrible happened here.

In the example above, the archaeologist was seeking to preserve the co-incidence of personal ephemera and human bone in the grave, which naturally juxtaposes the mundane and the frightening. The grave communicates the fragile line between routine daily life and horror (and therefore its proximity to us all) in a way that allows a charged moment of empathetic engagement with the suffering of another, a pleasing shock of compassion. It also allows us to safely flirt with the closeness of our own death as voyeurs of that of another. The same observation can be made of a great deal of popular media coverage of disaster, crime, and suffering, but the time dimension in this instance highlights the fact that the archaeological encounter with any artefact contains within it a benign version of this voyeuristic thrill. Archaeological theory now emphasises the way in which aspects of the archaeological and the forensic process accord with a prevailing modernist sensibility. Tilley (2000) characterises this sensibility as 'a sensitivity to the ephemeral, fleeting and contingent nature of the present... a sense of possibility: that the world could be changed, turned upside down.' The fragility of normal lives, as intimated by bones and quotidian objects in a mass grave, exemplifies this preoccupation. The photographic image of a mass grave allows this moment of encounter to be consumed by a much wider audience (see Fig. 12.3).

Some authors, in analysing the popular allure of both the forensic and archaeological aesthetic, have noted its ability to create meaning from destruction, or order from chaos. As Buchli and Lucas (2001) put it, to 'sanitize' our engagement with violence and decay. Or as a way of 'making good the loss' (Schnapp et al. 2004: 12). In the majority of media representations of the Spanish exhumations, there is a notable absence of images depicting archaeological, forensic, or even historical methodology in any detail. Although the scientific techniques used to identify human remains generally elicit great public interest and speculation from local visitors to the graves, the focus of media representation suggests that the same bodies and objects lose their

Figure 12.3 Skeletons in a mass grave with sandy fill from the Burgos region (Layla Renshaw).

visual power once transposed to the laboratory. If the media wished to feature investigative techniques, it would be possible to represent this to the viewer materially and visually – the insignia on a belt buckle, the medal of a patron saint from the victim's home village, or fracture patterns on the body of a victim brutalised prior to death – all conform to conventional notions of archaeological or forensic evidence. Yet the majority of visual representations of exhumation are of intact graves and in situ bodies, 'wide-angle' shots encompassing an entire scene. Their value for the viewer is not 'evidential' in the strict sense but iconic. Arguably, during this first stage in the long process of Spain's reckoning with its past, the Memoria campaign is not seeking to present its investigations as a process of creating order from chaos. Instead, it is more powerful to present the graves almost 'untouched' in a disordered state, resonant with violence, as a freeze frame of the agonising moment. This demands that the viewer reflect consciously, or subconsciously, on why the chaos of the past is still unresolved and presents the civil war as a loss yet to be 'made good'.

Shanks et al. (2004) have observed this process of 'archaeological metamorphosis' in which the 'mundane becomes allegorical', in relation to the Smithsonian's quest to assemble a material record representative of the events of 11 September 2001, particularly from 'Ground Zero'. 'More accurately, the museum curators and archaeologists sought material icons…. Each acts a touchstone; not so much illuminating the topics of political and forensic interest, the exhibits are material correlates for the intimate personal experiences, the individual stories. That is what we mean when we call things iconic' (2004: 61). Further analysis of the iconic properties of the September 11th material reveals the potential strategic value of a similar iconography for the Memoria campaign in Spain. 'Conventional historiography… slips away, is irrelevant in the confrontation between the banality of everyday life, sentimental association and the apocalyptic' (2004: 61). Spain's conventional historiography of the civil war – both the Francoist victor's history and the public's ingrained hostility to partisan claim and counter claim – is precisely what the Memoria campaign seeks to overcome.

Visual Image Production within the 'Pact of Silence'

Within the broader project of recuperating left-wing memory in Spain, there are several competing claims for time and resources, primarily the collection of oral history or testimony, documentary evidence in state archives, commemorative acts and monuments, and the exhumation of human remains. From a pragmatic point of view, the collection of oral testimony from elderly informants appears to be the most urgent activity as it is constrained by a biological time limit. Despite this, there is a concentration of limited resources on the recuperation of 'memory' from the graves. Part of the Memoria movement's urge to prioritise exhumation in its campaign agenda is a calculation of the strategic value of the visual images and symbolic associations produced by the act of exhumation. The value of this type of visual image production in contemporary Spain can only be fully appreciated by understanding the narrow constraints currently placed on oral and written political discourse, especially discourse on the past. The iconography of a mass grave is a useful political tool because it can say the un-sayable, and the un-sayable is still a surprisingly large category in contemporary Spain. Visual images of mass grave being opened can articulate a complex set of messages, without the archaeologists, exhumation coordinators, or journalists ever having to explicitly articulate these messages or be seen publicly to intentionally politicise the investigative process.

Across Spain's political spectrum, the consensus to draw a line under the past and enable the transition to a post-Franco democracy in the 1970s is referred to variously as the 'Pact of Silence', the 'Pact of Forgetting', and the 'Pact of Amnesia'. These phrases eloquently convey the impossibility of a reckoning with the past, yet they fail to show the degree to which the pact was a one-sided imposition, accepted by Spain's Left as the 'price' of democracy. The victors of the civil war had already used the intervening 40 years to enshrine their version of the past and commemorate their dead as 'Fallen for God and Spain'. In Desfor Edles's (2002) media-based study of this transition, she undertakes a close reading of newspaper commentary on the transitional process that established a stable democracy, to show how shared symbols and a restricted common vocabulary helped build the political consensus between former enemies. Within Spain, the fear of a future civil war is slight but still real and omnipresent in a way that outside observers cannot fully share. No organisation can be seen to be reviving the dichotomies of the civil war, and in this climate an interest group accused of being partisan, inflammatory, or backward looking is effectively silenced. This is obviously a problem for an organisation such as ARMH, dedicated to the recovery of the Left's memory of right-wing oppression, an inherently political process. In this prevailing climate, with a restricted, self-policed political vocabulary, material objects and visual images can sidestep these controls. By letting material evidence do nothing more than 'speak for itself', the Memoria campaign can transmit a political message while avoiding the accusation that it politicises the graves.

In seemingly allowing the photographs of mass graves to 'speak for themselves' without interference or intervention, the Memoria campaign is correctly judging not only the public's curiosity but its faith in both physical and photographic evidence, and a corresponding mistrust of words. As discussed, this is in part a specifically Spanish mistrust of any debate or analysis that threatens public consensus, a legacy of the 'Pact of Silence'. However, in this respect the Spanish public's mistrust of words accords with a more widely held hierarchy of belief that permeates contemporary society and privileges the material and photographic record over the verbal and written. This hierarchy has been instrumental in the birth of forensic archaeology as a discipline. In analysing the media's representation of death among America's urban poor, Klinenberg (2001: 121), highlights the significance of the body in this prevailing mood.

> It is difficult to verify the competing truth claims of antagonists in social conflicts, particularly in a moment of intellectual history when political leaders are as likely as postmodern professors to claim that truths are multiple, perspectival and partial, and when public relations and information management teams are standard features of every political organization. But there is one way... familiar to anyone who follows cases of political violence, in which adjudicators can establish definitive and reliable evidence: get to the dead bodies, the corpses whose materiality cannot be denied.

Archaeologists, well versed in the multiple meanings of all categories of material evidence (including burials), need to apply the discipline's critical and interpretive view equally to exhumation and not have it obscured by the prefix 'forensic'. Although the materiality of corpses means their existence cannot be denied, this does not equate to a 'definitive' meaning. The danger of suggesting that forensic evidence can unambiguously 'speak for itself' is explored in an article by Irina Paperno (2001) on a mass grave from the 1930s in the Ukrainian city of Vinnytsia. The same autopsy reports, exhibits, and photographed corpses are recycled and circulated among different documents for decades. The German occupiers who initiate the investigation are seeking evidence for 'the crimes of Stalin', yet this is picked up in an American McCarthy-era report as 'The Crimes of Khrushchev'; meanwhile, the bodies themselves are commemorated as the victims of Nazism. Over time, certain names are added and subtracted from the original document following political and ethnic tensions within Ukraine. The seemingly immutable and rigorous forensic evidence remains the same throughout, and in fact was collected to a high standard, but its meaning is far from definitive.

While violence and civil war are not unique to Spain, the persistence of mass *desmemoria* (a vacuum resulting from the absence of memory) surviving decades into the democratic era is particularly Spanish. Spain's Memoria campaigners have drawn upon the image of burial to critique the concealed histories of Republican suffering and the suppressed nature of public debate. There are countless metaphors that play with the thin surface layer that divides Spain from its past and talk about scratching or breaking this surface, sometimes as topsoil, sometimes as the surface of a wound. The president of the Memoria Network, Emilio Silva, used an arresting image in his contribution to a 2004 edited volume coordinated by ARMH: 'The transition to democracy in this country tiptoed over the surface of the mass graves.' The parallels between physical burial, concealment, and psychological repression are attractive to the media. This attraction is shown in headlines such as 'Spain Disinters Its Painful Past'[5] from the *New Yorker* in 2003, or 'Spain Digs over Painful Memories'[6] from the *London Times* in 2004. The use of these metaphors generates a kind of natural logic that equates exhumation with revelation, honesty, and catharsis, as if physically bringing material objects 'into the light' will drag feelings and memories along with them. This is echoed in accompanying photographs of the moment of exposure or revelation of the skeletons, the ground being broken, or bodies partially emerged from the ground.

During an exhumation, the media focus is intense. The bustle and movement of an exhumation is infinitely more televisual and photogenic than the quiet collection of oral histories or archive material that Memoria groups undertake throughout Spain. The progressive discoveries in the grave are dynamic, tantalising, and inherently suspenseful. There is also an undeniably morbid and voyeuristic quality to the media interest in obtaining images of the investigator and the body under investigation, based on the frisson produced by the unnaturally intimate interaction between the living and the dead. Media representations of the graves seek to maximise this contrast between flesh and bone by focusing on the exposure of the young – and often female – flesh of students and volunteers who participate in the exhumations. I have seen press photographers as well as news and documentary cameramen engineer this juxtaposition, moving female archaeologists around the grave, because they know it will draw the viewer's eye.

In the first phase of ARMH's campaign, it was possible to detect two parallel discourses at work. One was an internal discourse circulated among supporters, with a broadly left-wing agenda critical of the 'Pact of Silence', government apathy, and right-wing hypocrisy surrounding civil war memory. The second was an external discourse designed to attract the media, win a broad base of sympathy among 'Middle Spain', and force the government to engage with ARMH demands. Looking at the points where these two discourses diverge highlights the precise areas in which the Memoria message becomes taboo and the visual images of the mass graves can 'fill in the blanks', wordlessly transmitting messages from the campaign's internal discourse to a broader audience, without explicitly stating its agenda. In the Memoria campaign's internal discourse among members and supporters, the Republican identity of the dead is acknowledged and celebrated, and the campaigners present themselves proudly as the ideological descendants of the victims. Occupants of mass graves are given collective labels such as the 'Priaranza 13', reminiscent of the group names given to martyrs or imprisoned freedom fighters.

The external discourse of the campaign still presents its work as primarily based on the pursuit of inalienable human rights. These human rights are held by the individual rather than the collective, so ARMH emphasises the individual identities of the victims (as husbands, sons, or fathers) rather than their collective political identity as socialists, atheists, or trade union members. It is much more difficult for right-wing politicians and press to demonise a dead grandfather than a dead communist. There has already been a backlash in Spain's powerful right-wing press, with opinion pieces on the 'archaeology of rancour' and the inherent 'perversion' of this campaign for 'necrophilia'. In this climate, ARMH's discourse has focused largely on the human rights of the surviving descendants of the victims, their children or grandchildren. A generation removed, the relatives are innocent victims of historical circumstance. They do not bear any responsibility for the political actions of the dead, whose militancy 'caused' their own deaths, according to Francoist discourse. Their status as blood relatives gives them a vested interest that is not politically threatening to right-wing Spain. Their motivation is always presented as a quest for personal history, identity, 'closure', and the fulfilment of familial duty, making them immune from charges of political axe-grinding.

This disavowal of ideological motives among its membership is gradually lessening as the campaign gains in momentum, size, and confidence and is better able to weather charges of 'politicising' the bodies. Over the last two to three years, the internal and external message has coalesced as ARMH grows in self-belief fuelled by public recognition and is able to bring the inherent politics of the graves more explicitly into the public eye. Nevertheless, the explanatory discourse most frequently repeated in communications with the media focuses on the phrase 'dignified reburial'. This discourse builds on the idea of a post-mortem but universal human right to rest in peace achieved by a normalised burial ritual in an individual grave. It makes a plea for 'common' decency, a sensibility that crosses political lines, and it draws attention to the dead while managing to say very little about their life or death that might be politically inflammatory. It is significant that the only sustained and explicit critique of this tactic has come from a rival exhumation group, the Forum for Historical Memory or *Foro*[7]. The group is affiliated with the Communist party and endeavours to excavate the remains of victims on a more explicitly ideological basis, privileging the political identity of the deceased. The president of the communist *Foro* has accused ARMH of being the 'neoliberals of memory' who, through their focus on the individual, engage in the 'privatisation' of suffering.

The Components of a Memoria/Desmemoria Iconography

The victim's individuality is emphasised in the montage of photos that the Spanish press uses when covering an exhumation. Rather than use the countless images of Republican fighters, activists, or prisoners, the press selects portrait photos of the 1930s, showing romantic black-and-white characters in period costume. These often depict men and women in their Sunday best, on their wedding day, or with a child on their lap – a far cry from the 'red hoard' depicted by Franco's propaganda. These family photos emphasise the small personal narrative of the victims, not the events that overtook them. On newspaper pages, these portraits are juxtaposed with the freshly exposed skeletons, like 'before and after' photos. It has become almost a visual convention in the regional press to include both types of image in its coverage of exhumation. It shows the victims as individuals in life but robbed of this identity by death, and by their burial in a mass grave.

This is an active choice to distance the press coverage from the existing Republican aesthetic – the aesthetic of Orwell's *Homage to Catalonia* (1974 [1938]), highly developed during the 1930s and recognisable as prototypical images of doomed protest. The Spanish Civil War was an early meeting of modern warfare and modern media coverage with embedded photographers (such as Capa or Centelles) creating a permanent record of Spanish Republicanism, some of which constituted potent propaganda for their cause. The photos show informal groupings of fighters that communicate spontaneity and optimism, the eclectic clothing and weapons of the underdog, the egalitarian presence of both women and foreign volunteers. The absence of these images from the press, and by and large from the Memoria campaign, is not accidental. It depoliticises the dead, and to some extent, these representations can indeed be construed as a 'privatisation' of Republican suffering. Yet this decision is also a crucial part of turning debate away from the battles of the civil war, and focusing instead for the first time on the social 'cleansing' of unarmed civilians that took place in countless communities away from the front line.

The use of portraits of the dead recurs in another frequent representation, iconic in press coverage, of the surviving children of Republican victims holding up a photo of the dead parent. A comparison between the two faces conveys a sense of time reversed and borrows the now universally understood visual language of the vigils held for the Disappeared in Latin America, particularly by the Mothers of the Plaza de Mayo. The image of a survivor holding a portrait of a loved one, taken in a different era, now eloquently compresses the fact of disappearance in the mind of the viewer with all its ramifications of doubt, loss, and lives interrupted. In Spain, the role of parent and child in this symbolic pairing is reversed. The dead are frozen in their youth and are contrasted with the aged faces of the children left behind. This juxtaposition eloquently conveys the time that has elapsed and the long wait of the survivors, allowing the Memoria campaign to silently critique the procrastination of successive governments in Spain.

But at the same time, the old-fashioned photos securely place this repression in a different historical epoch, making it safe and palatable to the right-wing establishment. Colour photos of those imprisoned or executed for political reasons in the 1960s (and even into the early 1970s) would threaten those in power in the previous regime who can still make their influence felt. Media images that depict the trappings of archaeology – tools, tapes, sample bags – are equally a distancing mechanism. The archaeological method firmly situates the graves in the distant past, the proper concern of archaeology according to popular perceptions of the subject. Although often just glimpsed in a photograph, the paraphernalia of science 'dresses' the grave and lends gravitas and the assurance of a neutral objectivity. The scientific process can be used to 'sanitise', but more precisely here to neutralise or defuse the immediacy of the graves as objects to remember but not revive. The involvement of archaeology is comforting in that it establishes historical boundaries, compartmentalising the graves as distinct from the present. If representations of the exhumations were to elicit a sufficiently negative response from those with political power, a moratorium on this work is a real and constant threat. This shows the tightrope that ARMH walks with the media, seeking to subtly promote its agenda while avoiding a backlash of sufficient weight to kill off the incipient movement before it gains the momentum required to pursue its political agenda more explicitly.

A final iconic image, favoured by the Spanish press, uses the grave space as a frame or stage set to group three generations – the dead, the elderly witness (or child of the deceased), and the youthful investigator. One generation is notable by its absence: the middle-aged who are either tainted by Franco's regime or acquiesced in the flawed transition to democracy that sealed the 'Pact of Silence'. It appears that in contemporary Spain, memory has skipped a generation. This grouping allows the Memoria campaign to critique the generation that still holds power for its complicity and prevarication over the graves. It encapsulates the idealistic hope for left-wing regeneration, transmitting the spirit of Republicanism to a new generation, through the hearing of oral histories from the elderly, and – directly through the bones in the graves – through some kind of transubstantiation during the act of retrieval.

The Memoria campaign is a work in progress, still testing the political climate in Spain and the country's readiness to incorporate the Republican experience into its national narrative. In the face of such a deeply entrenched response of silence and denial, the exhumation process provides a bank of visual images with which to encode an alternative and long-suppressed version of the past that is still too threatening to the status quo to be verbalised explicitly. The images reach a wide cross-section of Spanish society, demanding attention and provoking reflection, opening a space for debate to begin.

Notes

1. ARMH web page http://www.memoriahistorica.org/ (accessed 15 November 2005).

2. *Independent*, 30 April 2004.

3. *Eccus*, Issue No. 206, 2 November 2004.

4. BBC News Online, 8 January 2004.

5. *New Yorker*, 22–29 December 2003.

6. *London Times*, 23 January 2004.

7. *Foro* web page http://www.nodo50.org/foroporlamemoria/ (accessed 15 November 2005).

PART V

ARCHAEOLOGY, THE MEDIA, AND THE DIGITAL FUTURE

13

THE PAST AS PLAYGROUND

The Ancient World in Video Game Representation

Andrew Gardner

Introduction: Archaeology, Media, and Video Games

Many kinds of media are engaged in the representation of archaeology, and most of them are more widely popular than those provided by archaeologists themselves. While analysis of these representations has become quite commonplace among some sectors of the discipline, there are still many areas of popular culture that remain neglected, and one of these is video or computer games. Some attention has certainly been given to the role of well-known game characters (particularly Lara Croft from the *Tomb Raider* series) in constructing stereotypes of the archaeologist/explorer, as part of the study of popular images of archaeological practice in the present (e.g., Holtorf 2005a: 42–45). However, with a handful of exceptions (see, especially, Watrall 2002a, 2002b), games have generally been ignored as modes of representation *of the past*, and thus the part they might play in shaping public understandings of specific periods or cultures is not well understood. This paper aims to tackle this problem in some detail, and to explore how games do what archaeologists themselves purport to do: construct working models of past worlds and narrate stories about them.

The ways in which media such as film and television portray the past have of course been the subject of wider interest, building upon the study of the public impact of earlier generations of archaeological narratives (see, e.g., MacDonald and Rice 2003; Russell 2002a; Winkler 2004; cf. Hingley 2000). In exploring this issue, archaeologists are rightly concerned that 'responsible' interpretations win out in the battle for public attention, and that seriously distorted visions of whatever historical realities on which we ourselves can agree do not contribute to social problems in the present. The case of Nazi archaeology is often cited in this context (e.g., Arnold 1990), but there are many more subtle examples of how the norms of the past are made to conform to those of the present, thus reinforcing the status quo (cf. Tilley 1989).

I will argue in this paper that a wide range of computer games do precisely this. The fact that such games are much more commercially successful than archaeological representations of the past – which are increasingly hoped to challenge the status quo (e.g., Thomas 2004: 238) – is salient, but the degree of influence they have on popular consciousness should not be simply assumed. I will return to the issue of whether the skewed representation of the past in games is something we should be concerned about, rather than merely interested in, at a later point in this paper. What should be stressed here, though, is that this is not a paper about 'the evils of video games'. I am by no means intending to add 'distorted historical consciousness' to a (spurious) list of the 'damage' that games do to young people, alongside increased aggression and slack morals. On the contrary, as a person who has played and enjoyed some of these games, as well as an archaeologist who has thought about them, I would hope to open up another area of critical engagement with an inadvertently educational medium.

The 'inadvertance' of the education that such games might provide is worth emphasising, as is the broad range of people whom it potentially affects. The subject of this paper is not overtly 'educational' software designed for use in schools or by school children at home. While I think that archaeologists should pay more attention to how their subject (usually disguised as 'History') is taught at levels below the universities in which many work, that is not my goal here. I will focus on games that are sold as entertainment but feature the past as the place in which to play. This is, in itself, a culturally idiosyncratic approach to the past that one might actually compare to the work of archaeologists (cf. Shanks and Tilley 1992: 7–28). It is also, and much more so than the practice/play of archaeology, a widespread and commercially lucrative one. The global revenue from sales of all games (for home computers and games consoles) has recently over-taken that generated by Hollywood (Gaudiosi 2003). In the United States alone, $7.3 billion worth of games were sold in 2004. Of the more than 248 million units sold, 45 million were computer games (as opposed to console games) and 26.9 per cent (nearly 67 million) were 'strategy' titles, which include most of those representing historical periods discussed in this paper (ESA 2005: 4, 9). While the compar-isons to movies are somewhat misleading since games are more expensive to buy than movies are to watch (Kimberly 2005), these figures are indicative of the success of the medium (cf. Newman 2004: 3–7). Moreover, according to the Entertainment Software Association, the average American gamer is 30 years old and 43 per cent of play-ers are female (ESA 2005: 2–3). In the UK, the BAFTA awards have recognised games since 1997 (http://www.bafta.org/site/page20. html). In short, games are now a pervasive cultural phenomenon and need to be taken seriously.

In this paper, I will look at a selection of the numerous games set in past contexts, particularly those of the ancient and classical old world. These examples all fall within the broad genre of 'strategy' games, which includes a range of variants. Although there are some 'action' games that are set in the past (one notable recent release being *The Shadow of Rome*, a combination of detective and gladiator stories), many more are set in the present or future (cf. Watrall 2002a). It seems that the past is an arena for a particular kind of play. Having outlined some of the main genre conventions across a number of examples, in the second half of the paper, I will look at the treatment of certain key themes: violence, cultural achievement, agency, cultural variability, and time. I will try to show that, through the consistent portrayal of these themes in particular ways, games present a very 'modern' past that largely obliterates any sense of the past as different to the pres-ent. Moreover, I will argue that this is not a necessary outcome of games designers' need to fill gaps in archaeological understandings of past cultures, nor of the requirements of a medium synonymous with high technology. As I will argue in the conclusion, there are other game genres that offer the potential to evoke different cultures in striking ways, though as yet these have not been used to explore the past. If games are seriously contributing to people's 'life-long learning', then it might be worth pursuing some of these options for creating more diverse and challenging visions of past societies.

Playing in the Past

Wargames

I will begin my survey of some of the main elements of games set in the ancient world with one of the simplest forms, concentrating on warfare. Computer wargames are in many respects based on the conventions and rules designed for table-top games involving miniature figures, but with all the mechanics handled by the computer (cf. Sabin 2002). As well as producing a more immediately entertaining experience for the player, the computer's processing power enables the possibility of all the action happening at once – in 'real time' – rather than by turns. This can involve either the player competing against a computer-controlled opponent or, as is increasingly common, having the option of finding human opponents on line. In either case, the continuous flow of activity generates a more superficially realistic sense of involvement in the events portrayed in the game. One recent example of this kind of 'real-time strategy' (RTS) wargame is *Praetorians*, in which the player controls Roman armies in the mid-first century BC Gallic and civil wars.

As with most strategy games, there are several different types of gameplay in *Praetorians*. Either players can progress through a series or 'campaign' of narratively structured missions against computer-controlled enemies, or they can play short, self-contained 'skirmish' games against the computer or online opponents. The former usually involve specific objectives such as building bridges over a river or rescuing characters from enemy forts, while the latter are simply about eliminating all opposing forces. The scale of the game is intermediate between single battles and strategic warfare, involving the control of several units of troops across varied terrain in each scenario (see Fig. 13.1). While units can be split or combined, the soldiers in each are not controllable on an individual basis and simply follow the orders that the player gives to the unit; leaders, medics, and scouts are the only individual characters. Civilians are not a big feature in this game. There are villages, which are important for the player to control as they provide the only resource that matters in this game: people. Any village (represented by a very small group of buildings with a few villagers moving around in them) can produce units of the types appropriate to the controlling player's 'civilisation' (on which more below), but these drain the village's population, which only replenishes itself slowly. The structures that players can build are limited to militarily useful things like siege engines and bridges. Gameplay

Figure 13.1 *Pretorians* (Eidos). A unit of cavalry and a 'legion' wait near a village.

largely consists, therefore, in trying to capture villages, recruit troops, and destroy the enemy while achieving whatever other objectives are involved in a particular mission. It's a lot more fun than it sounds.

There are numerous details of this game that could be explored in more depth, but all I want to draw out here – in addition to the obvious emphasis on warfare and lack of attention to any other aspect of life – are a couple of points about cultural difference. The scenarios involved in the main single-player campaign are quite chronologically well defined (58–45 BC) and range across a number of places in the Roman world: Gaul, Britain, Germany, Italy, Spain, Greece, Syria, Palestine, and Egypt. In terms of the background terrain, different regions are beautifully portrayed, and there are also animated 'cut scenes' – small cinematic vignettes – between certain missions that are dramatic and evocative. However, the player only controls the Romans in any of these scenarios, and the various opponents are either other Romans or, depending upon whether the action is happening in the west or east, 'Barbarians' or 'Egyptians'. One can only control these alternative factions in the 'skirmish' form of the game, except where some of their troops might be allied with the Romans in particular scenarios. Each of the three 'civilisations' has a similar range of available unit types to perform the key functions involved in combat: light and heavy infantry, spearmen, archers, cavalry, and horse archers. Every culture also has three unique 'special units' – including gladiators for the Romans, berserkers for the Barbarians, and chariots for the Egyptians – but again there is certain symmetry of functions between each group. The various siege weapons are also equally available to each civilisation.

On the one hand, then, each culture is more or less identical, and arguably this is for gaming reasons having to do with fair competition (itself a value-laden idea, of course). On the other hand, the Romans are clearly culturally superior. Their troops are the only ones who routinely walk around in neatly ordered lines rather than more random formations, and more importantly they seem to have a consistent identity, while each of the other two civilisations is really a mixture of peoples from wide areas (the 'Egyptians', used in all of the scenarios based in the eastern Mediterranean, also includes units described as Nubians and Parthians). One quite curious aspect of the game is the addition of a little magic to the otherwise quite realistic rendering (cf. *Age of Mythology*, an RTS involving ancient gods and heroes [see Schadla-Hall and Morris 2003: 213]). Each culture has two kinds of scout – 'wolf scouts' and 'hawk scouts' – with the ability to send their animal companion off for a look around, thus extending their own range of vision. Even more idiosyncratic are the different medic units. While the Roman physicians dispense rational medical aid, the Barbarian druids and Egyptian priests can do strange things like cast blinding spells on enemy troops. The Egyptian leader character can even create mirages of phantom units (the Roman leader's special skill, by comparison, is simply to speed up the recuperation of his troops after combat). These subtle touches reinforce the more obvious stereotyping of the non-Roman cultures, and turn a basic (and – I would still freely admit – immensely enjoyable) game into a fascinating exercise in orientalist cultural politics.

Fighting and Farming

This tendency, along with many more of interest, is present in other examples of strategy games that involve a greater degree of nonmilitary activity. The 'ancient world' segment of the *Age of Empires* series is particularly important here, although there are several other examples, including *Rome: Total War*. The *Age of Empires* series began with the eponymous game focused on the old world civilisations of Egypt, Babylon, and Greece, as well as Japan (an expansion pack entitled *The Rise of Rome* added an extra main civilisation). The player can control each of these cultures in separate multi-scenario campaigns (all RTS), as well as one-off 'skirmish' scenarios, in a similar basic structure to *Praetorians*. The content of the game is, though, rather different. Resource gathering and construction are much more important, with the player able to control villagers as well as soldiers (here all represented by individuals rather than whole units). These villagers are, curiously, all male, and their main functions are to collect the various materials needed to make the structures that in turn produce different kinds of warriors, and also enable 'research' into improved fighting and gathering skills (Fig. 13.2). These materials are also needed to 'purchase' new villagers and soldiers, and consist of wood, gold, stone, and food – all procured from the game's landscape or, in the case of food, potentially from farms built and worked by villagers.

Figure 13.2 *Age of Empires.* **An Egyptian settlement in 'Tool Age' – essentially Neolithic. Copyright © Microsoft Ensemble Studios.**

This adds several dimensions to the basic fighting gameplay of a wargame, but the goal of any particular scenario still invariably involves warfare against computer-controlled opponents representing various cultures that the main protaganist civilisations encountered historically. It is possible to win a 'skirmish' game by constructing a special type of building – a 'Wonder' (the Egyptians can build a pyramid, for example), but this takes a lot of time and resources and a certain level of technology. This brings us to another complication: technological progress. Embedded into the game's core mechanic is the idea that each civilisation has to proceed through certain stages – the Stone Age, Tool Age, Bronze Age, and Iron Age – with each development requiring resources and certain buildings, but unlocking new kinds of structures, soldiers, and improvements to fighting and resource-gathering efficiency. This demands a certain level of patience and commitment from players, at the same time as offering them some choice in how to shape their particular civilisation, and as such is a major feature of the game experience. From a historical point of view, though, it is rather curious – notwithstanding the built-in assumptions about technology and progress, on which more below. Because it is such a feature of *Age of Empire*'s gameplay, it tends to figure in all scenarios, even if they are supposed to represent historical events taking place in a single year, and even if all of the stages have been worked through in a preceding scenario. The struggle for technology is a perpetual feature of life in the *Age of Empires* world.

At the same time, and similarly to *Praetorians*, there is a great deal of flattening of cultural diversity. Each culture has the same potential range of buildings and units (albeit with different bonuses for producing certain types), and more importantly they are represented as the same, at least in terms of the people. There are some different graphics for architectural styles, but not for the villagers or different kinds of soldiers, so that the Japanese end up producing warriors that look like Greek hoplites. There are also no women. Some of these features were changed in *Age of Empires II*, set in the medieval world (spanning the fifth to the fifteenth centuries AD). Female villagers make an appearance, along with special 'culturally distinctive' units for each of the wider range of cultures represented in campaigns that tend to be more focused on the exploits of individual leaders (e.g., Joan of Arc, Genghis Khan) than 'civilisations'. These still, though, accompany generic types of soldiers. With the *Conquerors* expansion to this game, the new world was also included in a campaign based on Cortés' expedition to Mexico – and with the player controlling the

Aztec defence. It is notable that, in updating the basic game to produce *Age of Empires II*, a number of the designers' main 'improvements' were in authenticity of cultural representation, to the extent of forcing players to take on roles detached from Western culture – as in the case of the Cortés campaign and indeed that based on Attila, where the player controls the Huns, not the Romans. Nonetheless, many of the generic features – including the central emphasis on technological progress – remain, as does the focus on fighting as the most effective way of achieving this.

Building Civilisation

My final examples combine and emphasise several of the trends noted so far, while partially trying to steer away from the military emphasis of the games already discussed. Some such games, focusing on the city-building and management side of ancient governance – as perceived by games designers – are context-specific, such as the Egyptian-set *Pharoah* and the Rome-set *Caesar III* (discussed in Watrall 2002a: 166). These involve micro-management of a townscape, with the provision of fire and police stations being more important than the creation of military units, in a similar fashion to the modern urban development game *Sim City 4* (and earlier versions). Population control and progress are the main features of gameplay. These features are expanded cross-culturally in the most famous and extensive of this variant of the strategy game, *Civilization*. Having gone through three versions (with a fourth due out in late 2005; *Sid Meier's Civilization II* is discussed here), this game involves the player in developing one of a range of cultures from 4000 BC to the present. The choices are quite broad, but the difference made to gameplay is fairly minimal, as there are only four main styles of city architecture and these primarily affect the ruler's (i.e., the player's) palace. As with *Age of Empires*, the units and characters that the player can generate from available resources (tax income) are generic. This means that the Zulus or the Sioux will start producing Crusaders or Alpine Troops when they attain the appropriate stage of civilisation (Fig. 13.3).

Beyond such familiar cultural generalisation, the other major feature that we have met before, but which *Civilization* emphasises more than any other game, is progress. While it is possible to win the game by conquering the world, the game steers the player in the direction of another objective: developing the technology to get into space. This goal can certainly be expedited by warfare; as through the course of history, technologies can be stolen from opponents by conquest, and

Figure 13.3 *Sid Meier's Civilization II* **(Microprose/2k Games). It is AD 800 and Sioux Crusaders are heading out from the tower of Cedar Creek, avoiding some Carthaginian catapults.**

control of as many cities as possible is desirable to generate the income to pay for scientific research. Nonetheless, it is difficult to invest heavily enough in military units to be too aggressive, as there are many other things to do. Indeed, a wide range of 'technologies' is required to make progress, from chivalry and democracy to pottery and physics. The mixing of political, religious, and social developments with more conventionally technological ideas is notable, and adds to the impression that all cultures operate with a pick-and-mix list of all-time-great cultural features.

To further reinforce this, another element of the technological progress charted in the game is the construction of 'Wonders', major structures that add to income and generate specific advantages in acquiring other technologies but can only be built once. Again, all wonders are available to all cultures and the list includes quite a global selection. Nonetheless, this attempt at egalitarianism can also be read as a representation of globalised cultural imperialism. Twenty-eight wonders are available, seven each for antiquity, the Renaissance, the

Industrial Revolution, and the modern world – all significant periods, but mainly from a Western perspective. Moreover, when the Romans can build the Great Pyramids and the Chinese can create Leonardo's workshop, what place has cultural specificity and context? As with all of the games discussed so far, *Civilization* is just that: a game designed to entertain and to allow the player to shape the past. However, as we have begun to see, games only allow players to shape the past in quite particular ways and project many of the values that are stereotypically associated with modern Western society into the past (cf. Friedman 2002). How serious a problem this is will be discussed after we have reviewed the major thematic consistencies across the various subgenres considered.

Creating the Present

Violence and Conflict

A major theme in the historically set games discussed in this paper is violence. This is hardly surprising, given the popular reputation that video games have for representing bloodshed, but it requires more serious attention given the contexts depicted in these specific examples. Two questions are relevant here: is conflict a necessary part of the 'contest' that makes a game worth playing in the first place, and is the level of violence misrepresentative of life in the ancient world?

The first question takes us close to the wide, and unresolved, debate about the role of video game (and other media) violence in society, which I want to avoid in this paper – but on which there is a growing literature (e.g., Carter and Weaver 2003; Ravitch and Viteritti 2003; cf. Newman 2004: 61–69). Suffice it to say that, while the violence in the strategy games discussed is not of the graphic kind that gets the tabloid press most agitated (and, perhaps also significantly, is not viewed from a first-person perspective), it is an important part of most of them. It is quite possible to have engaging games that do not particularly prioritise warfare; *Pharaoh* and *Civilization* are examples of this. Competition – rather than experience – is still a part of such games, though, and as long as this remains the case, conflictual modes of competition are likely to remain dominant. Whether or not this is a socially 'healthy' thing is an extremely complex issue, involving many questions about innate aggression (or the lack thereof), reality, and escapism, and the differences between causes and symptoms of specific social problems. Again, these are too complex to be reduced to a short section of this paper, and I will restrict myself to considering whether or not the past is being misrepresented.

This is also rather a difficult question to answer, for slightly different reasons. With respect to the Roman world, the historical evidence is certainly full of accounts of military campaigns, and from these one does gain the impression that warfare was a major part of life not just for soldiers, but for anyone present in zones of conflict (Goldsworthy 2002: 24; James 2002: 1). The problem is that insofar as games follow these dominant concerns of the classical writers, it is clear that they only reflect the partial view of elite men who often had political or professional experience that foregrounded conflict (such as Julius Caesar). Archaeologists have been divided about the extent to which this dominant discourse should be imposed upon the material they use, which obviously speaks to a much wider range of activities and people. At some points in recent scholarship, the study of the Roman military has simply been unfashionable, rejected as a topic that is too closely tied to 'the tyranny of texts' (James 2002: 12–27; cf. Moreland 2001: 21). More recently, though, attempts have been made to rehabilitate the subject, on the basis that previous research largely ignored many of the most interesting things about the military – such as its role as a nexus of identity transformations in frontier provinces, which is evinced by a wide range of archaeological material (e.g., Allason-Jones 2001; James 2001, 2002). The way the military both contained and encouraged violent behaviour in different contexts has also been examined (e.g., Goldsworthy 1996). This work, and similar research in other periods (e.g., in Carman 1997), has brought out more of the complexity of violent behaviour in the past – as complex as it is in the present – and does seem to illustrate its pervasiveness, at varying scales, in human societies. From this perspective, the representation of violence in games about past societies is not necessarily a problem in itself.

What is perhaps a problem is simply its dominance over all other aspects of life, and at the same time its detachment from them – indeed, from any kind of social context. In games like *Age of Empires*, soldiers are the main kinds of people whom the player 'produces' and they are much more highly differentiated than the ubiquitous villagers. The majority of technological advances also relate to improving military attributes. In a way, I can accept that this is simply a concentration on the more 'fun' (i.e., competitive) aspects of a past society that are likely to appeal to more games buyers than the ability to produce a number of different types of pottery. I certainly do not think that this necessarily makes games players desperate to support increases in military expenditure in the present. What is troubling, though, is the flattening of cultural diversity and specificity that even the complex range of different units and soldiers produces. As we will see, this is a recurrent theme and perhaps the most important one to stress in this paper. Insofar as conflict is a universal feature of human social life, it is nonetheless always mediated in very particular ways, through symbolic, ritual, and other social filters: violence means different things in different societies (Aijmer 2000). One gets no sense of this in any of the games described – apart from the bogus example of the magical powers of Egyptian priests in *Praetorians*. On its own, this may seem like a small point of weakness, but it is part of a bigger problem.

Time and Space

Another key area of interest in terms of the themes behind the games is the representation of how societies work in time and space. In spite of the acronym, none of the games described above run in anything like 'real time'. Each has its own peculiarities of temporal manipulation (cf. Wolf 2001a). *Praetorians* is set within specific campaign periods, but the player has time to train as many new units as a village population will support (each takes a couple of minutes), and of course there is no night or day, or any other activity for the troops than waiting for or following orders. *Age of Empires* has a confusing pattern of technological ages that can succeed each other at a range of actual dates when scenarios are supposedly set – so, for example, one Egyptian scenario is set in 1450 BC, but the player starts in the Stone Age and has to develop through the other ages to get adequate technology to win. Again, activity is a constant, with no cycles of work and rest, and while farms only last for a certain period before needing to be reseeded, people have no fixed life-span. *Civilization* is the most interesting of all. It is turn based rather than 'real time', but the notional length of turns actually changes through history: at the start of the game, in 4000 BC, each turn is equivalent to 20 years; by the twentieth century, they have progressively reduced to one-year intervals. History literally gets more detailed as time passes.

What can we make of this temporal confusion? Some allowance must certainly be made for the necessary conventionalisation of the varying temporalities of social life in order to make a workable game. Nonetheless, the choices made by games designers reveal some interesting priorities on how time is valued. The most obvious have to do with linearity and progress. Technological advancement is a major feature of two of the examples discussed, requiring continuing investment of resources. Without new technologies, the player cannot keep up with opposing cultures. Of course, the available technologies are closely proscribed, so there is no genuine invention or divergence of cultures along different paths, according to their different social or political dynamics. Each game is in many ways the fulfillment of a modernising prophecy. Therefore, in spite of their potential to allow the player to create 'alternative' histories (indeed, this is often part of their marketing appeal), there is no sense of history unfolding as if for the first time. The fact that the Romans or the Chinese can build the pyramids in *Civilization* does not really make the world a very different place, just a jumbled-up version of the one that we have. The teleology of game time over the long term is complemented by a model of time at smaller intervals that is equally one dimensional. The inhabitants of the game (especially *Age of Empires*) are locked into an endless life of work, in a world with no or very few natural cycles. As with the progressive linearity of the quest for higher technologies, it is difficult not to see these features as characteristic of a stereotype of modern, Western time (cf. Shanks and Tilley 1987a: 127–129) – one that does not really do justice to our own experience in that culture, let alone those of the past.

A similar quality is apparent in the treatment of space in the games under analysis. Even though all of these games are linked by the use of maps as the dominant mode of representation, essential to the narrative drive of the story (Friedman 2002; Newman 2004: 113–115), these maps are of course constructed in quite particular ways. One major aspect of the past societies concerned that is effaced almost completely is the rural life-style of the majority of people. While *Praetorians* makes little attempt to model the civilian population at all, cities and towns are at the core of *Age of Empires* and *Civilization*. As such, they are required to grow and acquire more and more public buildings as well as houses. In the latter example, this growth can also generate problems of squalor and disorder, placing an emphasis on urban management, while farmers are not represented. *Age of Empires* is a little different, with farming among the tasks that villagers can perform, but this usually happens close to the village/town centre and within the defences. It is difficult to establish networks of farms across the landscape because these are too vulnerable to attack. This landscape is also, of course, purely a resource for the player. Trees are there to be cut down, stone to be mined, animals to be hunted. Often a game of *Age of Empires* ends with the map completely denuded of life apart from the virtual humans. Similarly, in *Civilization*, cities have a catchment of land that automatically supplies them with resources, and this can be transformed to improve the returns. The emphasis on urbanism and landscapes as material resources is as stereotypically modern as the idea of space travel as the logical culmination of all human achievement.

Individuals and Societies

This brings us to my final theme – humans themselves. The conventions of the genre mean that the real human player is very much in control of the virtual human characters and groups, with the power to create life and destroy it (players can kill off unwanted villagers or soldiers in *Age of Empires*, for example, if they want to create different units but have reached the game's population limit). This godlike position has been taken to an extreme in a fantastic context in the game *Black and White*, where the player is actually a god who must secure the continued worship of his or her dependent community. In games set in antiquity, there is no such conceit and the player's power appears to be merely a necessary convention of actually playing the game at all – indeed, as Friedman has noted, the player is almost assimilated to the computer's mode of thought, underlining the modernity of the experience (2002: 2). However, the subtext here is still that ancient societies were strongly hierarchical and that rulers were very powerful. This is reinforced by various aspects of gameplay. Some element of 'freedom' for the virtual humans is provided in *Civilization*, where citizens can rebel if they are unhappy, but they can be relatively easily quelled by either lowering taxes or building entertainment or religious structures. The only characters given individuated characteristics or graphic representations in *Age of Empires* are the rulers, while everyone else is anonymous. The picture of the ancient world in such games is thus one of ordered social systems governed by 'great men', with the player standing astride the action either as an eternal ruler or as the hidden hand of history itself.

The emphasis on social stability twinned with technological advance produces a very particular narrative about how societies work, one that sits rather well with some of the dominant ideologies of Western modernity (cf. Shanks and Tilley 1992: 46–67; Thomas 2004: 96–148). It also has the effect of decontextualising technological change, as this appears to have no social consequences. This destruction of context is even more evident in a theme that I have already mentioned several times: the flattening of cultural variation. As we have seen, there are aspects of each of the games discussed where some attempts have been made to distinguish different cultures, which range from the stereotypically exotic (Egyptian priests in *Praetorians*) to the more prosaic (architectural differences in *Age of Empires*). However, the overwhelming impression from such games – indeed, from their very inclusion within the universal logic of the game itself – is that past cultures are all pretty interchangeable. They follow the same rules, they do the same things, they look similar, and they have the same objectives. There is of course an argument in favour of general models for understanding society that might justify this approach to some extent, but this is certainly not an overt issue in the gaming context – nor would one expect it to be.

Rather, the balance in favour of universal cultural values is so overwhelming in the gaming context that the line between necessary conventions of a playable game and a vision of the past as the (modernised, globalised, homogenised) present is entirely blurred. Paradoxically, though, one of the universal values that these games also appear to endorse is the primacy of the nation-state (Friedman 2002: 7). One of the few things that distinguishes the different cultures in any of the games is their name, and most notably in *Civilization* this remains unchanged throughout history – as does that of the ruler. As a result, 'playing a single, unchanging entity from the Stone Age to space colonisation turns the often-slippery formation of nationhood into a kind of immutable racial destiny' (Friedman 2002: 7). The political values of the modern world are again imposed upon antiquity, even where they contain something of an apparent contradiction – modernity certainly accommodates, and even encourages, the formation of stable nations, as long as they all work in the same way and want the same kinds of things (rather like modern 'individuals' [Thomas 2004: 108, 137]). As noted above, this contradiction does relate in some way to a genuine dilemma in studying (and perhaps living as) humans – the balance between similarity and difference (cf. Gardner 2004: 120–121) – but this problem does not appear in the game world, only one particular modern solution to it. The possible consequences of, and alternatives to, this situation are the subject of the final section of this paper.

Conclusion

All the games discussed in this paper are a great deal of fun to play. As I noted at the outset, the criticisms levelled at the implicitly (and sometimes quite explicitly) ideological content of them do not mean that they should be banned, but rather engaged with both as a means to think about the popular representation of the past in the present, and in the hope that the rapid cycles of development in the video game industry will allow for future modifications. This critical engagement is all the more essential because of the lack of academic attention to games and their impact on the creation of social knowledge. Aside from the heated debate over violence, which has triggered research into this specific aspect of media representation – albeit still inconclusively and with limited understanding of the relationship between design and consumption (Newman 2004: 1–7, 66–69) – there has been very little serious study of this field. Games scholars are multiplying and gradually coming to grips with the way the medium works in terms of its similarities to, and differences from, other communicative and artistic media (Wolf 2001b; Wolf and Perron 2003).

As yet, it is very difficult to say how games players routinely consider or challenge the ideologies with which the games present them, especially when these are presented as somewhat 'educational' (an endorsement to this effect appears on the back of the *Age of Empires II* box and instruction manuals frequently contain some 'historical notes'). However, they are certainly capable of adopting different strategies within the rules (Friedman 2002: 6), and indeed of adapting the graphics to represent new cultures and create new scenarios through various software tools (see, e.g., *Age of Kings Heaven* [http://aok.heavengames.com/] for an *Age of Empires II* fan site with dozens of player-designed modifications). A game is much less of a 'finished product' than a film, and so the participation of the player in finishing it in different ways creates manifold opportunities for new kinds of learning experiences.

This potential can perhaps most intriguingly be developed with another genre of game than that discussed in this paper. This is MMORPGs – Massively Multiplayer Online Role-Playing Games – in which a complete game world is networked and hundreds, or even thousands, of players participate as particular characters in this environment. This genre includes titles such as *Everquest II* and *Star Wars: Galaxies*, which construct fantasy worlds in which players can effectively 'live' and are inspired by traditional role-playing games rather than board- or miniature-based wargames. Given their online nature, any one player can drop in or out of the game but it carries on continuously, and this – along with the possibility of playing a character from a wide range of different professions – gives the virtual world a much stronger sense of integrity than the abstractions discussed in this chapter.

Of course, there will always be particular ideologies represented in the rules of such games, and the degree of free identity play that they offer is perhaps distinctively postmodern (Filiciak 2003); it is probably no accident that they tend to involve fantastic, rather than historical, worlds[1]. The possibility, though, of archaeologists being involved in designing such a game, where the player could at least for a while live as a farmer in central Italy – rather than Tatooine – is enticing (the recently released *Immortal Cities: Children of the Nile* takes some steps in this direction, with new levels of detail for a city management game, but the player is still the Pharaoh). The potential popularity of simulations of mundane lives is hinted at by the success of *The Sims*, a family-level version of *Sim City* that has spawned several expansions, where players control the lives of a small group of suburban characters, living lives that are rather like their own. If these kinds of game ideas can be extended to reconstructing and re-imagining past contexts, they might have the potential to illuminate some of the ways in which those contexts were not like our own. The point of critically engaging with games, rather like playing them, is to move to the next level (Friedman 2002: 7). In this way, archaeologists might yet find a valuable tool to aid them in the task of creating challenging pasts for wide audiences.

Acknowledgements

I would like to thank Kathryn Piquette (UCL) for discussion of several of the themes in this paper, and the editors and referees for their helpful feedback on its contents.

Note

1. Between the drafting and proof stages of preparing this paper, a major large-scale historical MMORPG was launched: *Rome Victor*. Further details about this game can be found at http://www.roma-victor.com/ (accessed November 2005).

14

DIGITAL MEDIA, AGILE DESIGN, AND THE POLITICS OF ARCHAEOLOGICAL AUTHORSHIP

Michael Shanks

Two Topics Concerning the Character of Archaeology and Two Philosophies of (Information) Design

Two topics that have long been the focus of my archaeological interest form the context for this essay. Both topics focus on the intimate connections, often unrecognised, between media and information design and management. The first topic is archaeological method, how we move from the collection of data through description, explanation, and interpretation. My argument is that our orthodox archaeological methods – traditional, processual, and post-processual – have a tendency to predetermine the past, what we notice, gather, and say; they may even actually obscure the past. The second topic is the very way we think about archaeology. I argue that archaeologists work on what is left of the past; we do not discover the past. We set up relationships with what remains.

I am going to explore these topics in connection with two different philosophies of information, ways of classifying and organising data. I will draw on some recent research and thinking in science and technology studies, the sociology of information, to associate information, categories, and standardised infrastructures with media, through considering the design practices that work on data to produce information. This entails a rethinking of the way media are commonly conceived. Media – such as text, image, and video – are often understood simply as supplemental to real archaeology, having to do with communication, presentation, and the dissemination of findings and theories following excavation and data processing, for example. It has, however, also long been recognised that publication is one of the *foundations* of any archaeological knowledge. Nevertheless, it is commonplace to discuss the *representation* of archaeology in the media (such as popular trade publication and TV) to separate the communication of findings from the substantive content of those findings and the work in the field, laboratory, or library that generated them. I argue that a new understanding of media as the work of mediation and as modes of engagement, and the proposed reevaluation of some issues of information science in relation to archaeology, puts media(tion) at the heart of our discipline and requires us to reject this distinction between primary research and secondary dissemination.

So I will set up a contrast between a top-down approach to design and one that uses agile and adaptive rapid prototyping. While this contrast is overdrawn for illustrative and rhetorical purposes, it is rooted in direct ethnographic research into the information technology (IT) industry of Silicon Valley, the home environment of my Metamedia Laboratory in Stanford University's Archaeology Center. I suggest that the contrast prompts archaeologists to rethink the political economy of our archaeological media, the mode of production of information and knowledge - the very way we go about doing archaeology. I do hope it will nevertheless be clear that there are key components of what I propose embedded in our orthodox archaeological practices.

It will be clear from this short introduction that this is quite a broad and interdisciplinary field. To argue my points closely with full scholarly apparatus would make for a long and unwieldy contribution that could not fit into a collection such as this book. But because I believe that the issues are vital to a critical understanding of archaeology and media, I have adopted a looser style suitable to an engagement with ideas rather than detailed research. There will be no problems for readers wishing to explore this field of ideas further: they should simply perform a standard Internet search on keywords. Let me begin with two anecdotes about the way we design archaeological information.

Anecdote – A Large Archaeological Project in the Mediterranean: What to Do with Too Much Information

Last year, I spent an afternoon talking with some members of a large archaeological project in the Mediterranean. They face a quandary of how to organise and make available the things they are finding. It is a typical problem faced by many projects.

Use of current recording media and IT in the field has allowed the capture of considerable amounts of data of and about the excavations. Large storage devices enable the use of rich media like digital imagery, sound, and video. And the project is aiming to make all this as accessible as possible to any interest anywhere through a web portal. The project's guiding mission is one of open and plural voices of comment, critique, interpretation, and debate.

But the project is drowning in data: millions of digital images, hundreds of hours of video, vast and detailed databases. The task is how to make available relatively unprocessed data – not just the summaries, explanations, and interpretations of the excavators. While an overall goal of multivocality is assumed as given, there is some confusion over the role of local, folk, popular, and ethnic categories and interests in organising and accessing data about the excavations. There is a proliferation of possible categories to be applied to the data in a quest to hold on to the rich texture of what is being found at the site.

The project has taken the decision to farm out the design of a web-accessed database to a well-established professional archaeology unit, and also to a smaller outfit that was investigating possible data standards in archaeology. The brief was to design and implement an industry-strength database that would be relatively future-proofed, stable, and accessible. The task is quite colossal. It is to formulate and anticipate data standards, to use those standards to code the data that are to be organised in such a way that as many different possible and unanticipated inquiries may be made of the excavation findings, with meaningful results delivered. The choice had been made to go with a well-established hardware and software platform that offers apparent reliability because it is the infrastructure of many corporations and institutions, large and small. But it was looking like the task of coding all the data was infeasible if the data were not to be too closely defined, so limiting the richness of the interactions with these remains of a fascinating prehistoric community.

Anecdote – The Digital Future of the Humanities: Supergrids and Metadata Standards

At Stanford Humanities Laboratory[1], we are investigating the future of the digital humanities. The Humanities, Arts, Science, and Technology Advanced Collaboratory,[2] of which we are a founding member, is one of many of the collective organisations in the United States that is promoting discussion of how information technologies should affect research and teaching in the arts and humanities.

The growth of IT and the prospect of building ever more networked linkage and processing capacity across academic and research institutions is a powerful rhetoric for achieving the old Enlightenment dream of encyclopaedic scope in academic practice: great collections of sources and resources made instantly accessible. Organisations like Google have made a commitment to digitising multiple library and media collections. Supergrid infrastructures offer vast bandwidth access. The task, as it is so often interpreted by academic institutions (though not so much by Google, it has to be noted), is to take centuries of cataloguing effort, literally the filing cards in library catalogues, rework them into standardised metadata format, and attach them to the digitised resources with a means of inquiry and delivery. As in my first anecdote, the task is one of structuring data efficiently so that meaningful inquiries may be made. And again the task is daunting, in spite of the claims of information technologists to be able to do whatever is required of them, given current data storage and processing power. Even simply agreeing on metadata standards is intractably slow, because any agreement on standards will prejudice everything that may be desirable or possible in the future. If you are going to catalogue all of humanity's creativity to date, you need to make sure you will be able to research what really matters. But how do you know until you have completed that catalogue? Is a pilot, or even multiple pilots enough? And while scanning text according to a standard format such as PDF may be reasonably justified, what about the vast collections of artefacts in museums? How should they be documented? Is it at all feasible?

Top-Down Design: The Art of Anticipation

These anecdotal experiences are about a particular philosophy, a particular political economy of data and information. It exhibits:

- An emphasis upon top-down design.
- In the hands of experts.

- With a focus upon metadata standards and specification of information structure.
- In designing interaction with data and information.
- Design that usually happens before most of the work of collection and coding.
- Which is undertaken by operatives – people who did not design the information structure.
- And is then disseminated to non-expert and uninvolved client communities.

This expert-based design has to excel as an *art of anticipation* – anticipating needs, questions, distribution, the function of data, and information. So our archaeological information design anticipates the structure of the data world we expect to encounter (finds, features, and all the rest) and the kind of dissemination of information that will occur (different kinds of publication and access), as well as the kind of inquiries we and others unknown to us might want to make (how many, where, with what).

There is nothing intrinsically wrong with such a design process. It has been immensely successful and is central to most engineering projects. Its success is closely connected with the degree of control that is possible over materials, processes, and aims. In designing a bridge, it is possible to restrict the field of reference to the physics and properties of materials and a precisely specified purpose to span a particular gap and carry a particular weight, and within a particular budget. We know exactly what kind of world such a project is building. There is a clear hierarchy of designers, contractors, and clients; you would not, for instance, want an inexpert client public designing or building a suspension bridge.

It is not so straightforward with the design of information, for one reason just mentioned: top-down information design has to anticipate what the structure is meant to find and explore. Then in archaeology, there are all the uncertainties of data preservation. Data structures are incomplete; at the least, archaeological formation processes are an essential contributing factor to data structures. This is also the relevance of notions such as the hermeneutic spiral in archaeological method (Hodder 1992: 188–193), a fourfold hermeneutic, as Tilley and I outlined (Shanks and Tilley 1987b: 107–108). There is not space to go into this issue here. Suffice it to say that there are several nontrivial mediating factors in dealing with archaeological data.

There are also several other much more fundamental aspects of this particular political economy of data, apart from the hermeneutic problems of entropy and mediated access. They have to do with the materiality and politics of the process of information design.

I argue that a top-down approach to information design is rooted in the old Enlightenment dream of encyclopaedic scope and control of the world in great systems of categorisation and description. The spectacular success of such a vision in the sciences since the eighteenth century is arguably not matched by similar success in the social sciences and humanities. Most notably, there has been considerable reaction against universal systems of understanding that are not sensitive to local cultural difference; this, most recently in archaeology, is the post-processual agenda, closely connected with progressive politics in social and cultural anthropology of effacing ethnocentrism and embracing multivocality. A more general point is exemplified in the classic Foucauldian thesis (notably, Foucault 1973, 1982) that particular and extensive categorisation and classification projects are deeply embedded in modernist discourse.

Ironically, for a discipline of materiality, archaeology has not paid much attention to the *materiality* of these deeply embedded classification systems and projects. Information structure is not simply an abstract system of ordering, of algorithms for sorting out what we find. Data are not simply abstract qualities and qualities, however defined. That any project of building an information system has to take into account the feasibility of physically coding, recording, and logging data is one of the main concerns in both the anecdotes I have just described. This tacit and often hidden work (Bowker and Star 1999) of establishing and building an information system is often forgotten once it is done, or when it is sequestered as infrastructure 'maintenance' or 'support', or because it is not the high-profile work of design that attracts intellectual kudos. Information cannot exist in the abstract. It exists in material artefacts – filing cards, cabinets, storerooms and archives, computer hard drives. It is embedded in the things it organises. And information, in these material forms, requires work for it to endure. Information is a verb.

That I have termed this a political economy of information points to the politics of any such managed work. There are essential relationships of dominance and subordinance among designers, funding and sponsoring agencies, operatives who carry out the drudgery (rarely anything else), the alienated labour of coding, and different kinds of client user.

I will also argue below that media are essential components in the design of information. Just think of systems of recording and dissemination, the images, the graphic and textual forms, the modes of dissemination. Think of the instruments: cameras, pens, styli, forms, cards, computer keyboards, screens. For me, this prompts a rethinking of just how we understand media. Below, I discuss a reorientation around a more pragmatic understanding; in accordance with this focus on the design work that constitutes information, one that would have us conceive of media as *modes of engagement*.

To get us to this, let me introduce another anecdote. This one opens up the issue of the contingency and materiality of information structures. It is about the rapid changes that characterise the IT industry.

Anecdote – NASA Shops at eBay

From the *New York Times*, 12 May 2002[3]:

NASA needs parts no one makes anymore.

So to keep the shuttles flying, the space agency has begun trolling the Internet – including Yahoo and eBay – to find replacement parts for electronic gear that would strike a home computer user as primitive.

Officials say the agency recently bought a load of outdated medical equipment so it could scavenge Intel 8086 chips – a variant of those chips powered I.B.M.'s first personal computer, in 1981.

When the first shuttle roared into space that year, the 8086 played a critical role, at the heart of diagnostic equipment that made sure the shuttle's twin booster rockets were safe for blastoff.

This point is now commonplace, yet surprisingly little theorised. NASA played an instrumental role in building the computer chip industry in the 1960s. With all its resources and military-style strategic planning, the agency has had to resort to scavenging (NASA's word) to maintain what were only recently (arguably still are) state-of-the-art space ships. What chance do we, mere mortal individuals, have of keeping track of data and media formats – of shifting the floppy disk contents to CD or hard drive, of VHS to DVD (with even DVD destined for only 10 more years of ubiquity and industry support)? Never mind the problems I would now face of rerunning the principal components analyses I applied back in 1979 to the bones from prehistoric monuments. The programme and data were written and formatted in Fortran IV on an IBM mainframe. I would have to do it all again from scratch, literally starting with the old pen marks on paper.

The 8086 chips were chosen for reliability. They still work but the support they originally received has gone. There is, of course, a distinctive temporal cycle to artefact design – from emergence through popularity to the decline and disappearance of an artefact form. It is one of the premises of archaeological understanding. Here there is also a commonly found mismatch between the design cycles of integrated technologies: information processing and space flight, one fast, the other spread over decades.

Factors in this anecdote are the maintenance of material artefacts: physical media and machines to read and run them. But also consistency of standards: what future for .doc files, for .pdf, for .wav, for DVD-R?

The overall point: instrumentalities matter in the world of information and media. And information is a verb. Information requires maintenance.

What Has Information to Do with Media?

The following definition establishes the link between information and medium.

A medium is a formalised method for dealing in data and conveying processed data – structured information – to some participants (known or unknown). The manner in which this happens is subject to control and negotiation. Usually, there has to be some agreement over encoding and decryption.

A key point in this definition is that structured information requires infrastructures and standards. Following Star and Rohleder (1976: 246), medium requires infrastructures that are:

- Embedded – sunk into other structures, social and cultural arrangements and technologies.
- Transparent – infrastructures do not get in the way of communication by having to be constantly inspected, revised, reinvented.
- Consistent (relatively).
- Possess reach beyond the single interaction or communication event.
- Built (usually) on an installed base – e.g., optical fibres running along pre-installed telephone conduit.
- Connect with conventions of practice – e.g., the connection between text, keyboards, and new digital media.
- Embodiment of standards – standardised conventions, categories, and classifications at the heart of media (on standards, see Bowker and Star 1999: 13–16).
- Backed by agreements, the results of negotiations and political arrangements (including institutions and states).

Historically, the notion of medium has been intimately associated with material and technology – e.g., paint, paper, photography, etc.

And also certain institutional forms that control the technology, as in the notion of the mass media of TV and publishing. The definition of medium just given above takes us beyond this narrow (though quite legitimate) conception of medium because it incorporates more explicitly the points I have been making about the materiality of media and the work of design, manufacture, and maintenance of information systems.

Another way to think about this reorientation is to consider what has happened with digital media over the last 20 years. The increasing digital nature of communication is prompting a rethinking of the notion of medium. More and more worldly data and information is becoming fungible and so amenable to computational processing and translation. Therefore, media forms are proliferating. I can take the same image and embed it in a phone conversation, instant message, blog, wiki, web page, Powerpoint presentation, DVD slide show, poster on a wall, or conventional printed book. Indeed, more and more parts of society and culture are becoming available to digital computation and therefore can be considered as media – as acts and forms of mediation. This is all due to a series of new standards that were established in their first form in the eighteenth century (Bowker and Star 1999: 17–26).

So I propose that it is better to think of a medium as process of manipulation and translation, of mediation and interaction – as a *mode of engagement*. What is now foregrounded in our experience of IT and digital media is what was always essential to analogue media, but is obscured in conventional understanding that emphasises material and institutional form (oil paint and Hollywood). Medium conceived as mode of engagement emphasises the dynamic aspects of mediation. Reading magazines on the subway, listening to iBooks in the car, sharing photos at home and with friends, watching a movie on a large screen in a dark room with strangers – all are modes of engagement. And all encapsulate the dynamic, material, and embedded aspects of information systems that I have been introducing: classification and category systems, standards, infrastructures, material instrumentalities, mediated networks of people and things.

Before I return to archaeology, I want to introduce another kind of design of information structures.

An Alternative: Iterative Agile Design

This is another political economy of the design of media.

Let me move to Silicon Valley and its developer community, an extraordinarily creative pool, whatever is thought of the contemporary

IT industry. In the late 1990s came a reaction against top-down design of software. Below is the 'Manifesto for Agile Software development', produced by the Agile Alliance of software developers[4].

> We are uncovering better ways of developing software by doing it and helping others do it.
> Through this work we have come to value:
>
> - individuals and interactions over processes and tools;
> - working software over comprehensive documentation;
> - customer collaboration over contract negotiation;
> - responding to change over following a plan.
>
> That is, while there is value in the items on the right, we value the items on the left more.

Top-down software design is very familiar to anyone who has any experience with software. It involves large corporations with teams of designers building expensive and often now massive multi-feature tools for all purposes, anticipating what anyone might conceivably want to do in writing a report or making a movie. Design and scripting take precedence over close attention to local needs and people's particular desires. Such software production is expensive and often unwieldy.

Agile design is an iterative process based upon rapid prototyping (Highsmith 2004; Larman 2003). Do your ethnography and research into what people want and need, but do not anticipate too much. Get something out there and see what people do with it. Then adapt and try again.

This is an entirely different mode of design, though it is by no means a new one. Robert Austin of the Harvard Business School and theatre director Lee Devin have used performance rehearsal and improvisation to understand this way of designing work (Austin and Devin 2003). And it does imply a different political economy of media design, not least because it works best in self-organising teams with a networked rather than hierarchical structure and operating predominantly through real-time interaction.

This mode of design recognises the importance of the world of the user – his or her semantic field and the inevitable lack of fit between the categories of the designer and the user, the ubiquity and incongruity of more or less integrated systems of classification and standardisation, the real-world pragmatics of media use, the resistances to systems of classification, the essential and constitutive relationship between signal and *noise* that constitutes any medium (Bowker and Star 1999).

Archaeological Forms to Fill in

Let me return to archaeology.

In the anecdote of the archaeological project with which I began, and in most archaeology, you begin with ideas of data and information, collect bits of the past according to these, then interpret and explain. Archaeologists design forms and fill them in. While the view of archaeology presented in the discipline's textbooks is dominated by fieldwork and specialized techniques focused upon data recovery and analysis, I would argue that such method is work upon data that have predominantly been *predefined*. Fine pottery, lithics, features and structures, faunal remains, small finds, and all the other standard categories have been thoroughly defined *prior* to any contemporary excavation or other research project, defined by the weight of preceding experience and orthodoxy of method. This is a top-down approach to the design of information structure, as I have just defined it. The forms archaeologists fill in with field and laboratory observation have to anticipate the structure of data.

This is not necessarily bad, because we have lots of experience of what works well to guide our 'art of anticipation'. But there is an appropriate suspicion that we mostly find what we are looking for (see Shanks and Tilley 1987b). When did you last come across an archaeological narrative that really surprised you? Not just surprise at a new find found somewhere unexpected, but a challenge to the very narrative structures we employ in understanding human history, in explaining the shape of social change.

There are ways of cleansing data, of ensuring high quality. Attention to procedure of controlled observation and recovery is important. Random sampling of some sort is very useful in this regard: it makes us look where we might not otherwise. But we also need to tackle the issue of the *structure*, not just the quality, of information. The argument for a bottom-up agile approach to information design is simply that we should be sensitive to alternate ways of classifying and categorising, sensitive to alternative takes on that reality, and that this sensitivity should be rooted in a close attention to the empirical character of what it is we are studying. This is the argument for a methodology that arises from the object itself, from engagement with what it is we are studying. There is a long line of argument along these lines in critical theory; in our book *Re-Constructing Archaeology*, for example, Tilley and I followed sociologists Theodor Adorno and Max Horkheimer (Shanks and Tilley 1987a: 78–80).

How Might We Do It Differently?

What, in archaeology, does an agile approach to designing information structure look like? Here are three personal examples.

The Art of the Ancient Greek State:
The Question 'Where Do I Begin?'

For ten years between 1988 and 1998, I explored themes of society, art, and design in ancient Greece and the Mediterranean – a study of rather exquisite perfume jars made in Corinth in the eighth and seventh century BC, when the city was first being built (Shanks 1996, 1999). My primary archaeological focus was upon ceramics conventionally termed proto-Corinthian – a style associated with the key period of social change in the city of Corinth. The ubiquity of the proto-Corinthian perfume jar (*aryballos*) makes it a type fossil and chronological index for much of the Mediterranean in the mid-first millennium BC.

My data sample consisted of two thousand pots found in over 90 locations. I first began with familiar notions of pottery industry, distribution, and consumption. But immediately my work found the fine chronologies suspect because of the lack of independent stratigraphical substantiation. The phasing of the pottery is entirely dependent upon an art historical and a priori notion of stylistic development (early, mature, late). That is, it depends upon a narrow iconology that relates shape and imagery to largely internal stylistic categories (restricted to art style rather than referring outwardly to social and cultural context and meaning) and a model of art workshops commonly associated with post-Renaissance art history (workshops centred upon creative individuals expressing themselves through their works). While the categories applied to the pottery are arguably real and open to study and verification, I felt that the very way of organising the data – of categorising ceramic design – was prescriptive in a debilitating way. It would give no route to a social archaeology. This is the conventional critique of the likes of classical archaeology. I felt justified therefore in adopting a contextual treatment that looked at all issues relevant to the design, manufacture, distribution, and consumption of the whole sample. Outwardly this took the form of a study of an artefact life-cycle.

I found the traditional categories of rank, resource, trade, state formation, urbanisation, and manufacture closely connected with long-standing tendencies to emplot archaeological material in standardised metanarratives (here of the expansion of the city-state as a component of ancient imperialisms). Such interpretive and analytical categories are quite blunt and prefigure, I came to argue, the components of conventional narratives (economy, trade, colonisation, acculturation, stylistic expression of ethnic and political identities). So while I built a narrative of the early state (expansion of the polity), while I presented a systemic model of design in the early state (motivations related to class culture), I also developed what I have come to call a heretical empirics (Shanks 2003). I began again with a single artefact, rather than an information structure, and adopted an agglomerative and iterative strategy (Shanks 1999). I started again not with a system of classification, categories of data and attributes to be observed, forms to be filled in, but with an encounter, an empirical engagement – with a single perfume jar. I then tracked a spiral of associations (empirical, spatial, conceptual, metaphorical) through the material and its contexts. I was led into a very different category structure of faces, animals, corporeality, potters wheels and brushes, physical and imagined mobility, flowers, food and consumption, sovereignty, gender, ships, clothing. For me, this led to a different message about the ancient Greek state in these times. That message is not so important here as the point I am making about method (outlined in Shanks 1999).

Close attention to the richness of the data led me to find the orthodox paradigms of design and sociocultural archaeology and ancient history inappropriate and confusing. The project has forced me to consider radical alternatives to the conventions of writing and representing the archaeological past. One of these is what we have called theatre/archaeology.

Theatre/Archaeology: Collaborative Improvisation and Different Modes of Engagement

My collaboration from 1992 with the performance company Brith Gof (artistic directors Mike Pearson and Cliff McLucas, Dorian Llywelyn, and other members of the company) was, among other things, an exploration of well-developed techniques of collaborative improvisation (as a form of agile design) directed at interdisciplinary research (McLucas and Pearson 1999). This mode of working creatively is familiar to many of the studio arts and is embedded in the pedagogy of the modern Western art school. The collaboration led to many live works, several articles, the book *Theatre/Archaeology* (Pearson and Shanks 2001), and the Three Landscape Project at Stanford[5].

What I simply want to mention here are modes of engagement (as just defined) with archaeological sites and materials that are quite different than those normally encountered in the discipline and yet equally grounded in empirical research. They include:

- Tri Bywyd, a large-scale site-specific performance: a highly designed scenography and dramaturgy set in a ruined farmstead in the forest of western Wales[6].
- Performed lectures around the archaeology of a hillside in western Wales (Pearson and Shanks 1996).
- A series of experimental works that came out of the Three Landscapes Project at Stanford:
  - An artist's book in a room (using digital and semi-industrial composition processes)[7].
  - A deep map on a wall (a work in large format digital graphics)[8].
  - A list of 33 archaeological events that may have occurred in Salemi, Sicily, in summer 1999[9].
  - A katachrestic juxtaposition of the archaeology of three rooms in the way of an academic journal paper (Shanks 2004).

Social Software

Another medium or mode of engagement is the collaboratory, a collaborative authoring environment embodied in a new genre of media – social software.

What is social software?
Imagine:
What if a group of people could work together to gather, present, and explore information and experiences in a genuinely collaborative way (without anyone being in control), with the order in the information they share emergent, growing interactively and organically (rather than being pre-organised), with everyone able to explore and react to everything others are doing as they are doing it, with their authoring medium providing quick and intuitive text, image, graphics, and sound-based input and navigation, with the medium itself suggesting ways that the growing body of shared information might be conceived and organised? And if this was all a richly textured and rewarding experience?

This is a description of a wiki - an authoring space built upon a flexible database infrastructure. This genre of social software is all about content management - the collaborative process of structuring data and information. For three years, my lab at Stanford has been building and experimenting with blogs, wikis, personal content management systems, knowledge management systems. and the like because they offer a way of exploring the agile design of information[10].

We have run many quick and unpolished trials. They have culminated in two major research projects exploring, in addition to primary substantive research aims, the implications for research of these collaborative software environments. One is with DaimlerChrysler: a six-month collaborative research project in material culture studies modelling media design and use in car interiors. The other is Performing Presence: From the Live to the Simulated, an interdisciplinary study of forms and documents of presence (a project managed jointly by Exeter University, University College London, Stanford University, and fourteen performance artists)[11].

The primary principle is to reverse the direction of design effort. Instead of designing a structure of information that may then be applied to the real world to generate tightly structured data, social software and collaborative authoring environments use the high processing power and raw storage capacity of contemporary information technology to structure relatively loosely defined and more comprehensively captured data *dynamically, on the fly*. The emphasis is on smart searching tools and algorithms that find structure after data capture. Pattern emerges from interaction with data and from interaction with others in the collaborative effort of making sense of an encounter with data. Significant design effort goes into making membership work creatively, into the ecology (human, machine, data) of a collaborative research project. This is a contextualised design of information.

Now this philosophy of iterative and agile design of information leads to experiences – modes of engagement – that can be very disconcerting. Impermanence, and the incomplete and chaotic, are the background to nodes of clarity, narrative, and control. But these media are genuinely collaborative and subversive of cliches, easy answers, and corporate control[12]. They are genuinely pluralist in the absence of hierarchical control and through the frictionless technology (quick to learn and fast to use). Their architecture is one of free-form databases, entirely compatible with all forms of archaeological data. But they add the potential of dynamic data feeds and debate around such changing data. This makes their epistemology far more robust than conventional static data matrices standing alone.

Moveon.org threatened a major upset in early stages of the last U.S. elections. Blogs (2004 was the UK *Guardian*'s 'Year of the Blog') are a serious alternative to corporate journalism, with blog journalism blocked in many parts of the world because it promises grass roots mobilisation and freedom of information. Online and virtual communities and games are thriving. The World Wide Web itself is sometimes seen as threatening and dangerous because no corporate entity has designed and controlled it (for broad issues, see Lessig 2002, 2005).

These media are interesting for archaeology because they allow us to rethink our relationship with our data and information design. They are about data management and information creation, but from the bottom up – a group bootstrapping its way to insight, understanding, explanation, letting data define information structures and forms.

The Fundamentals in a Pressing Argument

The examples I have given are just a few ways of explaining how I have responded to what I consider to be a powerful argument for changing the way we do archaeology. To summarise: I suggest that archaeologists attend to three key points about media and their relationship to the design of information.

- Data are material.
- Information is a verb.
- Media are modes of engagement.

This is a pressing argument because of the scale of data collection and loss. Because decisions about data archives will shut down future options in research if they are not kept open. And because the cult of expert design and the efforts being made to classify, categorise, standardise, and apply notions of corporate intellectual property to everything are challenging a human right to communicate and create (Lessig 2004). This is that crucial point about information and media in archaeology: that we do not so much discover the past as mediate; we work creatively on what remains.

Notes

1. Stanford Humanities Laboratory http://shl.Stanford.edu (accessed 15 November 2005).

2. Humanities, Arts, Science, and Technology Advanced Collaboratory http://hastac.org (accessed 15 November 2005).

3. William J. Broad, *New York Times*, 12 May 2002, http://www.nytimes.com/2002/05/12/technology/ebusiness/12NASA.html?ex=1131685200&en=7570dcc58a08fb8e&ei=5070 (accessed 15 November 2005).

4. Manifesto for Agile Software development http://agilealliance.com (accessed 15 November 2005).

5. McLucas, Llywelyn, and Shanks (forthcoming); http://metamedia.Stanford.edu/projects/MichaelShanks/.

6. McLucas (2000); http://traumwerk.stanford.edu/projects/MichaelShanks/911 (accessed 15 November 2005).

7. http://traumwerk.stanford.edu/projects/MichaelShanks/893 (accessed 15 November 2005).

8. http://traumwerk.stanford.edu/projects/MichaelShanks/893 (accessed 15 November 2005).

9. Wiki hypertext, http://metamedia.Stanford.edu/~mshanks/traumwerk (accessed 15 November 2005).

10. http://metamedia.Stanford.edu/projects/traumwerk (accessed 15 November 2005).

11. http://presence.Stanford.edu (accessed 15 November 2005).

12. Rheingold (2002); http://en.wikipedia.org/wiki/Social_software (accessed 15 November 2005).

REFERENCES

3WE, Third World and Environment Broadcasting Project (2000) *Viewing the World: Production Study*, London: DFID, http://www.dfid.gov.uk (accessed 15 October 2005)

3WE, Third World and Environment Broadcasting Project (2001) *Losing Reality: Factual International Programming on UK Television, 2000–01*, http://www.ibt.org.uk/3WE/Research/LosingRealityTop.htm (accessed 15 October 2005)

Adorno, T (2005) *Minima Moralia: Reflections from Damaged Life*, Redmond, D (trans), http://www.efn.org/~dredmond/MinimaMoralia.html (accessed 10 February 2006)

Adorno, T, and Horkheimer, M (1972) *Dialectics of Enlightenment*, Cumming, J (trans), New York: Continuum International

Aijmer, G (2000) 'Introduction: The Idiom of Violence in Imagery and Discourse', in Aijmer, G, and Abbink, J (eds), *Meanings of Violence: A Cross-Cultural Perspective*, Oxford: Berg

Aitchison, K (1999) *Profiling the Profession: A Survey of Archaeological Jobs in the UK*, York: Council for British Archaeology, English Heritage, and Institute of Field Archaeologists

Aitchison, K, and Edwards, R (2003) *Archaeology Labour Market Intelligence: Profiling the Profession 2002/03*, Bradford: Cultural Heritage National Training Organisation and Institute of Field Archaeologists

Aldgate, A (1979) *Cinema and History: British Newsreels and the Spanish Civil War*, London: Scolar Press

Allason-Jones, L (2001) 'Material Culture and Identity', in James, S, and Millett, M (eds), *Britons and Romans: Advancing an Archaeological Agenda*, York: Council for British Archaeology (Research Report 125)

Allen, P, and Lazio, C (1983) *Archaeology on Film: A Comprehensive Guide to Audio-Visual Materials*, Boston: Archaeological Institute of America

Andrews, K (1999) 'University Archaeology: Ivory Tower or White Elephant?', in Beavis, J, and Hunt, A (eds), *Communicating Archaeology*, Oxford: Oxbow Books

Anonymous (2000) 'Telegraph Was Behind First Flood Finds', *Daily Telegraph*, 14 September, pp. 15–16

Arens, W (1979) *The Man-Eating Myth: Anthropology and Anthropophagy*, Oxford: Oxford University Press

Arnold, B (1990) 'The Past as Propaganda: Totalitarian Archaeology in Nazi Germany', *Antiquity* 64: 464–478

Ascher, R (1960) 'Archaeology and the Public Image', *American Antiquity* 25: 402–403

Ascherson, N (2002) 'Editorial', *Public Archaeology* 2(3): 129–130

Ascherson, N (2004) 'Archaeology and the British Media', in Merriman, N (ed), *Public Archaeology*, London: Routledge

Assmann, J (2002) *Das Kulturelle Gedächtnis*, München: C.H. Beck

Atkinson, R (1978) 'Silbury Hill', in Sutcliffe, R (ed), *Chronicle: Essays from Ten Years of Television Archaeology*, London: British Broadcasting Corporation

Auel, J (1991) 'Romancing the Public', in Smith, G, and Ehrenhard, J (eds), *Protecting the Past*, Boca Raton, FL: CRC Press

Austin, R, and Devin, L (2003) *Artful Making*, New York: Prentice-Hall

Bacon, E (ed) (1976) *The Great Archaeologists and Their Discoveries as Originally Reported in the Pages of the Illustrated London News*, London: Secker and Warburg

Bailey, G, Massung, E, and Piccini, A (2005) 'In View', *British Archaeology* 83: 56–57

Baines, A (2005) 'Using Photography in Archaeology', in Brophy, K, and Cowley, D (eds), *From the Air: Understanding Aerial Photography*, Stroud: Tempus

Baker, D (2002) 'Gaining More Value from Archaeology', *British Archaeology* 63: 26

Baker, D, and Morris, R (2001) 'Last Orders?' *Antiquity* 75(289): 608–611

Bamberger, S (1968) *Christentum und Film*, Aschaffenburg: Pattloch

Banks, M, and Morphy, H (1997) *Rethinking Visual Anthropology*, New Haven, CT: Yale University Press

BARB, Broadcast Audience Research Bureau (2003) http://www.barb.co.uk (accessed 23 October 2005)

Barrett, J (1995) *Some Challenges in Contemporary Archaeology*, Oxford: Oxbow Books

Barthes, R (1981) *Camera Lucida: Reflections on Photography*, Howard, R (trans), New York: Hill and Wang

Barthes, R (1986) *The Rustle of Language*, Howard, R (trans), Oxford: Blackwell

Baudrillard, J (1983) *Simulations*, New York: Semiotext(e)

Baudrillard, J (1988) 'Simulacra and Simulations', in Poster, M (ed), *Selected Writings*, Stanford, CA: Stanford University Press

Baxter, J (2002a) 'Popular Images and Popular Stereotypes: Images of Archaeologists in Popular and Documentary Film', *SAA Archaeological Record*, September, pp. 16–17, 40

Baxter, J (2002b) 'Teaching with "Indie": Using Film and Television to Teach Archaeology', *SAA Archaeological Record*, November, pp. 18–20

BBC, British Broadcasting Corporation (1972) *Principles and Practice in Documentary Programmes*, London: British Broadcasting Corporation

BBC, British Broadcasting Corporation (2004) 'Building Public Value: Renewing the BBC for a Digital World', http://www.bbc.co.uk/thefuture/bpv/prlogue.shtml (accessed 15 October 2005)

Beale, T (1975) Review of *The Dig*, *American Anthropologist* 77(4): 907–908

Beale, T, and Healy, P (1975) 'Archaeological Films: The Past as Present', *American Anthropologist* 77(4): 889–897

Benjamin, W (1969) *Illuminations*, New York: Schocken

Benjamin, W (1992 [1936]) 'The Work of Art in the Age of Mechanical Reproduction', in Harrison, C, and Wood, P (eds), *Art in Theory*, London: Academic Press

Benjamin, W (1999 [1935]) *The Arcades Project*, Eiland, H, and McLaughlin, K (trans), Cambridge, MA: Belknap Press/Harvard University Press

Bennett, T (1982) 'Media, 'Reality', Signification', in Gurevitch, M, Bennett, T, Curran, J, and Woollacott, J (eds), *Culture, Society and the Media*, London: Routledge

Berger, J (1972) *Ways of Seeing*, Harmondsworth: Penguin

Berger, J (1980) *About Looking*, New York: Pantheon

Berger, J (2002) 'The Ambiguity of the Photograph,' in Askew, K, and Wilk, R (eds), *The Anthropology of Media*, Oxford: Blackwell

Berggren, Å, and Hodder, I (2003) 'Social Practice, Method, and Some Problems of Field Archaeology', *American Antiquity* 68(3): 421–434

Bibby, G (1956) *The Testimony of the Spade*, New York: Collins

Biddle, M, and Kjøbye-Biddle, B (1997) 'Letter', *The Archaeologist* 29: 24

Blatherwick, S (2001) 'Saving the Rose', *Current Archaeology* 172(XV): 148

Blumler, J (1993) 'The British Approach to Public Service Broadcasting: From Confidence to Uncertainty', in Avery, R (ed), *Public Service Broadcasting in a Multichannel Environment*, New York: Longman

Bock, H-M, and Töteberg, M (1992) *Das Ufa-Buch*, Frankfurt am Main: Zweitausendeins

Bohrer, F (2005) 'Photography and Archaeology: The Image as Object', in Smiles, S, and Moser, S (eds), *Envisioning the Past: Archaeology and the Image*, Oxford: Blackwell

Bolter, J (2005) 'Preface', in King, G (ed), *The Spectacle of the Real: From Hollywood to Reality TV and Beyond*, Bristol: Intellect

Bolter, J, and Grusin, R (1996) Remediation, *Configurations* 4(3): 311–358

Bolter, J, and Grusin, R (1999) *Remediation: Understanding New Media*, Cambridge, MA: MIT Press

Borman, S (1978) 'Communication Accuracy in Magazine Science Reporting', *Journalism Quarterly* 55: 345–346

Bourdieu, P (1984) *Distinction: A Social Critique of the Judgement of Taste*, Nice, R (trans), London: Routledge

Bourdieu, P (1998) *On Television*, Ferguson, P (trans), New York: New Press

Bourdieu, P, Boltanski, L, Castel R, Chamboredon, J-C, and Schnapper, D (1990) *Photography: A Middle-Brow Art*, Whiteside, S (trans), Cambridge: Polity Press

Bourke, J (1995) 'Heroes and Hoaxes: The Unknown Warrior, Kitchener and "Missing Men" in the 1920s', *War & Society* 13(2): 41-63

Bowker, G, and Star, S (1999) *Sorting Things Out: Classification and Its Consequences*, Cambridge, MA: MIT Press

Bray, W (1981) 'Archaeological Humour: The Private Joke and the Public Image', in Evans, J, Cunliffe, B, and Renfrew, C (eds), *Antiquity and Man: Essays in Honour of Glyn Daniel*, London: Thames and Hudson

Bricker, H (1973) Review of *Advance into the Past: Modern Archaeological Methods* and *Archaeology in the Laboratory*, *American Anthropologist* 75(2): 598–600

Brill, D (2000) 'Video-Recording as Part of the Critical Archaeological Process', in Hodder, I (ed), *Towards Reflexive Method in Archaeology: The Example at Çatalhöyük*, Cambridge: McDonald Institute for Archaeological Research

Broadcasting Research Unit (1989) *Quality in Television*, London: John Libbey

Brooks, M (2005) 'Watching Alone: Social Capital and Public Service Broadcasting', http://www.bbc.co.uk/info/policies/pdf/watching_alone_text.htm (accessed 15 October 2005)

Bruzzi, S (2000) *New Documentary: A Critical Introduction*, London: Routledge

Bucchi, M (1998) *Science and the Media: Alternative Routes in Scientific Communication*, London: Routledge

Buchli, V, and Lucas, G (2001) *Archaeologies of the Contemporary Past*, London: Routledge

Buck-Morss, S (1989) *The Dialectics of Seeing: Walter Benjamin and the Arcades Project*, Cambridge, MA: MIT Press

Cappella, J and Jamieson, K (1996) 'News Frames, Political Cynicism, and Media Cynicism', *Annals of the American Academy of Political and Social Science* 546: 71–84

Carlson, W, and Gorman, M (1990) 'Understanding Invention as a Cognitive process: The Case of Thomas Edison and Early Motion Pictures, 1881–91', *Social Studies of Science* 20: 387–430

Carman, J (ed) (1997) *Material Harm: Archaeological Studies of War and Violence*, Glasgow: Cruithne Press

Carter, C, and Weaver, C (2003) *Violence and the Media*, Maidenhead: Open University Press

Caughie, J (1980) 'Progressive Television and Documentary Drama', *Screen* 21(3): 9–35

Caveille, S, Fox, K, and Piccini, A (2005) 'In View', *British Archaeology* 80: 44–45

Ceram, C (1980 [1951]) *Gods, Graves and Scholars: The Story of Archaeology*, Harmondsworth: Penguin

Champion, T (1996) 'Three Nations or One? Britain and the National Use of the Past', in Diaz-Andreu, M, and Champion, T (eds), *Nationalism and Archaeology in Europe*, London: UCL Press

Channel 4 (2005) *Channel 4 Statement of Programme Policy 2005–6*. London: Channel 4

Chomsky, N (1989) *Necessary Illusions: Thought Control in Democratic Societies*, London: Pluto Press

Christians, C, Ferre, J, and Fackler, M (1993) *Good News: Social Ethics and the Press*, New York: Oxford University Press

Clarke, C (2003) 'The Politics of Storytelling: Electronic Media in Archaeological Interpretation and Education', *World Archaeology* 36(2): 275–286

Clarke, D L (1973) 'Archaeology: The Loss of Innocence', *Antiquity* 47: 6–18

Clarke, D V (1981) 'Scottish Archaeology in the Second Half of the Nineteenth Century', in Bell, A (ed), *The Scottish Antiquarian Tradition*, Edinburgh: John Donald Publishers

Cleere, H (2000) 'Behind the Scenes at Time Team by Tim Taylor', *Public Archaeology* 1(1): 90–92

Clewlow, C, and Cowan, R (1975) Review of *The Survey*, *American Anthropologist* 77(4): 907

Cloître, M, and Shinn, T (1985) 'Expository Practice: Social, Cognitive and Epistemological Linkage,' in Shinn, T, and Whitley, R (eds), *Expositing Science: Forms and Functions of Popularisation*, Dordrecht: Reidel

Cole, J (1972) 'Motion Pictures as an Archaeological Data Source', *Programme in Ethnographic Film Newsletter* 4(1): 12–13

Cole, J (1980) 'Cult Archaeology and Unscientific Method and Theory', *Advances in Archaeological Method and Theory*, 3: 1–33

Coleman, C, and Dysart, E (2005) 'Framing of Kennewick Man Against the Backdrop of a Scientific and Cultural Controversy', *Science Communication* 27(1): 3–26

Colley, L (2002) *Captives: Britain, Empire and the World 1600–1850*, London: Jonathan Cape

Colley, S (2002) *Uncovering Australia: Archaeology, Indigenous People, and the Public*. Washington, DC: Smithsonian Institution Press

Conklin, B (1997) 'Body Paint, Feathers, and VCRs: Aesthetics and Authenticity in Amazonian Activism', *American Ethnologist* 24: 711–737

Cooter, R, and Pumfrey, S (1994) 'Separate Spheres and Public Places: Reflections on the History of Science Popularization and Science in Popular Culture', *History of Science* 32(3): 237–267

Copjec, J (1990) 'Dossier on the Institutional Debate: An Introduction', in Lacan, J (ed), *Television*, New York: Norton

Corner, J (2000) 'What Can We Say About "Documentary"?' *Media, Culture & Society*, 22: 681–688.

Corner, J (2001) 'Documentary Realism', in Creeber, G (ed), *The Television Genre Book*, London: British Film Institute

Corner, J (2002) 'Performing the Real: Documentary Diversions', *Television and New Media* 3(3): 255–269

Crandall, J (2003) 'Unmanned: Embedded Reporters, Predator Drones and Armed Perception', CTHEORY 4/9/2003, http://www.ctheory.net (accessed 15 October 2005)

Crane, V (1992) 'Listening to the Audience: Producer-Audience Communication,' in Lewenstein, B (ed), *When Science Meets the Public*, Washington, DC: American Association for the Advancement of Science

Crawford, O (1955) *Said and Done: The Autobiography of an Archaeologist*, London: Weidenfeld and Nicolson

Crossland, Z (2000) 'Buried Lives: Forensic Archaeology and the Disappeared in Argentina', *Archaeological Dialogues* 72: 72–101

Croton, G (1989) *From Script to Screen: Documentaries*, Borehamwood: BBC Television Training

Cunliffe, B (1981) 'Introduction: The Public Face of the Past,' in Evans, J, Cunliffe, B, and Renfrew, C (eds), *Antiquity and Man: Essays in Honour of Glyn Daniel*, London: Thames and Hudson.

Curran, J, and Seaton, J (1988) *Power Without Responsibility: The Press and Broadcasting in Britain, 3rd edition*, London: Routledge

Curtis, R (1994) 'Narrative Form and Normative Force: Baconian Story-Telling in Popular Science', *Social Studies of Science* 24: 419–461

Daggett, R (1992) Tello, the Press and Peruvian Archaeology. In Reyman, J (ed), *Rediscovering Our Past: Essays on the History of American Archaeology*, Aldershot & Brookfield: Avebury

Daniel, G (1950) *A Hundred Years of Archaeology*, London: Gerald Duckworth

Daniel, G (1964) *The Idea of Prehistory*, London: Pelican

Daniel, G (1967) *The Origins and Growth of Archaeology*, London: Penguin

Daniel, G. (1986) *Some Small Harvest*. London: Thames and Hudson

Danien, E (1997) 'Publicly Speaking: Notes from the Public Relations Committee', *SAABulletin*, March, http://www.saa.org/publications/saabulletin/15-2/SAA14.html (accessed 14 February 2006)

Darling, J (1999) 'Mass Inhumation and the Execution of Witches in the American Southwest', *American Anthropologist* 100: 732–752

Darvill, T, and Hunt, A (1999) 'PPG16 Has Quickened the Pace of Archaeological Investigations', *English Heritage Conservation Bulletin* April: 14–17

Day, D (1997) *A Treasure Hard to Attain: Images of Archaeology in Popular Film, with a Filmography*. London: Scarecrow Press

DeBoer, W (1999) 'Metaphors We Dig By', *Anthropology News* October: 7–8

Denzer, K (2004) 'FEDARCINE: Cooperation of International Archaeology Film Festivals', *Treballs d'Arqueologia* 10: 35–46

Desfor Edles, L (1998) *Symbol and Ritual in the New Spain*. Cambridge: Cambridge University Press

Desfossés, Y, and Jacques, A (2000) 'Vers une Definition et une Reconnaissance de L'archeologie de la Premiere Guerre Mondiale', *Actes des Colloques 'La Bataille en Picardie, Combattre de l'Antiquité au XXème Siècle', Amiens 16 Mai 1998 et 29 Mai 1999*: 203–220

Deuel, L (1978) *Memoirs of Heinrich Schliemann: A Documentary Portrait Drawn from His Autobiographical Writings, Letters, and Excavation Reports*, London: Hutchinson

Doane, M (1990) 'Information, Crisis, Catastrophe', in Mellancamp, P (ed), *Logics of Television: Essays in Cultural Criticism*, London: British Film Institute

Drößler, R (1988) *Flucht aus dem Paradies – Leben, Ausgrabungen und Entdeckungen Otto Hausers*, Halle-Leipzig: Mitteldeutscher Verlag

Dunwoody, S, and Ryan, M (1987) 'The Credible Scientific Source', *Journalism Quarterly* 64: 21

Earl, G (2005) 'Video Killed Engaging VR? Computer Visualizations on the TV Screen', in Smiles, S, and Moser, S (eds), *Envisioning the Past: Archaeology and the Image*, Oxford: Blackwell.

Efthymiadis, P, and Heinz, M (n.d.) 'Von Heinrich Schliemann bis Lara Croft', unpublished paper, Ausstellung in der Unibibliothek Freiburg

Eiselein, E, and Topper, M (1976a) 'Introduction', *Human Organization* 35(2): 111–112

Eiselein, E, and Topper, M (1976b) 'Media Anthropology: A Theoretical Framework', *Human Organization* 35(2): 113–122

Ellis, J (1990) 'What's the Point?' in Mulgan, G (ed), *The Question of Quality*, London: British Film Institute

ESA, Entertainment Software Association (2005) *Essential Facts About the Computer and Video Game Industry*, http://www.theesa.com/files/2005EssentialFacts.pdf (accessed 24 September 2005)

Evans, C (1983) 'Wildmen, Pulp and Fire: Archaeology as Popular Fiction', *Archaeological Review from Cambridge* 2(1): 68–70

Evans, C (1989) 'Digging with the Pen: Novel Archaeologists and Literary Traditions', *Archaeological Review from Cambridge* 8(2): 36–45

Eve, R, and Harrold, F (1987) 'Pseudoscientific Beliefs: The End of the Beginning or the Beginning of the End?', in Harrold, F, and Eve, R (eds), *Cult Archaeology and Creationism: Understanding Pseudoscientific Beliefs About the Past*, Iowa City: University of Iowa Press

Fagan, B (1996) 'The Arrogant Archaeologist,' in Vitelli, K (ed), *Archaeological Ethics*, Walnut Creek, CA: AltaMira

Fagan, B (2000) 'Education Is What's Left: Some Thoughts on Introductory Archaeology', *Antiquity* 74(283): 190–194

Fagan, B, and Rose, M (2003) 'Ethics and the Media,' in Zimmerman, L, Vitelli, K, and Hollowell-Zimmer, J (eds), *Ethical Issues in Archaeology*, Walnut Creek, CA: AltaMira

Fagan, G (ed) (2006) *Archaeological Fantasies: How Pseudoarchaeology Misrepresents the Past and Misleads the Public*, London: Routledge

Fawcett, C (1995) 'Nationalism and Postwar Japanese Archaeology,' in Kohl, P, and Fawcett, C (eds), *Nationalism, Politics, and the Practice of Archaeology*, Cambridge: Cambridge University Press

Feder, K (1984) 'Irrationality and Popular Archaeology', *American Antiquity* 41(3): 525–541

Felder, K, Hammer, I, Lippok, J, and Wulf, M (2003) 'Erkenntnisgewinn und Unterhaltungswert – eine Analyse von Archäologiebildern in den Unterhaltungsmedien', *Ethnographisch-Archäologische Zeitschrift* 44(2): 161–182

Filiciak, M (2003) 'Hyperidentities: Postmodern Identity Patterns in Massively Multiplayer Online Role-Playing Games', in Wolf, M, and Perron, B (eds), *The Video Game Theory Reader*, London: Routledge

Film Club Kiel EV (1994) (ed), *Cinarchea – Internationales Archäologie-Film-Festival 20-23/4/1996*, Kiel: Film Club Kiel

Film Club Kiel EV (1996) (ed), *Cinarchea – Internationales Archäologie-Film-Festival 24-28/4/1996*, Kiel: Film Club Kiel

Finn, C (1999a) 'Words from Kept Bodies: The Bog as Inspiration', in Coles, B, Coles, J, and Jorgensen, M (eds), *Bog Bodies, Wet Lands and Sacred Sites: Proceedings from 1996 Conference*, Exeter: Wetland Archaeology Research Project

Finn, C (1999b) *Fieldwork: Archaeology and the Poetic Past of WB Yeats and Seamus Heaney*, unpublished D.Phil. thesis, Oxford University

Finn, C (2000a) 'Ways of Telling: Jacquetta Hawkes as Film-Maker', *Antiquity* 74: 127–130

Finn, C (2000b) 'Art or Artefact: The Body as Image', in Campbell, F, and Hansson, J (eds), *Archaeological Sensibilities*, Gothenburg: University of Gothenburg

Finn, C (2001) 'Mixed Messages: Archaeology and the Media', *Public Archaeology* 1: 261–268

Finn, C (2003) 'Poetry and Archaeology: The Transformative Process', in Jameson, J, Ehrenhard, J, and Finn, C (eds), *Ancient Muses: Archaeology and the Arts*, Tuscaloosa: University of Alabama Press

Finn, C (2004a) *Past Poetic: Archaeology in the Poetry of W.B. Yeats and Seamus Heaney*, London: Duckworth

Finn, C (2004b) 'Art or Artifact? The Body Behind Glass', *Archaeological Review from Cambridge* 19(1): 132–138

Finn, C (2006) 'Bog Bodies and Bog Lands: Trophies of Science, Art and the Imagination', in Russell, I (ed), *Image, Meaning, Heritage: Movements Beyond Modern Approaches to Archaeology*, New York: Springer-Kluwer

Firstbrook, P (n.d.) 'Surviving the Iron Age: Planning and Making the Series', http://www.bbc.co.uk/history/programmes/surviving_ironage/intro_peter.s html (accessed 15 November 2005)

Fischer, M (2003) *Emergent Forms of Life and the Anthropological Voice*, Durham, NC: Duke University Press

Foucault, M (1973) *The Order of Things: An Archaeology of the Human Sciences*, New York: Vintage

Foucault, M (1980) *Power/Knowledge: Selected Interviews and Other Writings 1972–1977*, Gordon, C (ed), New York: Pantheon

Foucault, M (1982) *The Archaeology of Knowledge*, New York: Pantheon

Fowler, P (1981) 'Archaeology, the Public and the Sense of the Past', in Lowenthal, D, and Binney, M (eds), *Our Past Before Us: Why Do We Save It?* London: Temple Smith

Fowler, P (1992) *The Past in Contemporary Society: Then, Now*, London: Routledge

Fowler, P (2001) 'Time for a Last Quick One?' *Antiquity* 75(289): 606–608

French, H (2000) 'Meet a Stone Age Man So Original, He's a Hoax' *New York Times*, 7 December, p. 4

French, M (n.d.) 'Tomb Raiders: The Idea of the Adventurer', http://www.theraider.net/features/articles/tomb_raiders.php (accessed 29 June 2005)

Friedman, J (2001) 'Indigenous Struggles and the Discreet Charm of the Bourgeoisie', in Prazniak, R, and Dirlik, A (eds), *Politics and Place in an Age of Globalization*, Lanham, MD: Rowman and Littlefield

Friedman, T (2002) 'Civilization and Its Discontents: Simulation, Subjectivity and Space', http://www.game-research.com/art_civilization.asp (accessed 24 September 2005)

Gale, J (2002) 'Are We Perceived to Be What We Say We Are?' in Russell, M (ed), *Digging Holes in Popular Culture: Archaeology and Science Fiction*, Oxford: Oxbow Books

Galison, P (1996) 'Computer Simulations and the Trading Zone', in Galison, P, and Stump, D (eds), *The Disunity of Science: Boundaries, Contexts, and Power*, Stanford, CA: Stanford University Press

Garcia i Quera, O (2004) 'El Comic i la Història', *Treballs d'Arqueologia* 10: 79–86

Gardner, A (2004) Review of *Archaeology and Modernity* by J Thomas, *Papers from the Institute of Archaeology* 15: 118–121

Gaudiosi, J (2003) 'Games, Movies Tie the Knot', http://www.wired.com/news/games/0,2101,61358,00.html (accessed 24 September 2005)

Gero, J, and Root, D (1994) 'Public Presentations and Private Concerns: Archaeology in the Pages of *National Geographic*', in Gathercole, P, and Lowenthal. D (eds), *The Politics of the Past*, London: Routledge

Gibb, J (2000) 'Imaginary, But by No Means Unimaginable: Storytelling, Science, and Historical Archaeology', *Historical Archaeology* 34(2): 106

Giddens, A (1999) *Runaway World: How Globalisation Is Reshaping Our Lives*, London: Profile Books

Gifford, J (1974) 'A Survey of Shipwreck Sites off the Southwestern Coast of Turkey', *Journal of Field Archaeology* 1: 23–25

Ginsburg, F (1994) 'Embedded Aesthetics: Creating a Discursive Space for Indigenous Media', *Current Anthropology* 9(3): 365–382

Ginsburg, F (1991) 'Indigenous Media: Faustian Contract or Global Village?' *Current Anthropology* 6(1): 92–112

Girdwood, A (1984) 'The Imaginative Response to Archaeology in Late Nineteenth and Early Twentieth Century Literatures', *Archaeological Review from Cambridge* 3(1): 29–37

Girouard, L, Boivin, R, and Laberge, M (1973) 'Communication Audio-Visuelle en Archéologie', *Recherches Amérindiennes au Québec* 3(5): 7–58

Glob, P (1965) *Mosefolket: Jernalderens Mennesker Bevaret i 2000 Ar.* Copenhagen: Gyldendal

Glob, P (1974) *The Mound People: Danish Bronze-Age Man Preserved*, Bulman, J (trans), London: Faber & Faber

Goldsworthy, A (1996) *The Roman Army at War: 100 BC – AD 200.* Oxford: Clarendon Press

Goldsworthy, A (2002) *Roman Warfare*, London: Cassell

Gordon, W (1997) *Marshall McLuhan: Escape into Understanding – A Biography*, New York: Basic Books

Graichen, G (1993) 'Tagebuch der Antike', in Graichen, G, and Hillrichs, H (eds), *C14: Die Gebeine des Papstes – Neue archäologische Entdeckungen in Deutschland*, Munich: Bertelsmann

Graichen, G (1996) 'Raus aus der Mottenkiste', in Film Club Kiel EV (ed), *Cinarchea: Internationales Archäologie-Film-Festival 24-2/.4/1996*, Kiel: Film Club Kiel

Graichen, G (1999) 'Vorstoß in die Vergangenheit', in Graichen, G, and Hillrichs, H (eds), *C14: Vorstoß in die Vergangenheit – Archäologische Entdeckungen in Deutschland*, Munich: Goldmann

Graichen, G, and Hillrichs, H (eds) (1999) *C14: Vorstoß in die Vergangenheit – Archäologische Entdeckungen in Deutschland* [1992]. Munich: Goldmann

Graichen, G, and Siebler, M (eds) (1995) *Schliemanns Erben: Entschlüsseln Archäologen unsere Zukunft?* Mainz: Zabern

Grant, C (n.d.) 'Moving Image Resources for Archaeology Teaching, Learning and Research, Guides for Teaching and Learning in Archaeology, Number 2', http://www.hca/heacademy.ac.uk/resources/guides/archaeology/index/php (accessed 15 April 2006)

Gregory, J, and Miller, S (1998) *Science in Public: Communication, Culture, and Credibility*, Cambridge, MA: Perseus

Gregory, T (1983) 'The Impact of Metal Detecting on Archaeology and the Public', *Archaeological Review from Cambridge* 2(1): 5–8

Gripsrud, J (1999) 'Scholars, Journalism, Television. Notes on Some Conditions for Mediation and Intervention', in Gripstrud, J (ed), *Television and Common Knowledge*, London: Routledge

Habermas, J (1989 [1962]) *The Structural Transformation of the Public Sphere: An Inquiry into a Category of Bourgeois Society*, Cambridge, MA: MIT Press

Habermas, J (2003) *Truth and Justification*, Fulner, B (ed), Cambridge: Polity Press

Habu, J, and Fawcett, C (1999) 'Jomon Archaeology and the Representation of Japanese Origins', *Antiquity* 73(281): 587–593

Hall, M (2004) 'Romancing the Stones: Archaeology in Popular Cinema', *European Journal of Archaeology* 7(2): 159–176

Hall, S (1976) 'Television and Culture', *Sight and Sound* Autumn: 246–252

Hammond, N (1992) 'US Television Blow Away a Dusty Image: Archaeology', *London Times*, 25 September, p. 16

Hancock, G, and Faiia, S (1998) *Heaven's Mirror: Quest for the Lost Civilisation*, London: Michael Joseph

Hansen, M (1987) 'Benjamin, Cinema and Experience: "The Blue Flower in the Land of Technology"', *New German Critique* 40 (Winter): 179–224

Hanson, W, and Rahtz, P (1988) 'Video Recording on Excavations', *Antiquity* 62: 106–111

Hartle, R, Logan, M, and Piccini, A (2005) 'In View', *British Archaeology* 84: 56–57

Hartley, J (1999) *The Uses of Television*, London: Routledge

Hartley, J (2004) 'Television, Nation, and Indigenous Media', *Television and New Media* 5(1): 7–25

Hatley, R (1997) 'Picks, Shovels... and a Ton of Hi-Tech Tricks', *London Times*, 22 October, pp. 14–15

Hawkes, J (1946) 'The Beginnings of History: A Film', *Antiquity* 20: 78–82

Hawkes, J (1982) *Mortimer Wheeler: Adventurer in Archaeology*, London: Weidenfeld and Nicholson

Heaney, S (1972) *Wintering Out*. London: Faber & Faber

Heaney, S (1974) Review of *The Mound People* by P Glob, *The Listener* 91: 23–58

Heaney, S (1975) *North*, London: Faber & Faber

Heaney, S (1980) '"Feeling into Words": Lecture Given at the Royal Society of Literature, October 1974', in *Preoccupations: Selected Prose 1968–1978*, London: Faber & Faber

Heaney, S (1991) *Seeing Things*, London: Faber & Faber

Heaney, S (1999) 'The Man and the Bog', in Coles, B, Coles, J, and Jorgensen, M (eds), *Bog Bodies, Wetlands, and Sacred Sites*, Exeter: Wetland Archaeology Research Project

Hearst, S (n.d.) 'Artistic Heritage and Its Treatment by Television', unpublished paper

Henley, P (2005) 'Anthropologists in Television: A Disappearing World?' in Pink, S (ed), *Applications of Anthropology: Professional Anthropology in the 21st Century*, Oxford: Berghahn

Henley, P (1985) 'British Ethnographic Film: Recent Developments', *Anthropology Today* 1(1): 5–17

Henson, D (2004) 'Digging Ditched', *History Today* 54(10): 63

Henson, D (2005) 'Television Archaeology: Education or Entertainment?' http:// www.history.ac.uk/education/conference/henson.html, (accessed 18 October 2005)

Herman, E, and Chomsky, N (1988) *Manufacturing Consent: The Political Economy of the Mass Media*, New York: Pantheon

Highsmith, J (2004) *Agile Project Management*, New York: Addison-Wesley

Hilgartner, S (1990) 'The Dominant View of Popularization: Conceptual Problems, Political Uses', *Social Studies of Science* 20: 519–539

Hill, A (2005) *Reality TV: Audiences and Popular Factual Television*, London: Routledge

Hill, J (2004) 'UK Film Policy, Cultural Capital and Social Exclusion', *Cultural Trends* 13(2): 29–39

Hills, C (1983) *The Blood of the British*, London: George Philip/Channel 4

Hills, C (1997) 'The Dissemination of Information', in Hunter, J, and Ralston, I (eds), *Archaeological Resource Management in the UK: An Introduction*, Stroud: Sutton

Hills, C (2003) 'What Is Television Doing for Us? Reflections on Some Recent British Programmes', *Antiquity* 77: 206–211

Himmelsbach, S (2005) 'Blogs. The New Public Forum – Private Matters, Political Issues, Corporate Interests', in Latour, B, and Weibel, P (eds) *Making Things Public: Atmospheres of Democracy*, Cambridge, MA: MIT Press

Hingley, R (2000) *Roman Officers and English Gentlemen: The Imperial Origins of Roman Archaeology*, London: Routledge

Hodder, I (1992) *Theory and Practice in Archaeology*, London: Routledge

Hodder, I (1992 [1984]) 'Archaeology in 1984', in Hodder, I (ed), *Theory and Practice in Archaeology*, London: Routledge

Hodder, I (1997) 'Always Momentary, Fluid and Flexible: Towards a Reflective Excavation Methodology', *Antiquity* 71: 691–700

Hodder, I (1998) 'The Past as Passion and Play: Çatalhöyük as a Site of Conflict in the Construction of Multiple Pasts', in Meskell, L (ed), *Archaeology Under Fire: Nationalism, Politics and Heritage in the Eastern Mediterranean and Middle East*, London: Routledge

Hodder, I (1999) *The Archaeological Process*, Oxford: Blackwell

Hodder, I (2000) 'Developing a Reflexive Method in Archaeology', in Hodder, I (ed), *Towards Reflexive Method in Archaeology: The Example at Çatalhöyük*, Cambridge: McDonald Institute for Archaeological Research

Hodder, I (2003) *Archaeology Beyond Dialogue*, Salt Lake City: University of Utah Press

Hoggart, P (2004) 'Extreme Archaeology Tried to Be a Cross Between Charlie's Angels and Tomb Raider: TV Review', *London Times*, 21 June, p. 22

Hollander, B (1987) 'Do Technical Journal Editors Care About Style?' *Journalism Abstracts* 25: 64

Holtorf, C (2003) 'Has Archaeology Never Been So Much Fun?' *Public Archaeology* 3: 125–127

Holtorf, C (2005a) *From Stonehenge to Las Vegas: Archaeology as Popular Culture*, Walnut Creek, CA: AltaMira

Holtorf, C (2005b) 'Beyond Crusades: How (Not) to Engage with Alternative Archaeologies', *World Archaeology* 37(4): 544–551

Holtorf, C (2005c) 'The Portrayal of Archaeology in Contemporary Popular Culture', http://www://traumwerk.standford.edu:3455/PopularArchaeology/38 (accessed 18 March 2005)

Holtorf, C (forthcoming) *The Portrayal of Archaeologists in Contemporary Popular Culture*, Oxford: Archaeopress

Howard, P (1992) 'Introduction', in Daniel, G (ed), *Writing for Antiquity*, London: Thames and Hudson

Hudson, K (1981) *The Social History of Archaeology: The British Experience*, London: Macmillan Press

Hunt, T (2004) 'How Does Television Enhance History?' in Cannadine, D (ed), *History and the Media*, Basingstoke: Palgrave

Hunter, M (1981) 'The Preconditions of Preservation: A Historical Perspective', in Lowenthal, D, and Binney, M (eds), *Our Past Before Us: Why Do We Save It?* London: Temple Smith

Huxley, A (1994 [1946]) *Brave New World*, London: Flamingo

IFA, Institute of Field Archaeologists (2001) 'The Value of Archaeology', abstract for 10 April session at the Institute of Field Archaeologists' Annual Conference, Newcastle, conference brochure, 14

Irwin, A, and Wynne, B (eds), (1996) *Misunderstanding Science? The Public Reconstruction of Science and Technology*, Cambridge: Cambridge University Press

Jagodzinski, J, and Hipfl, B (2001) 'Youth Fantasies: Reading *The X-Files* Psychoanalytically' *Studies in Media & Information Literacy Education* 1(2), http://www.utpjournals.com/jour.ihtml?lp=simile/issue2/jagfulltext.html#citation (accessed 15 October 2005)

James, S (2001) 'Soldiers and Civilians: Identity and Interaction in Roman Britain', in James, S, and Millett, M (eds), *Britons and Romans: Advancing an Archaeological Agenda*, York: Council for British Archaeology (Research Report 125)

James, S (2002) 'Writing the Legions: The Development and Future of Roman Military Studies in Britain', *Archaeological Journal* 159: 1–58

Jameson, J (1997) 'What this Book is About', in Jameson, J (ed), *Presenting Archaeology to the Public: Digging for Truth*, London: AltaMira

Jenks, C (ed) (1995) *Visual Culture*, London: Routledge

Jenssen, T (2005) 'Cool and Crazy: Anthropological Film and the Point of Convergence Between Humanities and Social Science', *Visual Anthropology* 18: 291–308

Jones, B (1984) *Past Imperfect: The Story of Rescue Archaeology*, London: Heinemann

Jordan, P (1981) 'Archaeology and Television', in Evans, J, Cunliffe, B, and Renfrew, C (eds), *Antiquity and Man: Essays in Honour of Glyn Daniel*, London: Thames and Hudson

Jowell, T (2004) *Government and the Value of Culture*, London: DCMS

Kapff, D (2004) 'Journalisten und Archäologie', *Archäologisches Nachrichtenblatt* 9(2): 127–130

Kastner, J, and Wallis, B (eds) (2005) *Land and Environmental Art*, London: Phaidon

Kempen, B (1994) *Abenteuer in Gondwanaland und Neandertal: Prähistorische Motive in der Literatur und Anderen Medien*, Meitingen: Corian-Verlag

Kidder, A (1949) 'Introduction', in Amsden, C, *Prehistoric Southwesterners from Basketmaker to Pueblo*, Los Angeles: Southwest Museum

Kimberly, R (2005) 'News: 2004 Video Game Sales Figures Released', http://www.gamesarefun.com/news.php?newsid=4253 (accessed 24 September 2005)

King, G (ed) (2005) *The Spectacle of the Real: From Hollywood to Reality TV and Beyond*, Bristol: Intellect

King, T, Shenk, R, and Wildersen, L (1970) 'Audio-Visual Techniques in Emergency Salvage Archaeology', *American Antiquity* 35: 220–223

Kittler, F (1999) *Gramophone, Film, Typewriter*, Winthrop-Young, G, and Wutz, M (trans), Stanford, CA: Stanford University Press

Klesert, A (1998) 'You Too Can Write Good: Writing About Archaeology for Local Newspapers', *SAA Bulletin*, May, http://www.saa.org/publications/saabulletin/16-3/SAA17.html (accessed 15 November 2005)

Klinenberg, E (2001) 'Bodies That Don't Matter: Death and Dereliction in Chicago', *Body & Society* 7(2–3): 121–136

Kolbert, E (2003) 'Looking for Lorca: A Country Begins to Disinter Its Painful Past', *New Yorker*, 22–29 December, pp. 14–18

Korn, D, Radice, M, and Hawes, C (2001) *Cannibal: A History of the People-Eaters*. London: Channel 4/Macmillan

Korte, B (2000) 'The Reassuring Science? Archäologie als Sujet und Metapher in der Literatur Britanniens', *Poetica* 32: 125–150

Kossinna, G (1914) *Die Deutsche Vorgeschichte eine Hervorragend Nationale Wissenschaft*, Würzburg: Kabitzsch

Kracauer, S (1979) *Von Caligari bis Hitler*, Frankfurt: Suhrkamp

Kuhn, R (2002) 'Archaeology Under a Microscope: CRM and the Press', *American Antiquity* 67(2): 195–212

Kuhn, T (1962) *The Structure of Scientific Revolutions*. Chicago: University of Chicago Press

Kulik, K (2003) 'British TV Archaeology and the Public (1998–2002)', unpublished paper

Kulik, K (2005) 'Mediating Archaeology: The Relationship Between Archaeology, the Media and the Public in Britain (1996–2002)', unpublished PhD thesis, University of Southampton

Lacan, J (ed) (1990) *Television*, New York: Norton

Lambrick, G (2002) 'Government and Treasure Hunters', *British Archaeology* 68: 26

Large, D (1990) *Between Two Fires: Europe's Path in the 1930s*, New York: Norton

Larman, C (2003) *Agile and Iterative Development: A Manager's Guide*, New York: Addison-Wesley

Latour, B (1987) *Science in Action: How to Follow Scientists and Engineers Through Society*, Cambridge, MA: Harvard University Press

Latour, B (2002) 'What Is Iconoclash? Or Is There a World Beyond the Image Wars?' in Latour, B, and Weibel, P (eds), *Iconoclash: Beyond the Image Wars in Science, Religion, and Art*, Cambridge, MA: MIT Press

Latour, B (2005) 'From Realpolitik to Dingpolitik: Or How to Make Things Public', in Latour, B, and Weibel, P (eds), *Making Things Public: Atmospheres of Democracy*, Cambridge, MA: MIT Press

Lauring, P (1957) *Land of the Tollund Man: The Prehistory of Denmark*, London: Lutterworth

Leakey, R (1983) *One Life: An Autobiography*, London: Michael Joseph

LeMahieu, D (1988) A Culture for Democracy: Mass Communication and the Cultivated Mind in Britain Between the Wars, Oxford: Clarendon Press

Lessig, L (2002) *The Future of Ideas: The Fate of the Commons in a Connected World*, New York: Vintage

Lessig, L (2004) *Free Culture: How Big Media Uses Technology and the Law to Lock Down Culture and Control Creativity*, New York: Penguin

Lessig, L (2005) *Free Culture: The Nature and Future of Creativity*, New York: Penguin

Lindenbaum, S (1979) *Kuru Sorcery: Disease and Danger in the New Guinea Highlands*, Palo Alto, CA: Mayfield

Lioult, J-L (2005) 'Framing the Unexpected', 47 Jump Cut, http://www.ejumpcut.org/currentissue/index.html (accessed 15 October 2005)

Liu, C (1991) 'Telacan: Tiananmen', *Lacanian Ink*

Locke, D (1992) *Science as Writing*, New Haven, CT: Yale University Press

Lockwood, D (2005) 'Teratology of the Spectacle', in King, G (ed), *The Spectacle of the Real: From Hollywood to Reality TV and Beyond*, Bristol: Intellect

Lowenthal, D (1985) *The Past Is a Foreign Country*, Cambridge: Cambridge University Press

Lucas, G (2001) *Critical Approaches to Fieldwork: Contemporary and Historical Archaeological Practice*, London: Routledge

Lüger, H-H, and Schäfer, P (2004) 'Adressatenorientierung in der Deutschen und Elsässichen Regionalpresse', in Frenkel, C, Lüger, H, and Woltersdorff, S (eds), *Deutsche und Französische Medien im Wandel*, Munich: Landauer Schriften zur Kommunikations und Kulturwissenschaft

Lupton, D (1995) 'The Embodied Computer/User', in Featherstone, M, and Burrows, R (eds), *Cyberspace, Cyberbodies, Cyberpunk: Cultures of Technological Embodiment*, London: Sage

MacDonald, S, and Rice, M (eds) (2003) *Consuming Ancient Egypt*, London: UCL Press

Marcus, G, and Fischer, M (1986) *Anthropology as Cultural Critique: An Experimental Moment in the Human Sciences*, Chicago: University of Chicago Press

Marler, J, Marler, R, Reinhard, K, Leonard, B, Lambert, P, and Billman, S (2000) 'Microscopic Intermollecular Evidence for the Human Origin of the Coprolite from the "Cannibalism" Site at Cowboy Wash 5MT100100'. *Southwestern Lore: Journal of Colorado Archaeology* 66(4): 14–22

Massung, E, and Piccini, A (2006) 'In View', *British Archaeology* 86: 56–57

Masterman, M (1970) 'The Nature of a Paradigm', in Lakatos, I, and Musgrave, A (eds), *Criticism and the Growth of Knowledge*, Cambridge, Cambridge University Press

McAdam, T (1999) 'Talking to Ourselves', in Beavis, J, and Hunt, A (eds), *Communicating Archaeology*, Oxford: Oxbow Books

McArthur, C (1978) *Television and History*, London: British Film Institute

McAvoy, F (2005) 'Silbury Hill, Wiltshire: An Assessment of the Conservation Risks and Possible Responses Arising from Antiquarian and Archaeological Investigations. Deep into the Hill – Report for English Heritage Research and Standards Department', http://www.english-heritage.org.uk/upload/pdf/Risk_assessment052005.pdf (accessed 15 November 2005)

McCleneghan, J (1994) 'The 1993 Newspaper Science Reporter: Contributing, Creative, and Responsible', *Social Science Journal* 31(4): 467–477

McLucas, C. (2000) 'Ten Feet and Three Quarters of an Inch of Theatre', in Kaye, N (ed), *Site Specifics: Performance, Place and Documentation*, London: Routledge

McLucas, C, Llywelyn, D, and Shanks, M (forthcoming) *Three Landscapes: A Visual Primer*

McLucas, C and Pearson, M (1999) 'Clifford McLucas and Mike Pearson', in Giannachi, G, and Luckhurst, M (eds), *On Directing: Interviews with Directors* Stanford, CA: Stanford University Press

McLuhan, M (1960) 'Effects of the Improvements of Communication Media' *Journal of Economic History* 20(4): 566–575

McLuhan, M (1964) *Understanding Media: The Extensions of Man*, London: Routledge & Kegan Paul

McLuhan, M (1967) *The Medium Is the Message*, New York: Bantam

Mead, M (1967) 'A Force that Can Change the Nature of Society', In Christenson, R, and McWilliams, R (eds), *Voice of the People: Readings in Public Opinion and Propaganda*, 2nd edition, New York: McGraw-Hill

Meadows, M, and Molnar, H (2002) 'Bridging the Gaps: Towards a History of Indigenous Media in Australia', *Media History* 8(1): 9–20

Merriman, N (1991) *Beyond the Glass Case: The Past, the Heritage and the Public in Britain*, Leicester: Leicester University Press

Metz, C (1990) *Psychoanalysis and Cinema: The Imaginary Signifier*, London: Macmillan

Michaels, G, and Fagan, B (1998) 'Anthropology 3: A New Approach to Introductory Archaeology', *Archaeology and Public Education* 8(1): 4–5

Milanich, J (1999) 'Archaeology in the Sunshine: Grass Roots Education Through the Media and Public Involvement,' in Smith, G, and Ehrenhard, J (eds), *Protecting the Past*, Boca Raton, FL: CRC Press

Miller, D (1972) 'Archaeology and Film: A Conflict of Reality?' *Programme in Ethnographic Film Newsletter* 4(1): 7–8

Miller, J (1984) 'Montré à Premontré', *Analytica* 37

Miller, J (1990) 'Microscopia: An Introduction to the Reading of Television', in Lacan, J (ed), *Television*, New York: Norton

Mitchell, W (1986) *Iconology: Image, Text, Ideology*, Chicago: University of Chicago Press

Moore, B, and Singletary, M (1985) 'Scientific Sources' Perceptions of Network News Accuracy', *Journalism Quarterly* 47: 95–100

Moreland, J (2001) *Archaeology and Text*, London: Duckworth

MORI (2001) *Survey of Attitudes During the 2001 General Election Campaign*, http://www.mori.com/polls/2001/elec_comm_rep.shtml (accessed 15 June 2006)

Morley, D (1995) 'Television: Not So Much a Visual Medium, More a Visible Object', in Jenks, C (ed), *Visual Culture*, London: Routledge

Morris, D (1985) 'Gothic Sublimity', *New Literary History*, Winter, pp. 299–319

Morris, R (1996) 'Anthropology in the Body Shop: Lords of the Garden, Cannibalism, and the Consuming Desires of Televisual Anthropology', *American Anthropologist* 98(1): 137–150

Mortimer, N (2004) 'Spoilheap', *British Archaeology* 77: 33

Moser, S (1998) *Ancestral Images: The Iconography of Human Origins*, Stroud: Sutton Publishing

Mulvey, L (1975) 'Visual Pleasure and Narrative Cinema', *Screen* 16(3): 6–18

Murdoch, G (1999) 'Rights and Representations: Discourse and Cultural Citizenship', in Gripstrud, J (ed), *Television and Common Knowledge*, London: Routledge

Murphy, E and Mallory J (2000) 'Herodotus and the Cannibals', *Antiquity* 74: 388–394

Murray, T, and Walker, M (1988) 'Like WHAT? A Practical Question of Analogical Inference and Archaeological Meaningfulness', *Journal of Anthropological Archaeology* 7(3): 248–287

Nelson, M (2004) 'It May Be History, but Is It True?' http://www.iamhist.org/forum/it-may-be-history.doc (accessed 15 November 2005)

Newman, J (2004) *Videogames*, London: Routledge

Nixon, L (2001) 'Seeing Voices and Changing Relationships: Film, Archaeological Reporting, and the Landscape of People in Sphakia', *American Journal of Archaeology* 105(1): 77–97

Norman, B (1983) 'Archaeology and Television' *Archaeological Review from Cambridge* 2(1): 27–32

Normile, D (2001) 'Japanese Fraud Highlights Media-Driven Research Ethic', *Science* 291(5501): 34

Ofcom (2003) *Ofcom Review of Public Service Television Broadcasting*, http://www.ofcom.org.uk/consult/condocs/psb/psb/psb.pdf (accessed 10 October 2005)

Ofcom (2004) *The Ofcom Internet and Broadband Update*, http://www.broadbanduk.org/reports/Ofcom%20InternetandBroadband%200404.pdf (accessed 11 July 2005)

Ofcom (2005a) 'Draft Guidance Note for Broadcasters', in *Public Service Broadcasting: Statements of Programme Policy and Self-assessment Reviews*, http://www.ofcom.org.uk/consult/condocs/psb_selfasses/psb_self_asses/section2/?a=87101 (accessed 15 October 2005)

Ofcom (2005b) *Television Production Sector Review: A Survey of TV Programme Production in the UK*, http://www.ofcom.org.uk/consult/condocs/tpsr (accessed 20 February 2006)

O'Keefe, M (1970) 'The Mass Media as Sources of Medical Information for Doctors', *Journalism Quarterly* 47: 673–683

Olsen, B (2001) 'The end of history? Archaeology and the Politics of Identity in a Globalised World', in Layton, R, Stone, P, and Thomas, J (eds), *Destruction and Conservation of Cultural Property*, London: Routledge

Orwell, G (1974 [1938]) *Homage to Catalonia*, Harmondsworth: Penguin

Palmer, A (2000) 'Primitives Among Us: The Paradox of the Taraday and Other "Lost Tribes"', *Science Communication* 21(3): 223–243

Palmer, G (2003) *Discipline and Liberty: Television and Governance*. Manchester: Manchester University Press

Paperno, I (2001) 'Exhuming the Bodies of Soviet Terror', *Representations* 75: 89–118

Patzek, B, Hauses, R, and Dudde, A (2001) 'The detective and the archaeologist', in Trümpler, C (ed), *Agatha Christie and Archaeology*, London: British Museum Press

Pausch, M (2000) 'Seitenblicke', *Antike Welt* 4: 427–430

Paynton, C (2002) 'Public Perception and "Pop Archaeology": A Survey of Current Attitudes Toward Televised Archaeology in Britain', *SAA Archaeological Record*, March, pp. 33–44

Pearson, M, and Shanks, M (1996) 'Performing a Visit: Archaeologies of the Contemporary Past', *Performance Research* 2: 42–60

Pearson, M, and Shanks, M (2001) *Theatre/Archaeology*, London: Routledge

Pendergast, D (1998) 'The Bedfellows Are Less Strange These Days: The Changing Relationship Between Archaeologists and the Media', *SAABulletin*, November, http://www.saa.org/publications/saabulletin/16-5/SAA12.html (accessed 14 February 2006)

Percival, J (1980) *Living in the Past*, London: British Broadcasting Corporation

Pertti, A (1997) 'Why Does the Radio Go Unnoticed?' *Nordicom Review of Nordic Research on Media and Communication* (special issue *Radio Research in Denmark, Finland, Norway, and Sweden*) 1: 161–172

Peters, E (1981) 'Archaeology and Publishing', in Evans, J, Cunliffe, B, and Renfrew, C (eds), *Antiquity and Man: Essays in Honour of Glyn Daniel*, London: Thames and Hudson

Peters, H (1995) 'The Interaction of Journalists and Scientific Experts: Co-Operation and Conflict Between Two Professional Cultures', *Media, Culture & Society* 17: 31–48

Peter-Röcher, H (1998) *Mythos Menschenfresser: Ein Blick in die Kochtöpfe der Kannibalen*, Munich: C H Beck

Petersson, B (1994) Indiana Jones på Birka: Om Arkeologisk Popularisering och Forskning, unpublished thesis (D-uppsats), University of Lund

Pew Research Centre (2002) 'News Media's Improved Image Proves Short-Lived, Survey Report for the People's Press', http://people-press.org/reports/159.pdf (accessed 25 June 2005)

Pew Research Centre (2005) 'Public More Critical of Press, but Goodwill Persists: Online Newspaper Readership Countering Print Losses', http://people-press.org/reports/pdf/248.pdf (accessed 12 June 2005)

Phelan, P (1993) *Unmarked: The Politics of Performance*, London: Routledge

Phillips, J (2004) 'The Past and the Public: Archaeology and the Periodical Press in 19th Century Britain', unpublished PhD thesis, University of Southampton

Philo, G (2002) 'Television News and Audience Understanding of War, Conflict and Disaster', *Journalism Studies* 3(2): 173–186

Piccini, A (1999) Celtic Constructs: Heritage Media, Archaeological Knowledge and the Politics of Consumption in 1990s Britain, unpublished PhD thesis, University of Sheffield

Pickering, J (1997) 'Agents and Artefacts', *Social Analysis* 41(1): 45–62

Piggott, S (1989) *Ancient Britons and the Antiquarian Imagination*, London: Thames and Hudson

Pine, J, and Gilmore, J (1999) *The Experience Economy: Work Is Theatre & Every Business a Stage*, Boston: Harvard Business School Press

Pittioni, N (1936) 'Cinematography and Prehistory', *Antiquity* 10: 217–220

Pitts, M (2001) *Hengeworld*, London: Arrow

Pokotylo, D, and Guppy, N (1999) 'Public Perception and Archaeological Heritage: Views from Outside the Profession', *American Antiquity* 64(3): 400–416

Pokotylo, D, and Mason, R (1991) 'Public Attitudes Towards Archaeological Resource and Their Management,' in Smith, G, and Ehrenhard, J (eds), *Protecting the Past*, Boca Raton, FL: CRC Press

Portable Antiquities Scheme (2003) *Annual Report 2001/02-2002/03*

Praetzellis, A (2000) *Death by Theory: A Tale of Mystery and Archaeological Theory*. Walnut Creek, CA: AltaMira

Pratap, A (1988) 'To See or Not to See: Film in Ethnoarchaeology', *Archaeological Review from Cambridge* 7(1): 110–117

Pratchett, R (2005) 'Gamers in the UK: Digital Play, Digital Lifestyles, BBC Audience Research Report', http://crystaltips.typepad.com/wonderland/files/bbc_uk_games_research_2005.pdf (accessed 14 March 2006)

Preston, P (2004) 'The Answer Lies in the Sewer', *Science and Society* 68(3): 277–312

Price, J (2004) 'The Ocean Villas Project: Archaeology in the Service of European Remembrance', in Saunders, N (ed), *Matters of Conflict: Material Culture, Memory and the First World War*, London: Routledge

Price, S (1996) *Communication Studies*, Harlow: Longman

Prince, D, and Schadla-Hall, T (1987) 'On the Public Appeal of Archaeology', *Antiquity* 61: 69–70

Prouty, G (2005) 'Underwriting Program Takes Off', *The Archaeology Channel Newsletter* 1(3), http://www.thearchaeologychannel.org, (accessed 8 November 2005)

Pryor, F (2001) *Seahenge: New Discoveries in Pre-Historic Britain*, London: HarperCollins

Pryor, F (1996) 'Archaeology and the Public', British Archaeological Awards Lecture, http://www.britarch.ac.uk/awards/baalect.html (accessed 11 December 2004)

Pulford, D (1976) 'Follow-Up of Study of News Accuracy in Magazine Science Reporting', *Journalism Quarterly* 53: 345–346

Rahtz, P(ed), (1974) *Rescue Archaeology*, London: Penguin

Ramos, A (1987) 'Reflecting on the Yanomanni: Ethongraphic Images and the Pursuit of the Exotic', *Cultural Anthropology* 2: 284–304

Ramos, M, and Duganne, D (2000) 'Exploring Public Perceptions and Attitudes about Archaeology, report prepared by HarrisInteractive for the Society for American Archaeology', http://org/pubedu/nrptdraft4.pdf (accessed 6 November 2005)

Ramsey, S (1986) 'Communicative Competence for the Science Interview: Information Brokers and Authority Brokers', *Journalism Abstracts* 24: 18

Rao, N, and Reddy, C (2001) 'Ayodhya, the Print Media and Communalism', in Layton, R, Stone, P, and Thomas, J (eds), *Destruction and Conservation of Cultural Property*, London: Routledge

Ravitch, D and Viteritti, J (eds) (2003) *Kid Stuff: Marketing Sex and Violence to America's Children*, Baltimore: Johns Hopkins University Press

Renfrew, C (2003) *Figuring It Out: What We Are? Where Do We Come From? The Parallel Visions of Artists and Archaeologists*. London: Thames and Hudson

Reporters Without Borders (2006) 'Press Freedom in 2005', http://www.rsf.org (accessed 6 February 2006)

Richards, J (2004) 'Archaeology as a Media Experience', *Treballs d'Arqueologia* 10: 47–54

Roberts, K (2004) 'Leisure Inequalities, Class Divisions and Social Exclusion in Present-Day Britain', *Cultural Trends* 13(2): 1–15

Robinson, T (2003) 'Ploughing Through the Past', *New Statesman* (special supplement *Living History: The Present State of Our Past*), December: xviii–xix

Rodney, L (2005) 'Real Time, Catastrophe, Spectacle: Reality as Fantasy in Live Media', in King, G (ed), *The Spectacle of the Real: From Hollywood to Reality TV and Beyond*, Bristol: Intellect.

Rosaldo, R (1993) *Culture and Truth: The Remaking of Social Analysis, 2nd edition*, Boston: Beacon

Roscoe, J, and Hight, C (2001) *Faking It: Mock-Documentary and the Subversion of Factuality*, Manchester: Manchester University Press

Rouse, J (1987) *Knowledge and Power: Towards a Political Philosophy of Science*, Ithaca, NY: Cornell University Press

Ruby, J (2005) 'The Last 20 Years of Visual Anthropology – A Critical Review', *Visual Studies* 20(2): 160–170

Rudgley, R. 1998. *Lost Civilisations of the Stone Age*. London, Arrow

Russell, M (2002a) '"No More Heroes Any More": The Dangerous World of the Pop Culture Archaeologist', in Russell, M (ed), *Digging Holes in Popular Culture: Archaeology and Science Fiction*, Oxford: Oxbow Books

Russell, M (ed) (2002b) *Digging Holes in Popular Culture: Archaeology and Science Fiction*, Oxford: Oxbow Books

Sabin, P (2002) 'Playing at War: The Modern Hobby of Wargaming', in Cornell, T, and Allen, T (eds), *War and Games*, Woodbridge: Boydell Press

Salmon, M (2000) 'Art or Science? A Controversy About the Evidence for Cannibalism', in Pera, M (ed), *Scientific Controversies: Philosophical and Historical Perspectives*, Oxford: Oxford University Press

Sarraute, N (1960) 'Review Article', *Times Literary Supplement*, 10 June, p. 371

Saunders, N (2002) 'Excavating Memories: Archaeology and the Great War, 1914–2001', *Antiquity* 76(291): 101–108

Schadla-Hall, T (2003) Review of *Two Men in a Trench: Battlefield Archaeology – The Key to Unlocking the Past* by T Pollard and N Oliver, *Public Archaeology* 3(1): 54–57

Schadla-Hall, T, and Morris, G (2003) 'Ancient Egypt on the Small Screen: From Fact to Faction in the UK', in MacDonald, S, and Rice, M (eds), *Consuming Ancient Egypt*, London: UCL Press

Schama, S (2004) 'Television and the Trouble with History', in Cannadine, D (ed), *History and the Media*, New York: Palgrave

Scherer, J (1990) 'Picturing Cultures: Historical Photographs in Anthropological Inquiry', *Visual Anthropology* 3(2–3)

Schmidt, M (2000) 'Archaeology and the German Public', in Härke, H (ed), *Archaeology, Ideology, and Society: The German Experience*, Frankfurt: Lang

Schnapp, A (1999) 'Une Archaéologie de la Grande Guerre, est elle Possible? L'Archaéologie et la Grande Guerre Aujourd'hui', *Revue Annuelle d'Histoire* 2: 19–27

Scott, K, and White, A (2003) 'Unnatural History? Deconstructing the Walking with Dinosaurs Phenomenon', *Media, Culture & Society*, 25: 315–332

Selkirk, A (2003) 'Have the Treasure Hunters Won?' *Current Archaeology* 189: 389–393

Seymour, M (2004) 'Ancient Mesopotamia and Modern Iraq in the British Press, 1980–2003', *Current Anthropology* 45(3): 351–368

Shackel, P (2002) 'Broadening the Interpretations of the Past at Harpers Ferry National Historical Park', in Little, B (ed), *Public Benefits of Archaeology*, Gainesville: University Press of Florida

Shanks, M. (1996) *Classical Archaeology: Experiences of the Discipline*, London: Routledge

Shanks, M (1997) 'Photography and Archaeology', in Leigh Molyneaux, B (ed), *The Cultural Life of Images: Visual Representation in Archaeology*, London: Routledge

Shanks, M (1999) *Art and the Early Greek State: An Interpretive Archaeology*, Cambridge: Cambridge University Press

Shanks, M (2003) 'Archaeology: The Implications for Historiography', http://traumwerk.stanford.edu/~mshanks/traumwerk/ (accessed 15 November 2005)

Shanks, M (2004) 'Three Rooms: Archaeology and Performance', *Journal of Social Archaeology* 4: 147–180

Shanks, M, Platt, D, and Rathje, W (2004) 'The Perfume of Garbage: Modernity and the Archaeological', *Modernism / Modernity* (special issue *Archaeologies of the Modern*) 11(1): 61–83

Shanks, M, and Tilley, C (1987a) *Social Theory and Archaeology*, Cambridge: Polity Press

Shanks, M and Tilley, C (1987b) *Re-Constructing Archaeology: Theory and Practice*, Cambridge: Cambridge University Press

Shanks, M, and Tilley, C (1992) *Re-Constructing Archaeology: Theory and Practice*, 2nd edition, London: Routledge

Sherman, S (1998) *Documenting Ourselves: Film, Video, and Culture*, Lexington: University Press of Kentucky

Silva, E, Esteban, A, Castán, J, and Salvador, P (eds), (2004) *La Memoria de los Olvidados: Un Debate Sobre el Silencio de la Represión Franquista*, Valladolid: Ámbito Ediciones

Silverstone, R (1994) *Television and Everyday Life*, London: Routledge

Singer, A (2002) 'Beyond Primetime: Anthropology and Television at War', Forman Lecture 2002, Manchester Conference Centre', http://www.socialsciences.manchester.ac.uk/socialanthropology/research/forman/documents/forman2002-singerfinal.pdf (accessed 15 April 2006)

Smith, G (1990) *Epic Films: Casts, Credits, and Commentary on over 250 Historical Spectacle Movies*, Jefferson, NC: McFarland

Smith, L (2004) 'BBC Dig Wrecks Site', *London Times*, 22 December, p. 20

Spriggs, M (1994) 'God's Police and Damned Whores: Images of Archaeology in Hawaii', in Gathercole, P, and Lowenthal, D (eds), *The Politics of the Past*, London: Routledge

Staden, H (1929 [1557]) *Hans Staden: The True Story of His Captivity 1557*. New York: McBride

Stallworthy, J (1982) 'W.B. Yeats and Seamus Heaney: The Poet as Archaeologist', *Review of English Studies* XXXIII(130): 158–74

Star, S, and Ruhleder, K (1996) 'Key Steps Towards an Ecology of Infrastructure-Design and Access for Large Information Spaces', *Information Systems Research* 7: 111–134

Statistiska Centralbyrån (2002) 'Vad Betyder Kulturmiljön För Dig?' http://uxra-kmsap2.raa.se/opencms/export/agendakulturarv/dokument/ (accessed 10 September 2005)

Steele, J (2003) 'The Television Documentary and the Real', *Journal for the Psychoanalysis of Culture and Society* 8(2): 330–337

Stern, T (1992) 'Zu Neuen Ufern...', in Keefer, E (ed), *Die Suche nach der Vergangenheit. 120 Jahre Archäologie am Federsee*, Stuttgart: Württembergisches Landesmuseum

Stern, T (1993) 'Archäologie im Film', in Sommer, U, and Wolfram, S (eds), *Macht der Vergangenheit – Wer macht Vergangenheit*, Wilkau-Haßlau: Beier & Beran

Stern, T (1994) 'Das Verhältnis von Archäologie und Film', *Archäologische Informationen* 17(1): 9–13

Stern, T (1997) 'Zwischen Glotze und Lehrfilm', *Archäologische Informationen* 20(2): 1–7

Stern, T (2001) 'Le Marketing de la Propagande en Préhistoire: Le film archéologique sous le 3e Reich', in Schnitzler, B (ed), *L'archéologique en Alsace et en Moselle au temps de L'annexion (1940–1944)*, Strasbourg/Metz: Musées de Strasbourg

Stern, T (2002) 'Weltwunder und Wunderwelten: Schliemann's Erbschaft an Indiana Jones', in Jensen, I, and Wieczorek, A (eds), *Dino, Zeus und Asterix: Zeitzeuge Archäologie in Werbung, Kunst und Alltag heute*, Mannheim: Beier & Beran

Stern, T (2003) 'Der Propagandistische Klang Stummer Zeugen Deutscher Vorzeit – Archäologiefilme im Nationalsozialismus', in Kuhnen, H-P (ed), *Propaganda – Macht – Geschichte: Archäologie an Rhein und Mosel im Dienst des Nationalsozialismus*, Trier: Rheinisches Landesmuseum

Stern, T, and Tode, T (2002) 'Das Bild des Archäologen in Film und Fernsehen: Eine Annäherung', in *ARCHÄOLOGIE Virtuell: Projekte, Entwicklungen, Tendenzen seit 1995*, Bonn: Habelt

Stevanovic, M (2000) 'Visualizing and Vocalizing Archaeological Archival Record: Narrative vs Image', in Hodder, I (ed), *Towards Reflexive Method in Archaeology: The Example at Çatalhöyük*, Cambridge: McDonald Institute for Archaeological Research

Stocking, S (1999) 'How Journalists Deal with Scientific Uncertainty,' in Friedman, S, Dunwoody, S, and Rogers, R (eds), *Communicating Uncertainty: Media Coverage of New and Controversial Science*, Mahwah, NJ: Lawrence Erlbaum

Stoddart, S, and Malone, C (2001) 'Editorial', *Antiquity* 75(289): 459–486

Stone, J (2000) *Losing Perspective: Global Affairs on British Terrestrial Television 1989–1999*, London: Third World and Environment Broadcasting Project

Stone, P (1989) 'Interpretations and Uses of the Past in Modern Britain and Europe', in Layton, R (ed), *Who Needs the Past? Indigenous Values and Archaeology*, London: Routledge

Stone, P (1997) 'Presenting the Past: A Framework for Discussion', in Jameson, J (ed), *Presenting Archaeology to the Public: Digging for Truth*, London: AltaMira

Swain, H (1997) 'Mirroring Reality? Images of Archaeologists', *The Archaeologist* 30: 16–17

Swain, H (2001) 'No. 1 Poultry and the Excavation of High Street, Londinium', presentation at Institute of Field Archaeologists' Annual Conference, 12 April, Newcastle

Tacchi, J (1999) 'Radio Texture: Between Self and Others', in Miller, D (ed), *Material Cultures: Why Some Things Matter*, Chicago: University of Chicago Press

Tagg, J (1988) *The Burden of Representation: Essays on Photographies and Histories*, London: Metheun

Tankard, J, and M. Ryan (1974) 'News Source Perceptions of Accuracy of Science Coverage', *Journalism Quarterly* 51: 219–225, 334

Tarabulski, M (1989) 'Recording the Past: Capturing the History of Archaeology on Videotape', in Christenson, A (ed), *Tracing Archaeology's Past: The Historiography of Archaeology*, Carbondale: Southern Illinois University Press

Taylor, F (2001) 'Not Entirely What It Could Be: Historical Perspectives on Modern Archaeology TV Programmes', *Antiquity* 75(289): 468–748

Taylor, M (2001) 'PPG16: Success or Failure?' *CBA Southeast Newsletter* 19: 14

Taylor, T (1992a) 'The Gundestrup Cauldron', *Scientific American* March: 84–89

Taylor, T (1992b) 'Counting Your Change' *Scientific American* August: 5

Taylor, T (1992c) 'Culture by Inheritance? Archaeology and Race', in Jones, D (ed), *Down to Earth*, London: Channel 4

Taylor, T (1994) 'Thracians, Scythians, and Dacians, 800 BC-AD 300', in Cunliffe, B (ed), *The Oxford Illustrated Prehistory of Europe*, Oxford: Oxford University Press

Taylor, T (1996) *The Prehistory of Sex: Four Million Years of Human Sexual Culture*, London: 4th Estate

Taylor, T (2001a) 'Explanatory Tyranny', *Nature* 411: 419

Taylor, T (2001b) 'The Edible Dead', *British Archaeology* 59: 8–12

Taylor, T (2002) *The Buried Soul: How Humans Invented Death*. London: 4th Estate

Taylor, T (2005) Untitled Essay, in Brockman, J (ed), *What We Believe But Cannot Prove: Today's Leading Thinkers on Science in the Age of Uncertainty*, New York: HarperCollins

Thomas, J (2004) *Archaeology and Modernity*, London: Routledge

Thomas, G, and Arnold, G (1974) 'Rescue Archaeology and the Public', in Rahtz, P (ed), *Rescue Archaeology*, London: Penguin

Thompson, M (1977) *General Pitt-Rivers: Evolution and Archaeology in the Nineteenth Century*, Bradford-on-Avon: Moonraker Press

Tichenor, P, Olien, C, Harrison, H, and Donohue, G (1970) 'Mass Communication Systems and Communication Accuracy in Science News Reporting', *Journalism Quarterly* 47: 673–683

Tilley, C (1989) 'Archaeology as Socio-Political Action in the Present', in Pinsky, V, and Wylie, A (eds), *Critical Traditions in Contemporary Archaeology*, Cambridge: Cambridge University Press

Tilley, C (2000) 'On Modernity and Archaeological Discourse', http://archaeology. kiev.ua/meta/tilley.html (accessed 3 November 2005)

Tode, T, and Stern, T (2003) 'The Presentation of the Vaus Battle in Film', in Denzer, K (ed), *Funde, Filme, Falsche Freunde – Der Archäologiefilm im Dienst von Profit und Propaganda*, Kiel: Verlag Ludwig

Trigger, B (1989) *A History of Archaeological Thought*, Cambridge: Cambridge University Press

Tringham, R (forthcoming) 'Forgetting and Remembering the Digital Experience and Digital Data', in Boric, D (ed), *Excavating Memories*, Oxford: Oxbow Books

Trümpler, C (2001) '"A Dark-Room Has Been Allotted to Me...": Photography and Filming by Agatha Christie on the Excavation Sites', in Trümpler, C (ed), *Agatha Christie and Archaeology*, London: British Museum Press

Tunstall, J (1996) *Newspaper Power: The New National Press in Britain*, Oxford: Clarendon Press

Turner, C, and Turner, J (1999) *Man Corn: Cannibalism and Violence in the Prehistoric American Southwest*, Salt Lake City: University of Utah Press

Ucko, P (1994) 'Foreword', in Gathercole, P, and Lowenthal, D (eds), *The Politics of the Past*, London: Routledge

Van Der Sanden, W (2004) *Through Nature to Eternity: The Bog People of Northwest Europe*, Bradford: University of Bradford

Vaughan, D (1976) *Television Documentary Usage*, London: British Film Institute

Vaughan, S (2004) 'Photographer's Notes for *Opened Landscape* Exhibition', Photofusion Gallery, London

Von Daniken, E (1969) *Chariots of the Gods: Was God an Astronaut?* London: Berkeley Publishing Group

Wainwright, G (2000) 'Time Please', *Antiquity* 74: 909–943

Walker, D (2000) 'On the Slant', *Guardian*, 3 October, p. 21

Watrall, E. (2002a) 'Digital Pharaoh: Archaeology, Public Education and Interactive Entertainment', *Public Archaeology* 2(3): 163–169

Watrall, E. (2002b) 'Interactive Entertainment as Public Archaeology', *SAA Archaeological Record*, March, pp. 37–39

Webb, D (1996) 'Photographs by David Webb', *The Archaeologist* 27: 15–17, cover

Weigold, M (2001) 'Communicating Science: A Review of the Literature', *Science Communication* 23(2): 164–193

West, A (2004) 'Archaeology and Television', in Henson, D, Stone, P, and Corbishley, M (eds), *Education and the Historic Environment*, London: Routledge

Wheeler, R (1954) *Archaeology from the Earth*, Oxford: Clarendon Press

Wheeler, R (1955) *Still Digging*, London: Michael Joseph

Wheeler, R (1966) *Alms for Oblivion: An Antiquary's Scrapbook*, London: Weidenfeld and Nicolson

Whitley, R (1985) 'Knowledge Producers and Knowledge Acquirers,' in Shinn, T, and Whitley, R (eds), *Expositing Science: Forms and Functions of Popularisation*, Dordrecht: Reidel

Whittle, A (1997) *Sacred Mound, Holy Rings: Silbury Hill and the West Kennet Palisade Enclosures: A Later Neolithic Complex in North Wiltshire*, Oxford: Oxbow Books

Williams, S (1991) *Fantastic Archaeology: The Wild Side of American Prehistory*, Philadelphia: University of Pennsylvania Press

Willis, J (2001) 'Past Is Perfect,' *Guardian*, 29 October, http://education.guardian.co.uk/print/0,3858,4286861-108247,00.html (accessed 29 June 2005)

Wilson, M (2001) 'Tales from the Trenches: The People, Policies, and Procedures of Cultural Resource Management', *SAA Archaeological Record*, May, pp. 37–38, 44

Winkler, M (ed) (2004) *Gladiator: Film and History*, Oxford: Blackwell

Winston, B (2000) *Lies, Damn Lies and Documentaries*, London: British Film Institute

Witmore, C (2004) 'Four Archaeological Entanglements with Place: Mediating Bodily Experience Through Peripatetic Video', *Visual Anthropology Review* 20(2): 57–72

Wolf, M (2001a) 'Time in the Video Game', in Wolf, M (ed), *The Medium of the Video Game*, Austin: University of Texas Press

Wolf, M (ed) (2001b) *The Medium of the Video Game*, Austin: University of Texas Press

Wolf, M, and Perron, B (eds), (2003) *The Video Game Theory Reader*, London: Routledge

Woolley, L (1965 [1930]) *Digging Up the Past*, London: Pelican

Wynne, B (1992) 'Public Understanding of Science Research: New Horizons or Hall of Mirrors?' *Public Understanding of Science* 1: 37–44

Young, P (2002) 'The Archaeologist as Storyteller,' in Little, B (ed), *Public Benefits of Archaeology*, Gainesville: University Press of Florida

ZDF (1994) 'Sphinx - Geheimnisse der Geschichte', *ZDF Monatsjournal* 12: 10–11

Žižek, S (1991) *Looking Awry: An Introduction to Jacques Lacan Through Popular Culture*, Cambridge MA: MIT Press

Žižek, S (2004) *Organs Without Bodies: On Deleuze and Consequences*, London: Routlegde

Zotz, L-F (1933a) 'Vorgeschichte und Film', *Nachrichtenblatt für Deutsche Vorzeit* 9(8): 132–134

Zotz, L-F (1933b) 'Die Deutsche Vorgeschichte im Film', *Nachrichtenblatt für Deutsche Vorzeit* 9(4): 50–53

Zotz, T (1986) 'Wir Wandern mit den Ostgermanen: Filmbericht über Ausgrabungen in Schlesien 1932', in Institut für den Wissenschaftlichen Film (ed), *Publikationen zu Wissenschaftlichen Filmen*. 6(2), Film G 167. Göttingen: Institut für den Wissenschaftlichen Film

INDEX

ABOUT THE EDITORS AND CONTRIBUTORS

Marion Benz teaches at the Department of Near Eastern Archaeology, University of Freiburg, Germany. She wrote her doctoral thesis on the Neolithisation of the Near East. She is a freelance journalist and has written about archaeology for various Swiss and German newspapers.

Marcus Brittain writes about the sociopolitical accountability of prehistoric research in Britain, exploring concepts of practice and historiography. He teaches archaeological theory, history, and philosophy, and recently completed doctoral research with the School of Arts, Histories and Cultures, University of Manchester, UK, focusing on approaches to the Bronze Age of Wales and the Cambridgeshire Fens.

Timothy Clack is Lecturer in Archaeology and Anthropology at St. Peter's College, University of Oxford, UK. He recently completed his doctoral research at the School of Arts, Histories and Cultures, University of Manchester, UK, concerning religion and memory in human evolution.

Brian Fagan is Archaeology Professor Emeritus at the University of California, Santa Barbara, USA, where he has been Professor of Anthropology since 1967. His experience in the communication of archaeological issues through the media is extensive, with regular appearances on radio and TV including *Patterns of the Past* (NPR) and *Treasure Seekers* (National Geographic). He has also consulted for Hollywood.

Christine Finn was a print and TV journalist before studying at the University of Oxford, UK. She is currently Writer Fellow,

J. B. Priestley Library, University of Bradford, UK and a Visiting Fellow at the Department of Archaeology, University of Bristol, UK.

Peter Fowler was Secretary to the Royal Commission on Historical Monuments (England) and Professor of Archaeology at the University of Newcastle upon Tyne, UK and is now a World Heritage consultant, writer, and painter.

Andrew Gardner is Lecturer in the Archaeology of the Roman Empire at the Institute of Archaeology, UCL, UK. His publications include the edited volume *Agency Uncovered: Archaeological Perspectives on Social Agency, Power, and Being Human* (UCL Press).

Cornelius Holtorf is currently Assistant Professor in Archaeology at the University of Lund, Sweden. His recent books include *From Stonehenge to Las Vegas: Archaeology as Popular Culture* (AltaMira) and *The Portrayal of Archaeology in Popular Culture* (Archaeopress).

Karol Kulik worked in film/TV education and marketing for 20 years before pursuing postgraduate studies in archaeology and the media at the University of Southampton, UK, receiving her PhD in 2005. She lectures, writes, and consults in the field of archaeological communication.

Anna Katrien Liedmeier is a student at the Department of Near Eastern Archaeology, University of Freiburg, Germany. She researches into the history, art, and archaeology of the Near East.

Angela Piccini is a Research Councils Academic Fellow in Performativity, Place and Space at University of Bristol, UK. Her background is in transdisciplinary research across archaeology, media, and performance through mixed-mode research practices. She is co-editor with Cornelius Holtorf of *Contemporary Archaeologies: Excavating Now*.

Jon Price is Senior Lecturer in the Northumbria University Cultural Management Unit, UK, and has carried out major fieldwork on battlefield sites from the First World War in France and Belgium. He has centrally participated in major media projects funded by Maya Vision, Discovery Channel, and YAP Films. He is co-founder with Andrew Robertshaw of the international research team No Man's Land.

Francis Pryor is former President of the Council for British Archaeology and has directed the Fenland Archaeological Trust since 1987. He is also a founding member of the Institute of Field Archaeologists. His numerous TV credits include *Now Then* (BBC), *Time Team*, *Britain BC*, and *Britain AD* (Channel 4).

Layla Renshaw is Senior Lecturer in Forensic Science and Investigative Analysis at Kingston University, UK, specialising in human identification and forensic archaeology. In addition, having completed an internship with the International Criminal Tribunal in Kosovo, she is currently carrying out PhD research in anthropology at UCL, UK.

Michael Shanks holds the Omar and Althea Hoskins Chair in Classical Archaeology at Stanford University, USA, where he directs the Stanford Humanities Laboratory.

Tom Stern has researched Near Eastern Archaeology, Prehistory, and Sumerian Cuneiform texts at various German universities and has directed excavations in Turkey, Syria, and Germany. He is currently a curator at the Ruhrlandmuseum Essen, Germany.

Timothy Taylor is Reader in Archaeology in the Department of Archaeological Sciences, University of Bradford, UK. His research interests include materiality, gender, symbolism, and death-related behaviours, and he is a specialist on the later prehistory of Central and Eastern Europe.

Archaeology and the Media

PUBLICATIONS OF THE INSTITUTE OF ARCHAEOLOGY,
UNIVERSITY COLLEGE LONDON
Director of the Institute: Stephen Shennan
Publications Series Editor: Peter J. Ucko

The Institute of Archaeology of University College London is one of the oldest, largest and most prestigious archaeology research facilities in the world. Its extensive publications programme includes the best theory, research, pedagogy and reference materials in archaeology and cognate disciplines, through publishing exemplary work of scholars worldwide. Through its publications, the Institute brings together key areas of theoretical and substantive knowledge, improves archaeological practice and brings archaeological findings to the general public, researchers and practitioners. It also publishes staff research projects, site and survey reports, and conference proceedings. The publications programme, formerly developed in-house or in conjunction with UCL Press, is now produced in partnership with Left Coast Press, Inc. The Institute can be accessed online at http://www.ucl.ac.uk/archaeology.

ENCOUNTERS WITH ANCIENT EGYPT Subseries, Peter J. Ucko, (ed.)
Jean-Marcel Humbert and Clifford Price (eds.), Imhotep Today (2003)
David Jeffreys (ed.), Views of Ancient Egypt since Napoleon Bonaparte: Imperialism, Colonialism, and Modern Appropriations (2003)
Sally MacDonald and Michael Rice (eds.), Consuming Ancient Egypt (2003)
Roger Matthews and Cornelia Roemer (eds.), Ancient Perspectives on Egypt (2003)
David O'Connor and Andrew Reid (eds.), Ancient Egypt in Africa (2003)
John Tait (ed.), 'Never had the like occurred': Egypt's View of its Past (2003)
David O'Connor and Stephen Quirke (eds.), Mysterious Lands (2003)
Peter Ucko and Timothy Champion (eds.), The Wisdom of Egypt: Changing Visions Through the Ages (2003)

Andrew Gardner (ed.), Agency Uncovered: Archaeological Perspectives (2004)
Okasha El-Daly, Egyptology, The Missing Millennium: Ancient Egypt in Medieval Arabic Writing (2005)
Ruth Mace, Clare J. Holden, and Stephen Shennan (eds.), Evolution of Cultural Diversity: A Phylogenetic Approach (2005)
Arkadiusz Marciniak, Placing Animals in the Neolithic: Social Zooarchaeology of Prehistoric Farming (2005)
Robert Layton, Stephen Shennan, and Peter Stone (eds.), A Future for Archaeology (2006)
Joost Fontein, The Silence of Great Zimbabwe: Contested Landscapes and the Power of Heritage (2006)
Gabriele Puschnigg, Ceramics of the Merv Oasis: Recycling the City (2006)
James Graham-Campbell and Gareth Williams (eds.), Silver Economy in the Viking Age (2007)
Barbara Bender, Sue Hamilton, and Chris Tilley, Stone Worlds: Narrative and Reflexivity in Landscape Archaeology (2007)
Andrew Gardner, An Archaeology of Identity: Soldiers and Society in Late Roman Britain (2007)
Sue Hamilton, Ruth Whitehouse, and Katherine I. Wright (eds.), Archaeology and Women (2007)
Gustavo Politis, Nukak: Ethnoarchaeology of an Amazonian People (2007)
Sue Colledge and James Conolly (eds.), The Origins and Spread of Domestic Plants in Southwest Asia and Europe (2007)
Timothy Clack and Marcus Brittain (eds.), Archaeology and the Media (2007)
Janet Picton, Stephen Quirke, and Paul C. Roberts (eds.), Living Images: Egyptian Funerary Portraits in the Petrie Museum (2007)
Tony Waldron, Paleoepidemiology: The Measure of Disease in the Human Past (2007)
Eleni Asouti and Dorian Q. Fuller, Trees and Woodlands of South India: An Archaeological Perspective (2007)
Russell McDougall and Iain Davidson (eds.), The Roth Family, Anthropology, and Colonial Administration (2007)
CRITICAL PERSPECTIVES ON CULTURAL HERITAGE subseries, Beverley Butler (ed.)
Beverley Butler, Return to Alexandria (2007)